## LET THE FACTS SPEAK FOR THEMSELVES...

The problem with all the books on Chappaquiddick is ignorance. Specifically, the writers lack legal knowledge and are totally ignorant of forensic science... At most, these writers have been jurors who apply common sense and general knowledge to a problem. In the real world, however, juries usually consist of twelve individuals. They reach a decision based on the presentation of two sides of a question and considerable physical evidence, much of which has been explained by the experts. Who among us would turn our fate over to one individual who has not been fully informed?

"Intriguing...
The authors tackle the big mysteries of the case."
—*Kirkus*

# CHAPPAQUIDDICK

## THE REAL STORY

**JAMES E.T. LANGE** and **KATHERINE DeWITT, Jr.**

ST. MARTIN'S PAPERBACKS

CHAPPAQUIDDICK: THE REAL STORY

Copyright © 1992 by The Weird Construction Co., Grammatical Division.

Library of Congress Catalog Card Number: 92-41155

ISBN: 0-312-95276-7

Printed in the United States of America

St. Martin's Press hardcover edition/June 1993
St. Martin's Paperbacks edition/July 1994

10  9  8  7  6  5  4  3  2  1

*To Our Parents*
*and*
*William of Ockham*

# Contents

*Introduction*

The problem with all the books on Chappaquiddick is ignorance. Specifically, the writers lack legal knowledge and are totally ignorant of forensic science. Writers have claimed that participants are guilty of certain crimes when they themselves cannot say what the elements of those offenses are. They discuss drowning when they don't know what drowning actually is, in a medical sense. These authors claim to be investigators. Yet investigators are people who either discover facts or apply their knowledge, experience, and expertise to facts already known. Until now, authors of books on Chappaquiddick have found few new facts. Instead, new or bizarre theories have been their stock-in-trade.

At most, these writers have been jurors who apply common sense and general knowledge to a problem. In the real world, however, juries usually consist of twelve individuals. They reach a decision based on the presentation of two sides of a question and considerable physical evidence, much of which has been explained by experts. Who among us would turn our fate over to one individual juror who has not been fully informed?

James E. T. Lange, one of the authors of this book, is a practicing lawyer. He tries drunken driving and accident cases in the Maryland courts. Prior to becoming a lawyer, he was an investigator for other lawyers. He has been to the autopsy room and the criminalistics lab. In the 1960s, he worked on Capitol Hill, the milieu of Senator Kennedy and of the boiler room girls. His undergraduate background is history, and he has also published articles on legal medicine.

Katherine DeWitt, Jr. was an advertising copy writer and editor who, while a few years younger than Mary Jo Kopechne would have been had she survived, also moved in the Hill/Agency/Shared Georgetown House milieu in the late 1960s. Her academic background is history, biology, and geography. The writers have worked together before as writer and editor.

When they started, they felt that if they wound up proving anything, it would be the popular idea that Ted Kennedy was drunk and the accident was not reported until the next day because he needed the time to sober up. While they might not prove this beyond a reasonable doubt, they felt it likely that they would turn up clear and convincing evidence.

In fact, however, research led them to a theory that seems to have been buried under truckloads of political propaganda. Scientific knowledge was not as advanced in 1969 as it is in 1993, and perhaps the right experts were never called in. This new knowledge and information won't change anything. Too much time has passed for that. But the theories and the research should allow everyone to better understand what happened that July weekend, when the eyes of most Americans were cast heavenward toward the moon and the men who were about to land on it, not toward a small resort on the edge of the Atlantic Ocean.

*Prologue*

On the night of July 18–19, 1969, while the first men to land on the moon were speeding toward their destination, an event occurred on Chappaquiddick Island off Martha's Vineyard, Massachusetts. A black 1967 Oldsmobile sedan owned by Edward Kennedy, senator from Massachusetts, went off the Dyke Bridge. The body of a young woman, Mary Jo Kopechne, was found in the submerged car on the morning of July 19.

This event and the few unquestioned facts surrounding it have led to the speculation that Senator Kennedy was everything from an innocent bystander to a first-degree murderer.

"I can understand shock, but I cannot understand Mr. Gargan and Mr. Markham. They weren't in shock. Why didn't they get help? That's where my questions start."

—*Joseph Kopechne,,*
*father of Mary Jo,*
*1969*

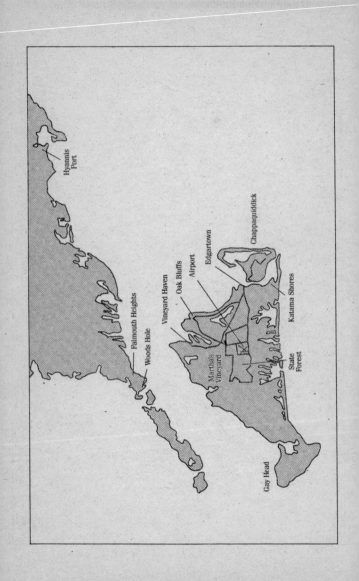

Hyannis Port

Falmouth Heights
Woods Hole

Vineyard Haven
Oak Bluffs
Airport
Edgartown
Chappaquiddick

Martha's Vineyard

State Forest

Katama Shores

Gay Head

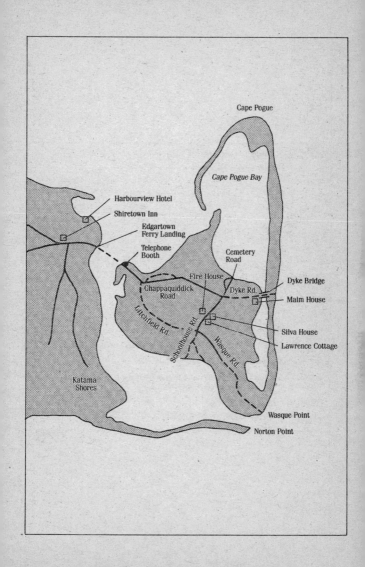

Cape Pogue

Cape Pogue Bay

Harbourview Hotel

Shiretown Inn

Edgartown
Ferry Landing

Telephone
Booth

Cemetery
Road

Fire House

Dyke Bridge

Chappaquiddick
Road

Dyke Rd.

Malm House

Litchfield Rd.

Schoolhouse Rd.

Silva House

Lawrence Cottage

Wasque Rd.

Katama
Shores

Wasque Point

Norton Point

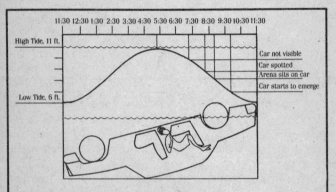

High Tide, 11 ft.

Low Tide, 6 ft.

11:30 12:30 1:30 2:30 3:30 4:30 5:30 6:30 7:30 8:30 9:30 10:30 11:30

Car not visible
Car spotted
Arena sits on car
Car starts to emerge

This chart was compiled using the following information:

1. Eyewitness accounts of water levels over the Oldsmobile on the morning of July 19, 1969.

2. Statement by Motor Vehicle Inspector Kennedy of low-tide water depth.

3. Interpolated tidal height based on readings at Nantucket, as the node of the basin, and readings at other specified distances from Nantucket.

4. Overall length of the Oldsmobile of 18 feet.

5. Farrar's description of Kopechne's position in the car.

# 1

*Edward Moore*

*(Ted) Kennedy*

Why would one traffic fatality out of over 56,000 in the year 1969 merit national headlines, spawn endless conjecture and dinner-table discussions, result in several civil and criminal court actions, and inspire several books?

The only reason this one was different from all the rest was that it involved a Kennedy: Edward Moore "Ted" Kennedy. Some thought him to be the "Last" Kennedy.

To understand just what that meant, you have to understand the past, the heritage and history that came together to create the Edward M. Kennedy who drove his car off a bridge one Friday night after a party.

The Irish carrying the genes that would become the living victim of Chappaquiddick all arrived in the United States and in Boston from Ireland between 1848 and 1852.

Bridget Murphy Kennedy, the widow of Patrick, the original Kennedy, prospered and brought the family from rags to middle class. Her only son, Patrick Joseph, went to work unloading freight at fourteen, saved enough money to buy a saloon and then a bank, and became part-time politician, Democratic ward heeler, state legislator, and candidate for street commissioner.

He prospered enough to send his son, Joseph Patrick Kennedy, to Boston Latin School and then to Harvard. By 1914 young Joe, Ted's father, had become the youngest bank president in the country at twenty-five.

In 1857, Thomas Fitzgerald of Boston married Rosanna Cox, a cousin. Their fourth son was John Francis "Honey Fitz" Fitzgerald. The first of his four daughters was Rose Elizabeth Fitzgerald, Ted's mother.

Around 1885, Honey Fitz embraced politics with the fervor of a young bridegroom. His career had begun in the commercial world as an insurance company president. He rose in politics the hard way, starting as ward heeler and rising to councilman, United States congressman, and mayor of Boston.

In 1913, Fitzgerald made an enemy of James Michael Curley, an alderman who had been elected from jail. Curley declared for mayor on the promise that Fitzgerald would not run. Fitzgerald ran anyway.

Just before the Boston mayoral election of 1913, Curley sent a letter to Mrs. Fitzgerald accusing Honey Fitz of marital infidelity with a cigarette girl. The affair with Elizabeth Ryan, known as Toodles, was exposed, and Fitzgerald was Gary Harted out.

Honey Fitz attempted to continue his career. He ran for Senate against Henry Cabot Lodge and was whipped. Although he attempted a number of comebacks—in 1916, 1918, 1922, 1930, and 1942—he never won another election.

Honey Fitz was first and foremost a politician. It was his major interest, his reason for being, and his claim to fame.

Fitzgerald fathered four daughters, but the eldest, Rose, was his favorite. It was she who would carry his political banner to his grandchildren.

When she was sixteen, Rose Kennedy fell in love with young Joseph Kennedy. Her father did not approve, and it took Joe eight years to prove to the Fitzgeralds that he was worthy of Rose's hand. They married in 1914. Careers in banking, shipbuilding, and stock brokerage made him a couple of fortunes before and after World War I. In 1929, Kennedy decided his stock values were extremely inflated and liquidated his stocks. Many on Wall

Street questioned his judgment until the October crash. He had escaped just in time.

Rumors persist that Joe Kennedy made a fortune in bootleg liquor during prohibition. While he may have brought in a little good-quality liquor from Canada, he was not in the rotgut and beer market, where the big money was. He made a killing legally, after prohibition ended, by holding the import licenses for several good Scotch whiskies.

Financially comfortable, Joe then entered the fringes of politics by supporting Roosevelt's 1932 presidential campaign with money, time, and talent. He was rewarded with several positions in Roosevelt's administration, culminating with the appointment as Ambassador to the Court of St. James.

As a politician and statesman Kennedy was a great business tycoon. He did a decent job as ambassador until Britain declared war on Germany. He never understood Hitler or the Nazis and did not like Winston Churchill, Britain's prime minister. The British soon opened a file on his "anti-British" activities, and Kennedy was recalled.

His career included making more money, inventing the concept of the rental automobile firm, playing around the edges of Hollywood, and earning a reputation for womanizing that eclipsed that of his father-in-law.

Meanwhile, Rose was training the children to be politicians. She began with the oldest, Joe, Jr., who was born in 1915. John Fitzgerald was born in 1917, Rosemary in 1918. After that came Robert, Kathleen, Eunice, Patricia, Jean, and Edward Moore.

Rose knew what her family should be. To realize those ideals, she set out to educate her children. She systematically took them to historic places in Boston, to political rallies, speeches, parades, processions, and public ceremonies. She clipped the day's events from the papers and posted them on a bulletin board. At dinnertime, the children were quizzed on those events, and they were expected to be able to answer correctly.

The Kennedy childhoods were also filled with athletic activities, from touch football and tennis to swimming. All the children were strong swimmers and swam regularly in the ocean off Hyannis Port.

Joe, Jr., was to be the model for all those who followed. He was the favored and the favorite. The best looking of the boys, he was a perfectionist, the setter of example, the disciplinarian, the third "parent." Rose wanted him to be the perfect one, to show the others how Mother wanted them to be. He was the the one Mother loved best.

Jack, Son Number Two, was the one everyone else loved best. He was ill off and on most of his life, and when he was ill, he had his mother to himself. She would read to him: fairy tales and adventure stories, legends and lore. Jack found something at which he was better than Joe—the world of the intellect.

Rosemary, mentally handicapped since birth, had a tragic fate. Rose attempted to raise her with the other children and, until she became a young adult, the strategy was successful. Then the young woman's behavior became erratic, with episodes of violence. Her doctors recommended that a new technique, a lobotomy, be performed to calm her down. Joe consented, but the surgery was botched. Rosemary had to be institutionalized.

Kathleen was known as Kick. Because Rosemary was handicapped, Kathleen was treated as the eldest daughter. She was happy and energetic. She could get along with anybody. She was Rose's favorite child.

Eunice, the fifth child, was particularly close to Rosemary. She was very mature even as a child and was considered nervous and highly conscientious.

Patricia was the prettiest of the girls. She was considered lazy for a Kennedy, but that wouldn't be lazy for most people. She was the best at athletics, better than her brothers. She grew up to be taller than her brother Bobby.

Jean was only four years older than Teddy and grew up with him in London and at Hyannis Port, away from the New York social scene the others had experienced.

Eventually the Gargans joined the crowd of Kennedy children. Mary Jo, Ann, and Joey Gargan were the children of Rose Kennedy's sister, Mary Agnes, and her husband, Joseph, a consultant to the War Department. Mary Agnes died in 1936, and Joe Gargan, Sr., died in 1946. From 1941 on, when their father was traveling extensively, the Gargan children spent a great deal of time with the Kennedys. After their father's death, they joined the Kennedy family permanently.

Ted was nine and Joe was eleven when the Gargan children began to merge with the Kennedys. Ted was delighted. Robert was a surrogate parent, but Joey was a friend. Teddy finally had a "brother" close to his own age. By the time Joey was sixteen and Ted was fourteen, the merger became permanent. They were the best of friends and remained so until 1982.

The war saw changes in the family makeup. Joe, Jr., and Kathleen did not return from the war. Joe was killed and Kathleen stayed on with her dead husband's father, to be killed in a plane crash in 1948. Jack had been badly injured in the highly publicized loss of his PT boat in the Pacific.

Robert, Jean, and Teddy were still in school. Because the family moved so often, Teddy had attended ten different schools by 1948 and was called "Fat Stuff," but he was good natured and lovable. His childhood as the baby hadn't been all easy. He was very close to his brother Bobby, who was seven years older, but felt more remote from Jack, who was fifteen years his senior, and from Joe, Jr., Bobby had been Ted's surrogate parent, much as Joe, Jr. had been for the older children. Teddy was the last male duckling in the row, bemused and easygoing, falling behind and then having to work like mad to catch up with the brood.

After the war, the influences that continued to shape Ted Kennedy were totally dominated by his family's political ambitions.

Although Papa Joe had committed political suicide as England woke up, and Roosevelt had cut his throat and drained the body, his sons were still very viable. Rose had inherited her father's political genius and ambition, and lavished it on her children. Her work was not nearly finished.

Jack was thirty-three years old, Robert was twenty-five, and Edward was eighteen. The young Ted was about to enter Harvard. It wasn't immediately evident that Ted would follow in what would seem to be the family business. Looking at it now, it is obvious why Ted once answered the question "Why did you go into politics?" with "What else would I have done?" He was a Kennedy and was given no choice but to follow the family vocation.

In 1952 Jack Kennedy ran for the Senate seat held by Henry Cabot Lodge, Jr. Partway through the campaign, Bobby became campaign manager and Jack's right hand. Their mother, Rose, campaigned for Jack with the women voters, and their father, Joe, helped with money and aid behind the scenes. The sisters and Ted spent many hours working with volunteers and getting out the vote for their brother, setting a pattern that would last for years. Jack won, and the campaign strengthened the bond between him and Bobby.

While Ted was a student at Milton Academy, he was a hard-working, pleasant person, a team player and always dependable. After graduation in 1950, he went off peacefully and obediently to Harvard.

The infamous Spanish exam is a good example of hanging with the wrong crowd that parents are always warning against. No one had ever accused Ted of having an overdeveloped brain so he gravitated to the similarly endowed jocks at Harvard. Sliding by on the gentleman's "C," taking the easiest courses, and a bit of genteel cribbing were the mores of this group. In the spring of 1951 another jock suggested that a mutual friend, who was a language whiz, should take the exam for Ted. No one agreed or disagreed. On the morning of the exam, the first jock woke up the Spanish expert and sent him down to the test while Ted was still getting ready. Ted heard this and didn't go himself. This was a case of going with the flow more than it was of deliberately planning to cheat. It was an early indication of his tendency to let others make his decisions for him. They were caught immediately, both were expelled from Harvard, and reentry could not be considered for a year.

Ted apparently felt worse about the expulsion of the other young man than about his own. Joe, Sr., tried to make things right for the other young man, who refused help. Instead, they formed one of those cross-generation friendships that some-times occur.

Ted went off and enlisted in the army. When Joe, Sr., found out his inattentive son had signed up for four years, he made a telephone call and cut it back to the more usual two-year hitch. He also arranged for Ted to serve in Europe rather than Korea, where war was raging.

The army experience seems to have broadened Teddy. After his service he did such un-Kennedy-like things as coach basket-ball at a Boston settlement house, spend a summer as a forest ranger, and spend another summer as a crewman on a trans-Pacific yacht race to Honolulu. Finally Ted turned to Harvard and graduated in 1956.

At Harvard he built a reputation as a womanizer, making his intentions quite clear to every girl he dated, and he wasn't so much offended as amazed on the few occasions when he was turned down.

After Harvard Ted went to the University of Virginia law school in Charlottesville. He gained admission only with some difficulty and afterward UVA passed a rule that no one could be admitted who had violated the honor code at any other university, as Ted had done at Harvard.

During his time in law school Ted ran up a number of driving violations, including speeding, reckless driving, and running a red light. In one often-recounted incident, a sheriff chased his car (a disreputable Oldsmobile convertible) and when he caught up with Teddy, he found him scrunched up under the steering wheel, hiding. While this report is unsubstantiated in official documents, several sources do repeat it.

Ted's friends were a little worried about this penchant for speed and recklessness in an otherwise fairly placid person. His law school years seem to have been an unusual time in his life. To make the grade, he had to study at least twice as hard as most of his classmates. The whole experience was very stressful.

He was also courting Joan Bennett, whom he married in 1958.

After law school graduation in 1959, Ted Kennedy went to work as Assistant District Attorney for Suffolk County (Boston),

Massachusetts. He is reported to have been an uneven prosecutor, good at oratory but sloppy in case preparation.

The adult Ted Kennedy was shaped by his mother's political ambitions and the womanizing of his grandfather, father, and at least one of his brothers.

In 1960, John Kennedy was elected President of the United States, leaving his Senate seat empty. A Kennedy loyalist, Benjamin Smith, a former Harvard classmate of John's, filled the remainder of the term, thereby "holding" it for Ted, who ran for it in 1962, as soon as he was old enough to do so. He won.

When Senator Edward M. Kennedy arrived in Washington in 1963, his brother John Fitzgerald was President and his brother Robert was Attorney General.

It was an incredible feat to have three brothers in Washington in these positions at the same time. Rose had done her work well. (Leaving out city and state government, the Kennedy–Fitzgerald families have produced one ambassador, two congressmen, three senators, a president, an attorney general, and, now, a third congressman, Robert's son, Joseph P. III.)

Ted played the Senate game very well. He was much better at it than Jack had been before him or than Bobby would be later. Always a team player, he was quick to recognize the rules. He worked hard, and he kept his nose clean.

After he arrived in Washington, Ted seldom drove a car. Senators work harder than most of their constituents realize. It is the custom for senators and many congressmen to work in their cars between home, the office, speaking engagements, and airports. Having someone drive not only allows more work time but avoids wasting time looking for parking spaces. Ted did, and still does, follow the custom of having a staff member serve as driver in addition to other staff duties. He was working the customary fourteen-hour days and trying to make time for his children. Even at home in Massachusetts, he used a driver most of the time.

Jack Kennedy's personal presidency was flavored by constant back pain, Addison's disease, and the entertaining of women other than his wife in the White House. The rocking chair that he used in the Oval Office to ease his back pain became a popular home fashion accessory. The Addison's disease was kept from the public, though this may be hard to accept in the days when we crawl up the president's colon with gun and camera. Most of Washington was at least vaguely aware of the women, the Secret Service and the CIA were having fits about them, and they were discreetly overlooked by the press.

Kennedy's official presidency started with an inaugural address in which he said, "Ask not what your country can do for you. Ask what you can do for your country," and a promise to put a man on the moon by 1970. This promise would be fulfilled with ironic, perhaps convenient timing, for his younger brother Ted. Other features were a tax cut; the Kennedy round of tariff talks; the botched attempt to invade Cuba at the Bay of Pigs; and the successful handling of the Cuban Missile Crisis. Foreign initiatives included the Alliance for Progress; the Peace Corps, sending idealistic Americans to underdeveloped countries; and the Green Berets, in case idealism wasn't enough.

On November 22, 1963, John Kennedy took a bullet to the brain stem, and became the fourth president of the United States to be assassinated.

The accused assassin was murdered on live television three days after the assassination. The Warren Commission issued a long but exceptionally confusing and confused report on the assassination, which was widely doubted and debated. These extensions of the event burned it into the national memory.

The youth, charm, and hope of the Kennedy Thousand Days ended, and with no period of adjustment the country had old, crude, and vulgar Lyndon Johnson as chief of state.

The "Camelot" years, the assassination, the Warren Report, and the contrast with his successor created a magical aura around Kennedy and, by extension, all Kennedys.

In 1964 Ted suffered a broken back in a plane crash. While lying on the ground, badly injured with three vertebrae broken in seventeen places, several broken ribs, and a hemorrhaging punctured lung, he insisted that the other survivors be treated and taken to ambulances before he would allow himself to be transported. It was a week before his doctors were sure he would live. He managed, nevertheless, to be reelected to the Senate, campaigning from a hospital bed.

Ted's Senate career went well, yet he used other people's talents and ideas and relied heavily on aides. This was partly necessitated by his bad back.

In early 1968, by the end of Johnson's first elected term, the country was in chaos. LBJ declined to run again. His administration had such an unsavory aura that whoever the Democrats nominated could well have been a sacrifical lamb.

Robert Kennedy was the third son. The Kennedy magic was still strong enough so that he might have had a chance to be elected, even on the Democratic ticket. He had been attorney general under his brother, then served as senator from New York. In 1968 Robert Kennedy declared himself a candidate for president. He waged a vigorous campaign, with Ted working hard, as was the family's tradition, culminating in a victory in the California primary on June 5, 1968. That evening Robert was shot and killed by Sirhan Sirhan, an anti-Israel Muslim fanatic who had been kicked in the head by a horse and who is still serving his sentence in California.

Coming within three months of the murder of Martin Luther King, Jr., the acknowledged head of the black civil rights movement, the death not so much shocked as battered again a nation stunned by the murder of its president and one of its leading political figures in the space of less than five years.

Coming as they did as part of the concern for the seemingly unending war in Vietnam, the assassinations of Robert Kennedy and Martin Luther King led a number of people to conclude that the country was literally coming apart.

Robert's assassination devastated Ted. Ted, the fourth son, the "baby," was now the only one left. He was de facto head of the family, as his father was ill and disabled from a stroke. The events and extra responsibilities proved too much for Ted.

He had worshiped his brother Bobby, and he barely managed to keep himself together through the funeral and aftermath. Soon he went into a severe depression and was seen weeping in public.

Eventually Ted went into seclusion at his house on Squaw Island, in the family compound at Hyannis Port, Massachusetts.

In late July Joe Gargan and Dave Hackett (Bobby's college roommate and later close friend and advisor) talked Ted into giving a three-day thank-you party for the women who had worked on Bobby's campaign. The women went to Hyannis Port and stayed with various family members in the compound. Gargan took them for a sail, and Ted and Joan hosted a cocktail party at their house. That cocktail party was the only event Ted attended.

By November 1968 Ted had recovered enough to return to the Senate, where he was elected Senate Majority Whip. He was also being considered as the hot Democratic prospect for the 1972 presidential race. The Democrats had no one else to turn to. Generations of political Kennedys and Fitzgeralds and his mother's ambition made it clear to Ted that, as the only adult male Kennedy left, it was his duty to run.

Ted Kennedy was drinking hard, but probably not much harder than most. In the early 1970s sophisticates still drank hard liquor instead of the white wine or bottled water so popular today. Such drinks as planter's punch were considered effete. Real Men drank beer, bourbon and water, scotch and soda, rum and Coke (and didn't call it Cuba libre, either), or just took it straight. Hard drinking and fast driving were considered manly, not antisocial.

Some people, looking back at the events leading up to Chappaquiddick, have seen an almost inevitable foreshadowing of tragedy. There is very little question that Ted Kennedy had a terrible choice: He could let his family and supporters down by not running for the presidency, or he could become the youngest dead candidate or dead president in United States history.

The Kennedy family, while being rightly credited with their record of public service, had also been hyped by the press to mythic proportions. These *nouveau riche arrivistes* were regularly touted in the media as America's "Royal Family." Serious, rational people took this with a grain of salt and slight distaste. The population of potential assassins, however, is not made up of serious, rational people. It is composed of people who believe they are receiving messages from Venus in the fillings of their teeth and that a regicide somehow takes on the power and aura of the king he kills

Ted Kennedy's fear was in no way irrational.

Hanging around the fringes of much of the Kennedy partisan writing is a sort of half-formed, rarely articulated theory that Ted Kennedy tried to avoid that choice, or at least thinking about it, by drink and carousing. He may have hoped that by living on the edge, something might happen that would remove the choice. To say that Kennedy subconsciously caused the accident at Chappaquiddick would be to take a Freudian leap of faith analogous to saying that John Wilkes Booth shot Lincoln to resolve his oedipal conflict. If Kennedy wanted to avoid the presidency, more likely he would have chosen to get caught with one of his very real mistresses or in a drunken public scene rather than to kill someone accidentally.

## 2

*Mary Jo Kopechne*

The often-overlooked victim of the accident at Chappaquiddick was a young career woman named Mary Jo Kopechne.

She was born July 26, 1940, in Wilkes-Barre, Pennsylvania. Her mother was Gwendolyn Jennings, a first-generation Welsh American. Her father was Joseph A. Kopechne, of Polish extraction.

The family moved away from Wilkes-Barre when Mary Jo was only a year old. At the time of the accident, the family was living in Berkely Heights, New Jersey, the edge of the New York metropolitan area.

Mary Jo seems to have been a good child and had a trouble-free youth. After graduation from high school, she attended the Dominican Caldwell College for Women in Newark, New Jersey. Hardworking, she was employed every summer and saved her money.

Caldwell girls were encouraged to give a year of their lives to God, and after graduation Mary Jo took a position as a teacher at the Mission of St. Jude in Montgomery, Alabama. Though she made only fifty dollars a month, she never asked her parents for money. It was her duty to her faith to live in near poverty and work for God, and she obeyed not only the letter but the spirit of the commitment.

Mary Jo called herself a novena Catholic. Novena refers to the practice of repeating a prayer or observance nine times in order to make a point with God. In other words, she was more than an observant Catholic, she was a serious Catholic.

After her year at the mission, Mary Jo sought employment in the nation's capital. When she first arrived in Washington in 1963, Mary Jo worked in the office of Senator George Smathers of Florida. She had worked for John Kennedy's presidential campaign in college and idolized Robert Kennedy.

Smathers convinced Kennedy to hire Kopechne as an aide and secretary in 1965. She was a dedicated worker, often staying up nights to work on speeches and papers for him. She frequently helped Robert's wife, Ethel, with social correspondence.

Mary Jo lived at 2912 Olive Street N.W. in Georgetown, a stylish section of Washington that was much like New York's Greenwich Village, with more money and without the sleazy self-consciousness. She shared the place with three other Washington career women, including Ann "Nance" Lyons, one of the other women at the party on Chappaquiddick. She drove an unpretentious blue Volkswagen bug.

Mary Jo was an attractive, five-foot, two-inch blonde with good legs. She enjoyed dancing and liked popular music. Miniskirts were the uniform of the day for career girls in Washington. They implied a fashion sense and the desire to blend in.

Hairstyles of the time were still teased and sprayed, with a flip quite popular. Mary Jo and most of her friends, however, wore similar, close-cropped, practical hairstyles.

Called "Salomé" because of her dancing and "Twiggy" for her figure, after an emaciated model of the day, old friends knew her as MJ.

She took an occasional social drink. Her friends testified that she was never a heavy drinker. Unusual for the time and place, she did not smoke. She never swore.

Mary Jo dated only rarely when she worked for Robert

Kennedy. At the time of her death, she had agreed to become engaged to a career foreign service officer. Contrary to some reports, either they had not told their parents, or there was no notice in the newspapers, or no rings had been exchanged, or some combination of those conditions was true because the engagement was not official. It was only an agreement. Her mother was not aware that the relationship was that serious. She was not lonely and looking for handouts from a married senator. As a good, observant, practicing Catholic, she would have avoided any personal involvement with him. She had a life of her own, quite apart from her job and the people she worked with.

Mary Jo Kopechne was not your standard-issue Washington G-girl (short for the government girl, a common Washington term) of the time. Instead of working for an obscure agency, she worked on "the Hill" and, later, with campaign consultants. Instead of being just a secretary, she had been an aide to a glamorous senator and was still working in politics rather than the bureaucracy. Instead of being in Washington to find a husband, she was apparently in Washington to make a real contribution. Her days of working with the poor had instilled a sense of a job to be done from within the system. Instead of being politically vague, as so many G-girls were at the time, she was committed and active.

She worked long and hard on Robert Kennedy's campaign. She and the others who attended the party on Chappaquiddick were called the "boiler room girls" (they worked on the telephone banks making campaign calls). They were so intelligent, competent, and hardworking that, as a Kennedy staffer said, people brought *them* coffee. This was high praise indeed at a time when young women had a harder time being taken seriously than they do now.

Mary Jo and the other women who attended the party were serious political operatives on their way to professional level. They were working toward goals, and that meant working long, hard hours. They had little time for or inclination to frivolity.

Kopechne wrote letters over Robert's signature, and once encouraged a woman who wanted an army-owned island in Long

Island Sound to be made available to the mentally retarded. Bobby had other ideas, but he treated her error as a joke. Kennedy and Ted Sorensen, chief speech writer, even consulted with her on key phrasings for speeches and press releases. Her devotion to Bobby and Ethel Kennedy was such that, when a boyfriend asked her to choose between him and the Kennedys, she did not choose him.

In 1968 her work was directed toward the nomination of Robert Kennedy as a presidential candidate at the Democratic National Convention. She served as the key Washington contact in charge of keeping track of the convention delegates and voter sentiment in Indiana, Pennsylvania, Kentucky, and the District of Columbia.

Each woman in the boiler room maintained files on the backgrounds (personal and political), voting records, sentiments, persuadability, and much more of all the delegates within her designated area. Each had to assess what the actions of the various opposition candidates meant so that Democratic supporters would know what to say about them. One of the spins put out was that Robert Kennedy was being "ganged up on" by various southern governors, organized labor, Wall Street and oil interests, Republican newspapers, and presumably Venusians and Alpha Centaurians who were sending mind waves. The idea was to create the underdog mentality—a little difficult with a Kennedy as your candidate.

This is heavy-duty work requiring toughness and intelligence.

After Robert Kennedy's assassination, Mary Jo stayed on for two months closing the office, helping to pack things up and helping Ethel Kennedy deal with correspondence that flooded Hickory Hill, Ethel's northern Virginia home, following the funeral.

In her next job Mary Jo worked with a political action group registering black citizens to vote in Florida; later she helped set up a campaign headquarters for Democratic presidential candidate George McGovern. In September 1968 she was given another job, this one also in the political arena, with Matt Reese Associates, a firm of campaign consultants who set up offices for

Democratic candidates. She was employed by Matt Reese at the time of her death. She had agreed to work on the New Jersey campaign of Thomas Whelan with the understanding that her plane fare home for Washington weekends be paid so that she could visit her foreign service officer.

Mary Jo Kopechne was spending her weeks working in a high-pressure, time-consuming job and her weekends with the man she was planning to marry. Between November 1968 and July 1969 she had absolutely no time to play around with Ted Kennedy.

Ted Kennedy knew Mary Jo only slightly. After the accident, he couldn't remember how to spell her last name. He had met her when she worked for his brother, had seen her at Robert's home helping Ethel, and had talked to her at a couple of parties for the boiler room girls—at the cocktail party at Hyannis Port in late July 1968, and another party in January 1969—but Ted didn't know her well at all, in spite of rumors to the contrary.

In late spring, the women gave their own reunion party and Ted had not shown up. Nance Lyons, one of the women who worked for Ted in the Senate, chided him for it and he regretted not having made it.

Ironically, Mary Jo was almost unable to attend the party on Chappaquiddick. She had an assignment in South Carolina, but at the last minute she found someone else to take her place.

Like all the other women at the party, Mary Jo had been hired by the Robert Kennedy campaign for discretion, brains, loyalty, humor under strain, and enough fast-thinking ability to stay ahead of things. The women were intelligent, ambitious, and politically aware—qualities that in 1969 were often considered the antithesis of sex appeal.

After the accident, reporters invented characters for all of the women. For the most part, they were wrong. To be fair, they may have been misled by Ted Kennedy himself, who referred to Mary Jo as a "secretary." The press made the women out to be giggling ingenues, invited to a party to pair off with the married men.

The party on Chappaquiddick was just one more "thank you" for the women, and Ted's attendance was virtually required. It was given in honor of the women. The men were there to express the thanks of the Kennedy family and the Democratic political machine for the women's hard work.

In short, Mary Jo Kopechne was no dizzy blonde.

We are not campaigning for Miss Kopechne's beatification. Nor do we discount the fact that there may have been a sexual motive behind Kennedy and Kopechne's departure from the party. Ted Kennedy, at thirty-seven, was rich, semipowerful, reasonably good looking, and a celebrity, a combination of aphrodisiac qualities that few young women could resist, especially one devoted to his political ideals and his family. Mary Jo Kopechne was, of course, not one of the pedigreed or vaguely famous blondes who were often linked with Senator Kennedy. Some writers have even suggested that she was far below his standards. We prefer to think that she fell outside his known preference. However, his philosophy that night might well have been "Any port in a storm."

Given Senator Kennedy's reputation and habits, a sexual motive is likely. Given his tiredness and depression that night, romance was probably not his highest priority. Given Miss Kopechne's character and habits, a sexual motive for her is unlikely. The facts will forever remain unproven.

July 19, 1969, was one week before Mary Jo Kopechne's twenty-ninth birthday.

## 3

*Party on Chappaquiddick*

In April 1969 Ted Kennedy traveled to Alaska to investigate the plight of Eskimos. It was an exhausting and depressing trip. On the scheduled commercial airliner on the final leg of the return journey, after he had a few drinks, a pillow fight started. He led the travelers in shouts of "Eskimo Power!" Reporters on the plane refrained from splashing the incident all over the papers.

By mid-1969 the senator had developed a code that he used when he felt he was under too much pressure. He would say "TMBS" to an aide, meaning "Too many blue suits." That meant to get those people out. He was drinking heavily. John Lindsay of *Newsweek* circulated an internal memo expressing the opinion that Kennedy was cracking up, but no one embarrassed the senator with that allegation either.

Most working reporters and a few editors and publishers were still in thrall to the Kennedys. The secret was access. There seemed to be no barriers between the family and the press. Great photo ops were always provided, and someone was always available to chat with a reporter.

Ted had been subjected to considerable flack for his brief appearances at the previous parties for the boiler room staff and his nonappearance at the last party. When Joe Gargan planned another party for July 1969, the senator's presence was absolutely required. To ensure his attendance, the party was timed and placed to coincide with the Edgartown Regatta, an event the Kennedys never missed.

Joe Gargan and his wife, Betty, had rented a cottage on Chappaquiddick for the whole week, through Sunday night. They planned to vacation there and host the party over the weekend. Betty Gargan's mother was taken ill and she was unable to attend.

Joan was three months pregnant and had been warned by her doctors not to travel. She had suffered two miscarriages between her second and third children, and she was at a difficult stage in this pregnancy. She stayed at Squaw Island in the Hyannis compound.

The invitation was extended to many people who had been at the core of Bobby's campaign. Many were unable to attend. It was only coincidence that the party wound up being six men and six women. Those without close family ties to the Kennedys but invited because of their work for Bobby included the women, Raymond LaRosa, and Charles Tretter.

That set the scene for the party.

## Those Involved in the Action

### Townies in Edgartown

**Mr. and Mrs. John Chirgwin and son,** innkeepers, Doggett House.
**Manuel Francis DeFrates,** charter boat skipper, *Bonnie Lisa.*
**Estey Teller,** secretary-receptionist to Dr. Mills.
**Jared Grant,** ferryman.
**Russell Peachy,** innkeeper of Shiretown Inn.
**Frances Stewart,** day clerk, Shiretown Inn.
**Antone "Tony Cocky" Silva,** fire chief.
**Lawrence Mercier,** fireman.

**Ewing and Hewitt,** ferrymen.

**Robert Samuel, Joseph Capparella,** fishing buddies.

**Robert "Bobby" Carroll,** Democratic selectman, real estate entrepreneur, owner of the Seafood Shanty and Harbor View Hotel, and pilot of his own plane.

## Chappaquiddick Residents

**Dodie and Foster Silva,** rental agents on Chappaquiddick; unofficial watchmen.

**Sylvia Malm and daughter,** also named Sylvia, summer tenants at Dyke House, overlooking Poucha Pond and Dyke Bridge.

**Anthony "Tony" Bettencourt,** Edgartown fireman and life-long expert on tides and Poucha Pond.

## The Law, etc.

**Dominick "Jim" Arena,** chief of police, three years; thirteen-year veteran state policeman.

**Christopher "Huck" Look,** special officer for Edgartown Police and Parks Department; deputy sheriff of Dukes County, fifteen-year veteran.

**Carmen Salvador,** policewoman on telephones.

**Robert Brugier,** summer temporary Edgartown police officer.

**Dr. Robert Mills,** general medical practitioner.

Dr. Mills was one of five doctors on the island (a shortage during the summer season when the tourists and summer residents swell the population) and the associate medical examiner. On Saturday, July 19, he was standing in for the regular ME, who was having his one day a week off, making Mills the only acting medical examiner available. He was also a contract physician for the U.S. Public Health Service, medical examiner for the Federal Aviation Agency, and held various board memberships and advisory positions. He had served with the Army Medical Corps in the Pacific and was an experienced medical examiner who had seen numerous drowning victims.

**David Guay,** licensed funeral director and embalmer.

**Eugene Frieh,** licensed funeral director and embalmer.

**Dun Gifford,** lawyer, Kennedy legislative aide.

**Walter Steele,** forty-three years old, Boston lawyer. He had been for fourteen years a top assistant in the Boston District Attorney's office. Had been for six weeks Dukes County special prosecutor, a part-time job. The position was a recent creation. He was also an attorney in private practice.

**John Farrar,** manager of the Turf 'N Tackle Shop, captain of the Edgartown Volunteer Fire Department and head of the Scuba Search and Rescue Division. While an experienced diver, Farrar had only recently become diver for the fire department.

**Edmund Dinis,** District Attorney, Southern District of Massachusetts. His district included Barnstable, Bristol, Nantucket, and Dukes counties. He was reputed to be a brilliant but erratic attorney whose mouth was a natural resting place for his foot.

**Lieutenant George Killen,** Massachusetts State Police; District Attorney Dinis's chief investigator. Killen had cracked the case of serial killer Tony Costa and was, at the time of the Chappaquiddick incident, still involved in developing the case for the prosecution. His duties included more than just investigating the suspect and gathering evidence; one of his most important duties was attempting to keep Dinis from giving incorrect information to the press.

**Lieutenant Bernie Flynn,** Massachusetts State Police, Killen's chief assistant. He was also still deeply involved in the Tony Costa case.

**Judge James A. Boyle,** justice of the District Court.

**Judge Wilfred J. Pacquet,** justice of the Circuit Court.

**Leslie M. Leland,** grand jury foreman.

**Antone "Tony" Costa,** accused murderer of four women,

held in Provincetown jail. At the time, the Costa case was the most important case on the docket in southern Massachusetts. The four young women had not been just murdered; they had been hung in trees and partially skinned and partially gutted before being buried in two graves close together. The prosecution was trying to develop leads, handle the media, and make sure they had a case that would keep Tony Costa off the streets permanently.

## The Party

**Edward Moore Kennedy.**

**Jack Crimmins,** sixty-three, general factotem and Kennedy's frequent driver; retired legal aide and investigator for the state police. He had a small house behind Gargan's at Hyannis Port.

**Paul Markham,** thirty-nine, former U.S. Attorney for Massachusetts, Assistant U.S. Attorney under Robert Kennedy. He was a close friend of the Kennedys, socialized with them, sailed with them, played touch football at the Kennedy compound.

**Joseph Gargan,** thirty-nine, lawyer and hanger-on, first cousin to Senator Kennedy. Former assistant U.S. Attorney in Boston.

**Raymond LaRosa,** forty-one, professional fireman, Massachusetts Civil Defense Officer.

**Charles C. Tretter,** thirty, counsel, Northeast Regional Commission. Served as a constituent aide to Kennedy from 1963 to 1966.

**Mary Jo Kopechne.**

**Esther Newburgh,** twenty-six, employed as a special assistant to the president of the Urban Institute in Washington. She had worked for Senator Abraham Ribicoff of Connecticut before moving to Kennedy's staff in 1968. She was efficient and down to earth.

**Rosemary Keough,** twenty-three, worked at the Children's

Foundation, a Kennedy project, in Washington. She had
worked as a campaign volunteer for John Kennedy and went
straight into Robert Kennedy's office on her graduation from
Manhattanville College in 1967.

**Maryellen Lyons,** twenty-seven, administrative assistant to
Massachusetts State Senator Beryl Cohen. Devotee of Ted
Kennedy.

**Anne "Nance" Lyons,** twenty-six, sister of Maryellen. At
the time of the party, she was the only one of the women
working for Ted Kennedy. She had been a volunteer in 1962
and 1964. She was a legislative aide, drafting bills for Ted.
Robert had borrowed her from Ted to work in the boiler
room. Later she had gone on detached service to help set up
Hubert Humphrey's boiler room. Helped run fund-raising
dinners to pay off the RFK campaign deficit, then returned to
routine duties in Ted Kennedy's Senate office.

**Susan Tannenbaum,** twenty-four, worked on the staff of
Representative Allard Lowenstein of New York. She had
worked for Robert Kennedy starting in 1967.

### Present in Edgartown

**Joseph Kennedy III,** student, nephew of Ted Kennedy, son
of the late Robert, present in Edgartown for the regatta.

### Damage Control in Hyannis Port

**Burke Marshall,** Kennedy's personal attorney, a member of
the bar of the District of Columbia but not Massachusetts,
and former Assistant U.S. Attorney under Robert Kennedy.
**Judge Robert Clark, Jr.,** a Kennedy family attorney in Mas-
sachusetts and former district court judge in Massachusetts.
**Robert Clark III,** his son, also a Massachusetts attorney.
**Richard J. McCarron,** Edgartown attorney.
**Robert McNamara,** president of the International Bank for
Reconstruction and Development; former chairman, Ford Motor

Company; former Secretary of Defense in the John Kennedy administration.

**Theodore Sorensen,** former Harvard teacher, author, Kennedy speechwriter, and hanger-on.

**Kenneth O'Donnell,** old friend and advisor of Robert's; Ted's Senate campaign manager.

**David Hackett,** football player with Bobby at college, campaign worker for Bobby. He had been instrumental in setting up previous thank-you parties for the boiler room staff.

**David Burke,** Kennedy's administrative assistant.

**John Tunney,** U.S. Congressman from California, son of Gene Tunney, world heavyweight boxing champion.

**John Culver,** longtime friend of Ted and U.S. Congressman from Iowa.

**Stephen Smith,** Kennedy's brother-in-law and president of the Park Agency, the Kennedy family holding company.

**Sargent Shriver,** another Kennedy brother-in-law, and a member of the Kennedy political machine.

**Milton Gwirtzman,** lawyer and speechwriter, overall Kennedy liaison on Ted's Senate staff.

**Frank O'Connor,** Kennedy assistant.

**Richard Goodwin,** lawyer, special assistant to President Kennedy.

Also present at the Hyannis Port compound during the week following the accident were Joan Kennedy, Joseph P. Kennedy, Jacqueline Kennedy Onassis, Rose Kennedy, Rita Dallas (nurse to Joseph), and Joe Gargan's sister Ann; Joe Gargan and Paul Markham arrived with Kennedy or shortly thereafter.

Arriving before Kennedy's nationwide television address were Jean Kennedy Smith, Eunice Kennedy Shriver, and Patricia Kennedy Lawford; all were in the room during the address. Also in the house were members of the next generation: Joseph III, Robert, Jr., and Bobby Shriver.

# THE 1967 OLDSMOBILE

The exact model was an "88," also called a Delmont that year. A four-door sedan, it was a midsize family car. It was over eighteen feet long, six and a half feet wide, and four feet seven and a half inches tall. The wheel base was 123 inches, the distance between the wheels was 63 inches. It weighed in at just over two tons. New, it had cost $3,600 to $3,700.

Like most 1967 cars, it was a far cry from anything we drive today. It was larger than any car on the road now except a Grosser Mercedes or a stretch limousine. The turning radius was over forty feet.

It had none of the safety equipment we associate with even the cheapest car today. Seat belts and headrests had not been installed. Dual braking systems, energy-absorbing bumpers, energy-absorbing front end, door reinforcements, roof supports (roll bars), and even side lights were innovations not yet required.

For a car with a trunk that would sleep six, the leg room in the rear seat was surprisingly small.

# THE SITE

Southeast of Boston, Cape Cod thrusts into the sea. The Cape and the two major islands to its south, Martha's Vineyard and Nantucket, were formed of an underlayment of glacial moraine and alluvial clays and were given a final shaping, like most of the barrier islands from there to Florida, by confluences of the Labrador current and the Gulf Stream. Currents sweeping the small peninsulas of Martha's Vineyard and Chappaquiddick into right angles with themselves left ponds as small bays or sounds between the beaches and the main parts of the islands.

The Labrador current sweeps the coast north and east to Boston, keeping it rocky and harsh. The long, beckoning arm of Cape Cod is the first of the great sandy capes of the Atlantic coast and, some argue, the greatest. It protects the shore, moderating the effects of dangerous storms on the mainland. Though Cape Cod is not naturally an island, the Cape Cod Canal, part of the Inland Waterway that cuts through between Cape Cod Bay and Buzzards Bay, has detached Cape Cod from the mainland.

The cold Labrador current moderates temperatures along the coast of New England and as far south as Delaware. The water in the Gulf of Maine seldom exceeds 50 degrees Fahrenheit, and then not until August. The cool summers attract hordes of summer visitors and residents, called "summer people" by the permanent residents.

Due south of Cape Cod are the two large offshore islands of Martha's Vineyard and Nantucket. Both can be reached by ferry and air from Cape Cod. Summer ferries run from Hyannis Port to both islands. The year-round auto ferry runs from Woods Hole to Vineyard Haven and Oak Bluffs on the north shore of Martha's Vineyard, then on to Nantucket. A passenger ferry runs from Falmouth Heights to Oak Bluffs, and a summer-only passenger ferry from Hyannis Port also puts in at Oak Bluffs. Oak Bluffs is now home to a state police barracks.

The airport on Martha's Vineyard is at about the middle of the island, on the edge of the state forest. It is about six miles west of Edgartown.

Edgartown, Massachusetts is a small fishing village/summer resort situated at the eastern end of Martha's Vineyard proper. It is a very pretty town, though quite small, and Shiretown Inn, where most of the men of the Kennedy party had rooms, is about a block from the ferry landing.

Due south of Edgartown is a new "town" called Katama,

named for Katama Bay, which it overlooks. Before development, Katama was traditionally used for beach parties. It is now mostly resort facilities, motels and restaurants and the supporting businesses. The six women included in the party were staying at Katama Shores Motel, a new structure there.

Due east of a line from Edgartown to Katama is a smaller offshore island called Chappaquiddick, which means "Refuge Island" in Wampanoag. During the winter in 1969, only seven people lived there. During summer, more Edgartown residents moved there, and summer people arrived. Some stayed all season, some only a week, some only a few days. All reached the island by private boat or by way of the small car ferry that runs from early morning to about midnight.

The road system on "Chappy" was a scant network. The pavement formed a Z starting at the ferry and going along Chappaquiddick Road to the intersection with Schoolhouse Road. Chappaquiddick Road became Dyke Road and continued, graveled with dirt shoulders, east and over the Dyke Bridge. At the time of the accident, there were no lights on the road or the bridge. The bridge was wood, 10 feet 6 inches wide and 81 feet long. It was at an angle to the road, making a left-hand bend of about 27 degrees going toward the ocean. There were no guard rails, only "rub rails" about 4 inches high resembling curbing. Schoolhouse Road ran paved from the intersection (Cemetery Road was the unpaved continuation of Schoolhouse Road that ran north from the intersection to Cape Pogue Bay) south to its intersection with Wasque Road.

Schoolhouse Road continued unpaved to the shore of Katama Bay. Wasque Road ran east toward Poucha Pond, but the paving gave out before it reached the water. Wasque Road was called Litchfield Road where it ran, unpaved, back west and north to the ferry from Schoolhouse Road.

The Lawrence Cottage, owned by a Scarsdale, New York, lawyer, stood about halfway along the paved section of Schoolhouse Road. The cottage was a one-story structure with a living room, two bedrooms, one bath with a tub, a kitchen, and an outbuilding locked against renters. There were only two beds in the house and a sofa that could be made into a bed. The only person who planned to stay overnight on Chappaquiddick Island was Crimmins, Kennedy's driver and helper. Directly across the road was a tiny firehouse, unmanned but with a lighted emergency button on it. Next to the Lawrence Cottage was the house occupied for the summer by Foster and Dodie Silva. The Silvas moved out to their cottage every summer and served as "resident managers" for several of the rental cottages on the island, including the Lawrence Cottage. Down the dirt extension of Chappaquiddick Road, called Dyke Road, were the cottages occupied by the Sylvias Malm, mother and daughter, and the Smiths. Both overlooked Poucha Pond.

Poucha Pond is a channel that runs north and south from Cape Pogue Bay at the north to a blind wide spot at the south. It is long and narrow, not a pond but an impoundment of tidal flow. At one time there was a dike separating the saltwater bay from the freshwater impoundment, and the Dyke (from the old spelling) Bridge crosses the narrow channel that was cut to join them. When the tide runs, all of Cape Pogue Bay tries to get into Poucha Pond and then back out again, with particular speed and force right under the bridge.

The whole New England coast is ruled by the summer season, and the residents resent it.

The great Triangular Trade—rum to Africa for slaves, slaves to the Caribbean for sugar, sugar to New England to be made into rum—died long ago.

The days when Herman Melville sailed out for unnamed whales under an Edgartown skipper are the stuff of legend and literature.

Fishing isn't what it used to be. The great schools of cod no longer rule the oceans, and the fortunes that were made in fish are now invested in other sources of income or lost. The golden cod that overlooks a pulpit in Boston is a relic of the past. Summer people are now the main source of new income.

When summer comes, the rates go up. Summer is so short, and money so scarce, that the permanent residents have to make it while they can. They gouge the summer people whom they hold in such contempt.

Martha's Vineyard isn't unique. In 1969 the winter income for people along the entire New England coast averaged $25 per month. Many other resort areas around the world have the same problems. The season is the season, and you make as much money as you can while it lasts so that starvation and repossession don't overtake you out of season.

The Kennedys may have ruled Boston. They may have had time in grade in Hyannis. At Edgartown they were just summer people and, by definition, nuisances.

# CHRONOLOGY I: JULY 16-19, 1969

## WEDNESDAY, JULY 16

**9:32 A.M.**

*Apollo 11* with astronauts Neil Armstrong, Michael Collins, and Buzz Aldrin lifts off from Cape Kennedy, Florida, to fulfill the inaugural promise made by Ted's brother John F. Kennedy in 1961 to put a man on the moon within the decade.

Some time during the day, Jack Crimmins arrives at Edgartown in Kennedy's black 1967 Oldsmobile 88. He has booked three rooms at Katama Shores Motel and uses one of them that night.

Also during this day, serial killer Tony Costa is being interviewed in Provincetown by a panel of psychiatrists.

# THURSDAY, JULY 17

### Afternoon

Young Joe Kennedy checks into Dogett House with a friend. The owner sees him and, because Kennedy is young, insists that he leave. When young Kennedy asks the owner's son about the towels they used, he is told not to worry about it. They are not charged for the room.

Four young women arrive in Edgartown for the rooms Crimmins had booked: Esther Newburgh, Rosemary Keough, Susan Tannenbaum, and Mary Jo Kopechne. They are driven in by Charles Tretter, who then goes over to Shiretown Inn and checks in. Newberg and Keough sign the register at Katama Shores, Tannenbaum and Kopechne do not. The four of them share two rooms, and Crimmins uses the third. The Lyons sisters do not arrive until Friday.

Jack Crimmins buys steaks, hors d'oeuvres, and other tidbits for the party. He has previously purchased, at sale prices in Boston, the following alcoholic supplies: three half-gallons of vodka, four fifths of scotch, two bottles of rum (size unspecified), and several cases of canned beer. He planned to keep the leftovers for his own use at home.

### Evening

Newburgh, Keough, Tannenbaum, and Kopechne stroll around Edgartown, dine quietly on seafood, visit the cottage on Chappaquiddick, and retire to Katama Shores early.

### Late Night

Young Joe is seen at Seafood Shanty, an inexpensive restaurant.

# FRIDAY, JULY 18

Joe Gargan had originally rented a small cottage, Lawrence Cottage, for a vacation with his wife and family. His wife's mother was taken ill, and he volunteered the use of the cottage for the party.

Gargan had also booked three rooms at the Shiretown Inn for the following people: Senator Kennedy and himself, who were sharing a room; Charles Tretter, Raymond LaRosa, John P. Driscoll, Harry Carr, and Ross Richards. Paul Markham was to stay at Lawrence Cottage on Friday night with Jack Crimmins, who gave up his room at Katama Shores for the Lyons sisters. Driscoll, Carr, and Richards did not attend the party at the Lawrence Cottage.

### 3:00 A.M.

Young Joe Kennedy is in attendance at a party on Norton Street. A local policewoman is also at the party.

### Midmorning

The Lyons sisters arrive at Katama Shores and take the third room booked by Crimmins.

### 12:10 P.M.

The junior heat of the regatta starts with young Joe at the helm of the *Resolute*.

The young women change into swimsuits at Katama Shores, and all six pile into the Oldsmobile, which Crimmins drives to Chappaquiddick and the Lawrence Cottage. They are then driven over the Dyke Bridge to the beach to swim.

### 1:00 P.M.

Ted Kennedy arrives at Martha's Vineyard airport. Crimmins picks him up and drives him to Edgartown. They take the ferry to

Chappaquiddick at about 1:20, and they both get into a car on the Chappy side. Ted is a passenger, not the driver.

Ted is driven to the Lawrence Cottage, changes, and is driven over Dyke Road and the Dyke Bridge to the beach where the young women are swimming. To get there, Crimmins drives Kennedy down Schoolhouse Road, turns right onto the dirt road, and crosses the Dyke Bridge. It is broad daylight.

After the swimming party, the women return to Katama Shores to change. They are next seen at 3:00 P.M. Kennedy was driven and ferried back to Edgartown.

### 2:50 P.M.

The senator starts the race at the helm of the *Victura*, his brother Jack's old boat, with Joe Gargan as crew.

### 3:00 P.M.

Six young women show up at *Bonnie Lisa* and tell Manuel Francis DeFrates, the skipper, to chase the *Victura*. Someone the others refer to as "Mary Jo" says she's a friend of Gargan's.

### 4:00 P.M. or so

Paul Markham pays DeFrates for the boat charter.

### 5:00 P.M. or so

Kennedy and company return to the Shiretown Inn and sit around talking on an upstairs porch. Eight to twelve men consume about eight beers. Joe Gargan and Jack Driscoll are among the crowd.

### 6:00 P.M.

Charles Tretter goes into Edgartown for more party supplies.

### 7:00 P.M.

Kennedy and Gargan cross to Chappaquiddick. Gargan drives back to the ferry to pick up more guests.

The party begins. Gargan lights the charcoal and starts preparing hors d'oeuvres. The men prepare and grill the steaks in shifts, because there isn't enough room on the grill to cook them all at once.

The party develops into storytelling, joking, and singing.

**8:00 P.M.**

Tretter returns with his supplies to find the party going strong.

**10:00 P.M.**

Joe Kennedy and friends make a date with several waitresses at the Colonial Inn.

Tretter and Rosemary Keough return from a trip to Edgartown in the Oldsmobile to pick up a portable radio. Keough leaves her handbag in the car.

Dodie remarks to Foster Silva, "Boy, they must be having a heck of a time. I hope they don't wreck the place."

**10:30 P.M.**

In Edgartown, the waitresses join Joe and friends for drinks after work. Joe's group now totals eight or ten young men and women.

**11:15 P.M.**

Kennedy, claiming to be tired, gets the keys to the Oldsmobile from Crimmins. Mary Jo Kopechne says she doesn't feel well and asks Kennedy to drive her back to Katama.

*Kennedy says he drove down Main Street, turned right onto Dyke Road, and drove off the bridge. He further states that he saw no one, that no one saw him. He says he dove on the wreck several times without success, then walked, trotted, and stumbled back to the cottage. He then had Gargan and Markham take him back to the bridge, all of this taking a little over an hour.*

**11:30 P.M.**

Low tide in Poucha Pond. Raymond LaRosa, the Lyons sisters, and Susan Tannenbaum take a walk, going away from the ferry. Esther Newburgh stays inside.

Tretter and Keough go for a walk. It must have been a long one, because they apparently didn't return until after 2:00. (See below.)

### Just Before Midnight

The Malms hear a car go past, traveling fairly fast. They hear no splash.

Joe Kennedy and friends go to a dance at the yacht club.

### Midnight

The yacht club dance ends and Joe and his friends leave. Miss Malm turns out her light, and the Malms to go sleep.

# SATURDAY, JULY 19

**12:20 A.M.**

*Kennedy claims to see the "clock in the Valiant" saying twelve-twenty, as Markham and Gargan were diving on the wreck to see if they could do anything to help Mary Jo. Kennedy's statement goes on to say that Gargan and Markham were busily diving on the wreck for some forty-five minutes.*

**12:30 A.M.**

Deputy Look takes the yacht club launch over to Chappaquiddick, where he lives during summer months. He picks up his personal car.

LaRosa takes another walk, with just the Lyons sisters, this time toward the ferry. Shortly after they leave the cottage, they are passed by a car that slows but does not stop, also going toward the ferry.

### 12:45 A.M.

Look sees a black car with a man, a woman, and a shadow (in the back) drive onto Cemetery Road. When he approaches, it backs out, turns, and goes down Dyke Road. He makes a mental note of a partial license tag: L7 _____ 7.

Look next encounters a man and two women on foot and asks if he can help. One of the women, thinking he was trying to pick them up, makes a remark and the man apologizes for it. Look then drives on home.

Joe's party goes to the Shiretown Inn for a couple of drinks; then they borrow a rowboat and row around the harbor for a little while.

### 1:00 A.M.

Foster Silva's dogs bark. He goes out to check on them, and hears singing from the Lawrence Cottage. Silva's dogs bark only at pedestrians; they never bark for any other reason.

### 1:20 A.M.

Jared Grant leaves the ferry for the night, one hour and twenty minutes later than his usual midnight closing. It was Regatta weekend and the steamer from Woods Hole has docked late. He has stayed on for possible late arrivals. He really didn't mind because rates trebled after midnight.

### 1:30 A.M.

Joe and party return the borrowed boat, and two of the waitresses they were with retire for the night. Joe and the other two girls start a "slow stroll" around the town.

Silva's dogs bark again.

### 2:00 A.M.

*Kennedy says he swam the five hundred feet across Edgartown Channel about this time (or somewhat earlier). He dove in before Gargan and Markham could stop him, not considering his exhaustion. It took a maximum of eight to ten minutes.*

Tretter and Keough return to find the cottage apparently deserted except for Crimmins, who is asleep in one of the small bedrooms. Neither car is there. Tretter had seen the Valiant pass him, going toward the ferry, while they walked. They then start to walk to the ferry, but give up and return to the cottage. On the way back, they see the Valiant pass them going back to the cottage. It is standing in the yard when they arrive.

**2:15** A.M.

Markham and Gargan return to the cottage.

Joe Kennedy and his friends are asked to leave the area of the Shiretown Inn. They do, and go to Harbor View Hotel to sneak a swim.

**2:25** A.M.

Ted Kennedy, appearing to be calm and sober, goes out onto the balcony of his room at Shiretown Inn and asks Russ Peachy, the innkeeper, the time.

**3:00** A.M.

Young Joe takes the last two waitresses back to their rooms and a little later is spotted alone by an old buddy.

**5:30** A.M.

High tide in Poucha Pond, eleven feet.

# 4

*After the Party*

---

## CHRONOLOGY II: JULY 19, 1969-MAY 27, 1970

---

### SATURDAY, JULY 19

**7:00 A.M.**

Robert Samuel and Joseph Capparella arrive at the ferry landing and cross to Chappaquiddick. They are looking for good fishing.

**7:15 A.M. or so**

Samuel and Capparella cross the Dyke Bridge and notice nothing. The tide is running out heavily. They cross over to the beach and try surf fishing but catch nothing.

**7:52 A.M.**

First recorded telephone call on Kennedy's credit card. This telephone call was not reported until 1980, although Kennedy testified that he had made a phone call "shortly after eight" to

David Burke. He was looking for his brother-in-law, Stephen Smith, who was out of the country, and Burke had the telephone number where Smith could be reached. He may also have been trying to find the Kopechnes' telephone number then or later.

### 8:00 A.M. (approximately)

Ted Kennedy borrows a dime from Frances Stewart, day clerk at the Shiretown Inn, to use the telephone. He is dressed in "knockabout," slightly faded, workmanlike yachting clothes: polo shirt, sneakers, and summer pants. When Mrs. Stewart inquired as to how he had placed in the previous day's race, he couldn't really remember. He thought he placed sixth or seventh. She found his handshake to be weak, his hand cold and clammy. Other witnesses say his handshake was weak, and he seemed calm but preoccupied.

Tretter, Keough, Tannenbaum, Markham, and Gargan take the Valiant to the ferry, cross, and walk to the Shiretown Inn. Markham and Gargan do not tell the others about the accident.

Tretter looks for the keys to LaRosa's car in the room they share so he can drive the women back to Katama Shores. He doesn't find them.

Gargan and Markham collect Kennedy from the hotel lobby and return to his room.

### 8:15 A.M. OR SO

Samuel and Capparella, having given up surf fishing and started back to town, cross the bridge again and spot the submerged car, which is bottom up in the water. They stop at the first house they come to and knock on Sylvia Malm's door. Mrs. Malm calls the police.

### 8:20 A.M.

The call from Mrs. Malm comes in to the police station. Jim Arena, chief of police, answers the call at the station, then crosses to Chappaquiddick. He drives to the Dyke Bridge and tries to dive to the wreck. He has to borrow a pair of swim trunks from Mrs. Malm. Even though he is a strong swimmer, the current is so strong Arena is unable to get down far enough to determine if there is anyone in the car. He has to swim at an angle even to reach the car. To attempt a dive, Arena must hold tightly onto some part of the car that is underwater. When he manages to submerge, the current almost instantly pulls him loose from his handhold. He sees nothing but the vague outline of the car as the current tumbles him away. He is carried quite a distance from the car before he finally comes up.

Because of the strong current, when Arena calls for a face mask, he warns the civilians on shore not to attempt to row out, but says he will swim to shore for it. He decides not to try to get into the car. The tide is going out all this time and Arena is able to sit on the rear end of the car, which is still underwater, while he waits for Tony Silva.

# POSITION OF THE CAR

Midway along the bridge, rear end about twelve feet from the bridge, front end facing the bridge. Upside down.

### 8:30 A.M.

Markham, Gargan, and Kennedy return to Chappaquiddick and use the telephone booth at the ferry landing. Ferryman Ewing's son asks Kennedy if he knows about the accident.

### 8:45 A.M.

Fire Chief Antone "Tony Cocky" Silva arrives with two firemen, Lawrence Mercier and Anthony "Tony" Bettencourt; John Farrar, diver; and Edgartown policeman Robert Brugier.

By then the rear license plate on the submerged car is visible.

Arena leans over to read it and calls out the number, L 78 207, for Brugier to call in and get a registration name. It is ID'd to Edward Kennedy.

Farrar, already dressed in a wet suit, dons mask, tanks, and flippers; takes the end of a rope Arena hands him; and dives.

# CONDITION OF THE CAR

The rear window on driver's side is closed tight, the driver's side window is open. The windshield is badly cracked but still intact because of the bonding used in the glass. Both windows on the passenger side are completely broken in with only fragments of glass remaining around the edges.

Farrar sticks his head in the window and sees the body of a blonde young woman submerged, her hair floating eerily in the current.

# POSITION AND CONDITION OF THE BODY

The woman's head was in the foot well, neck craned back. The tops of her thighs were pressed against the seat, her feet jammed against the rear window. Her hands were still holding tight to the edge of the seat. Even a touch told Farrar she was in rigid rigor mortis: Her flesh was rock-hard.

Farrar has a difficult time getting the body out of the car: The body is so stiff that he has to maneuver her out carefully around the obstacles and through the smashed window. Because of the strong current, Farrar secures the rope around the body's neck so it would not wash out to sea. He then guides it to the surface to wait for the medical examiner's arrival.

# THE BODY'S ATTIRE

Black slacks, white long-sleeved blouse. All buttons buttoned, very neat. A chain belt had been fastened around the waist, but had dropped off when the body was raised. The woman was also wearing sandals and three gold bangle bracelets. Under her blouse, she was wearing a dressy blue bra. She was not wearing panties.

# FOUND IN THE CAR

A handbag containing odds and ends, a U.S. Senate pass and an automobile registration in the name of Rosemary Keough, and two keys to Katama Shores motel. The ID items lead to some confusion about the victim's identity.

**9:00 A.M.**

Medical Examiner Dr. Mills hears about the drowning from Mrs. Teller, his receptionist, then gets the official call to come over. At that time, he had a patient in labor at the hospital and had planned to go over and attend her, but heads for Chappaquiddick instead.

Gargan goes to the cottage and informs Crimmins, LaRosa, and the women who are there of the accident. He then drives the women to the ferry, leaving LaRosa and Crimmins to tidy up the cottage.

### 9:30 A.M.

Tony Bettencourt goes to the ferry to fetch Dr. Mills. He sees Kennedy and two other men near the telephone booth and tells him about the girl in the car.

*Kennedy says he telephoned Burke Marshall, his attorney and longtime friend, from here.*

Dr. Mills arrives with undertakers Frieh and Guay. They had met at the ferry. Rather than take two vehicles on the tiny boat, Dr. Mills had gotten into the undertakers' wagon.
The tires and bumper of the submerged car begin to emerge.

### 9:45 A.M.

Ted Kennedy is told about the accident one more time by Dick Hewitt, deckhand on the ferry.

### 10:05 A.M.

Kennedy calls the police station and is patched through to Jim Arena by radio telephone. Arena tells Kennedy to meet him at the Edgartown police station. Kennedy takes the ferry back to Edgartown.
Dr. Mills examines the body on the beach.

# MEDICAL EXAMINER'S FINDINGS

Female, late twenties. There was white foam around the mouth and nose and a webbing of blood at the nose. The body was totally rigid. External examination showed no abrasions, no broken bones, fingernails intact and neatly manicured, a small bruise on one upper arm. Palpation of the abdomen showed the uterus to be normal, no enlargement. Palpation of the rib cage brings up water. One of the undertakers thought it came from the stomach, but Mills said he was pressing on the rib cage and the water was from the lungs. He remarked, "Why, she's the most drowned person I've ever seen." When the body is tipped over to check the back for abrasions, more water gushes forth.

He reports no swelling or abrasion on the head.

(Later, back at the mortuary, Frieh put the body over the barrel used to compress water from the lungs of drowning victims and was surprised that no more than a cupful or so came out.) A blood sample was taken and later tests revealed a blood alcohol level of .09 percent. Semen tests on her clothing were negative.

### 10:30 A.M. (approximately)

Kennedy and Markham arrive at the Edgartown police station and begin using both telephone lines. Gargan goes off to tell the others what happened.

Arena arrives at the police station. During a conversation with Kennedy, he learns that Kennedy was the driver, the girl wasn't Rosemary Keough after all but Mary Jo Kopechne (which, since Kennedy didn't know how to spell it, Arena jotted down as Copachini), and that her parents had already been notified. Arena puts Kennedy and Markham into a small room so that Kennedy could write a statement. Arena then calls Inspector George Kennedy, supervisor of the Registry of Motor Vehicles in Oak Bluffs.

### 10:57 A.M.

The telephone calls charged to Kennedy's credit card begin.

Kennedy calls David Burke, "four or five times" according to Burke; Mrs. Onassis's house at Hyannis Port; Burke Marshall; and others. These telephone calls were never a secret.

Approximately sixteen telephone calls on the list of charged calls were introduced as evidence at the inquest. The calls include the first call to Mrs. Kopechne in New Jersey. Kennedy got her number from Burke during one of the earlier calls.

### 11:00 A.M.

Lawyer Walter Steele arrives at the Edgartown police station. Arena asks him to stick around awhile in case he's needed.

George Kennedy and an assistant, Inspector Molla, arrive at the police station and accompany Arena back to Chappaquiddick.

Back at the bridge, when the wrecker tries to pull the car out, it starts to swing toward the bridge because of the strong current. The wrecking crew decides to wait until slack tide, only a half hour away, to pull the car in.

### 11:30 A.M.

Slack (low) tide in Poucha Pond. Six feet of water.

The car is pulled out and righted.

Deputy Sheriff Huck Look arrives at the scene and identifies the car as the one he saw the night before.

Arena calls off the search of Poucha Pond because he now knows that no one else was in the car when it went into the water.

# MORE ON THE CONDITION OF THE CAR

There was glass all over the floor of the car. The door on the driver's side was locked; the headlight switch was in "on" position, the gear shift lever was in "drive," and the ignition key was turned to "on." There was a hairbrush on the seat, old and battered. A copy of the *Boston Globe* for Friday, July 18, 1969, was on the driver's seat. In the glove compartment were a package of tissues, an automobile registration for the 1967 Oldsmobile 88 sedan made out to Edward M. Kennedy, and a few papers. The right side was caved in between the door supports; the edges of doors buckled outward beyond the supports. The front of the roof was dented "downward" and, judging from the breakage pattern, caused the windshield breakage. There were some scratches across the front edge of the hood and front fenders.

# THE ACCIDENT SITE

Inspectors Kennedy and Molla investigate the scene. Kennedy finds skid marks starting at the edge of the bridge and on the dirt and continuing straight to the right and over. The skid marks are five feet apart. One skid mark measures 18 feet; the other 33 feet 2 inches; both went straight over the bridge. There are gouges in the "rub rail," curblike planks 10 inches wide and 4 inches high that were the only barriers at the edge of the bridge.

Arena then returns to Edgartown.

Markham and Steele go to Senator Kennedy's hotel room at the Shiretown Inn and strip it. A young man who looks like a Kennedy asks if he can help.

### Noonish

The second heat of the regatta starts without either Kennedy racing.

Arena asks Bobby Carroll, Democratic selectman and owner of the Harbor View Hotel, if Carroll can fly the Kennedy party out of town in his plane, a Piper Comanche. Registry Inspector Robert Molla drives Kennedy and Markham to the airport. On the drive to the airport, Kennedy keeps asking "What happened?" He is confused and seems depressed. Molla hears these disjointed questions but doesn't have a clear idea what is going on, and has no idea why the atmosphere is so gloomy. The flight is silent. Carroll lands Kennedy and Markham at Hyannis and returns to Martha's Vineyard.

The reporters have descended on Edgartown and are making it very difficult for anyone, including Arena and Dr. Mills, to get on with either the case or their own other concerns—in the case of Dr. Mills, a busy general medical practice.

*Hyannis Port*

Damage Control begins to assemble even before Kennedy arrives. Burke Marshall, who had been at Waltham, Massachusetts, and Dick Goodwin, a Bobby Kennedy aide, arrive first. The house belonging to Jacqueline Onassis (formerly Mrs. John Kennedy) is used as headquarters.

When Ted Kennedy calls his girlfriend Helga Wagner in California, his wife Joan picks up an extension telephone, thus learning about the accident. Ted breaks the news of the accident to his father.

Some time that afternoon or evening, someone finally calls a doctor for the senator. Edward Kennedy is examined by Dr. Robert Watt and found to have suffered "a half inch abrasion and hematoma over the right mastoid, a contusion of the vertex, spasm of the posterior cervical musculature, tenderness of the lumbar area, a big spongy swelling on the top of his head." Impairment of judgment and confused behavior are consistent with such injuries. Taken together, they constitute serious injury.

Dr. Watt also takes subjective history from the patient. Patient describes retrograde amnesia and current confusion.

The diagnosis is concussion, contusions and abrasions of the scalp, acute cervical strain.

Dr. Watt prescribes a neck brace, a muscle relaxant, heat, and bed rest. The advisors were present at the examination.

*Edgartown*

Gargan pays off DeFrates for the unused charter of his boat for Saturday.

Dr. Mills calls the police barracks at Oak Bluffs. He asks a trooper to call District Attorney Dinis's office in New Bedford and ask whether an autopsy is necessary. He repeats the message to make sure the trooper understands it.

A trooper calls back with a message from Lieutenant George Killen, the DA's chief investigator. Killen is deeply involved in the investigation of Tony Costa, the serial killer. His message to the medical examiner is that if Mills is satisfied that the cause of death is drowning and there's no evidence of foul play, there is no need to do an autopsy. A request for a routine blood sample was relayed as well.

Dr. Mills immediately calls Frieh and tells him to go ahead and embalm. Dr. Mills then responds to an emergency call from one of his patients.

Killen calls Chief Arena. Killen asks if Arena sees any reason for an autopsy. Arena is satisfied that if Dr. Mills thought it was a drowning, then it probably was. He has no further reason to request an autopsy. Killen's closing words lead Arena to think that the case was all his and didn't belong in Dinis's office.

Local prosecutor Steele and Chief Arena check the Massachusetts law and discover that leaving the scene of an accident is a crime in the Commonwealth of Massachusetts. Steele asks Arena if he has notified Dinis, and Arena says no, only Killen. Steele insists that Arena notify Dinis directly, even though it's a Saturday.

When Dinis is told that Kennedy signed a statement, he says his office is taking over the case completely.

Killen calls Arena again, to tell him to go ahead and handle it, that he (Killen) has talked to the DA and it's okay.

Steele studies the medical examiner's statute and later calls Killen back. Killen is unenthusiastic about the whole case and gives the impression he doesn't want to be bothered.

Steele says that they (Steele and Arena) have done all they could do, and the DA's office wants no part of it.

Crimmins and LaRosa leave the cottage cleaned and neat, and take away two full bottles of vodka, three full bottles of scotch, and most of the beer. In inquest testimony, Crimmins stated there were some partial bottles that were either discarded or taken away, but the disposition isn't clear.

## Late Afternoon

*Edgartown*
Foster Silva, the real estate agent, finds the cottage orderly and neat. All the glasses are washed; no empty bottles or trash is left around.

Tony Bettencourt, burning trash at the dump on Chappaquiddick, notices three *unopened* bottles of gin. There is no evidence that the gin came from the Lawrence Cottage. It was found in the dump.

Someone checks out all parties from Katama Shores.

David Guay, undertaker, and Dun Gifford, one of Senator Kennedy's aides, bring a death certificate to Dr. Mills to sign. Gifford says he's seeing that the body is flown to Pennsylvania that afternoon.

## 11:30 P.M.

*Edgartown*
Chief Arena has written out the citation on Kennedy for leaving the scene of an accident. He goes home after telling the night shift that he is taking his phone off the hook and that if they really need him, they will have to knock on his door.

# SUNDAY, JULY 20

## Morning

*Edgartown*
The news breaks, and the reporters continue to converge on the town.

Dr. Mills is besieged by telephone calls. Among them was a technician reporting on Mary Jo's blood alcohol level: 0.09 percent. Other tests showed negative for barbiturates or organic bases (heroin and cocaine) and a carbon monoxide level of less than 5 percent.

### 10:00 A.M.

Dinis calls Killen to have him order an autopsy. Killen informs Dinis that the body has been flown out. However, it has not actually left the airport.

### Noon

Chief Arena arrives at the police station.

### 12:30 P.M.

Mary Jo Kopechne's body was scheduled to leave Martha's Vineyard airport at this time.

### Afternoon

Dr. Mills calls Killen to get some help handling the press. Killen tells him that if reporters keep bothering Mills, to hang up on them. He seems not to hear a request for help with the phones. Killen still indicates that Dinis's office doesn't want to get involved.

#### Hyannis Port

Gargan is talking to his sister when Rita Dallas, Joseph Kennedy's nurse, notices that he is moving stiffly and asks him about it. He says he hurt his arm diving for Mary Jo.

Little if anything else happens here that day. Perhaps those present were watching the moon landing.

### 4:00 P.M. (approximately)

#### Moon

"The *Eagle* has landed." The lunar module touches down to a soft landing on the moon's surface. The landing site is called

Tranquility Base. At that time the moon certainly was more tranquil than Edgartown or Hyannis Port.

**8:56 P.M.**

Neil Armstrong steps off the end of the ladder from the *Eagle*, saying "That's one small step for man, one giant leap for mankind." The event is broadcast live worldwide.

Television and radio are focused nonstop on the moon landing. Only the print media are covering Chappaquiddick with any enthusiasm, and the reporters are being kept away from the family and advisors at Hyannis Port.

# MONDAY, JULY 21

**Morning**

*Edgartown*
Jim Arena files charges of leaving the scene of an accident without reporting it against Kennedy. A Kennedy lawyer is already there.

Arena calls Killen and asks him to help out with the investigation. Killen gives the impression that he would be glad to. Arena asks Killen to visit the Hyannis compound and interview the principals.

*Hyannis Port*
Kennedy is still walking around in a daze. He makes a second telephone call to the Kopechnes, reaching Mary Jo's father, but breaks down after only a few words. The senator is unable to take part in the various meetings and councils going on. He spends much time at his own home on Squaw Island.

Kennedy and a group of advisors travel by car to Cape Cod Hospital, where Dr. Watt is joined by Dr. Brougham. X-rays and an electroencephalogram were performed and a lumbar puncture, or spinal tap, was attempted. The diagnosis is the same as

Dr. Watt's previous diagnosis: cerebral concussion, contusions and abrasions of scalp, acute cervical strain. Kennedy is fitted with a cervical collar and Watt's previous prescription of heat, rest, and oral muscle relaxants is repeated.


# TUESDAY, JULY 22

*Larksville, Pennsylvania*
Mary Jo Kopechne is buried near her birthplace four days before she would have celebrated her twenty-ninth birthday. Ted and Joan Kennedy (over the objections of Joan's doctors) are in attendance. So are Joan's old friend and sister-in-law Ethel Kennedy, Lem Billings (Kennedy hanger-on), Dave Hackett, and Dun and Bill vanden Heuvel. The Kennedys return to Hyannis Port the same day.

*Hyannis Port*
Ted Sorensen and Robert McNamara arrive to take part in the Damage Control Conference. Stephen Smith flies in from Majorca. McNamara advises them to hold a news conference and go public. This advice is not heeded, and McNamara discovers sudden business elsewhere.

For the first time in memory, the Kennedys ignore or keep away reporters. They were left outside the compound, and no Kennedy or Kennedy minion came out to them. There were no cozy chats. The Kennedy forces didn't even give any press conferences.


# WEDNESDAY, JULY 23

*Edgartown*
Local prosecutor Walter Steele reports to Arena that Killen is maintaining a strictly hands-off policy and isn't doing any of the interviews Arena asked him to do. The reporters are behaving

abominably. They are harassing not only the police and Dr. Mills, but innocent townspeople. Steele and Arena are giving twice-daily news briefings that they have no news. These are called the "Walter and Dominick Show." The reporters have nothing to report, their editors are getting upset, and they are taking it out on the locals.

### Steele's Fishing Camp

In a remote rental cabin near the fishing camp, Steele and Arena have a conference with the Clarks, Kennedy's representatives, to work out how they will proceed. Judge Clark, the senior of the father-and-son team, proposes that Kennedy would plead guilty to leaving the scene of an accident. Arena then opens the bag and types out a statement of exactly what the prosecution had.

This is perfectly normal and routine. The public could never afford for every charge filed to go to trial. We will go into more detail on this subject later. What is not normal and routine is that this conference was held at a remote fishing camp to avoid the press. The men could never have gotten anything done had they tried to hold the meeting in Edgartown.

# EVENTS DURING THAT WEEK

### Hyannis Port

In attendance at the Damage Control Conference: John Culver, U.S. congressman; John Tunney, a U.S. congressman from California (and son of Gene Tunney, boxer); Judge Robert Clark Jr. and Robert Clark III (father and son law partners and the Kennedy lawyers for this purpose); Sargent Shriver, brother-in-law; Paul Markham; Joe Gargan; Frank O'Connor, Kennedy aide; Milton Gwirtzman, liaison; and David Burke, Kennedy's administrative aide.

Burke Marshall twice telephones an expert in Massachusetts motor vehicle law.

Rita Dallas, Joseph Kennedy's nurse, expresses the opinion that Senator Kennedy should be hospitalized.

Ted Kennedy spends the week in an apparent daze, sometimes talking lucidly, then drifting off in the middle of conversations. He is very little help to Damage Control, seeming to be unable to make up his mind, finally insisting on the "guilt" theme.

Damage Control writes the television address that (it was decided after much discussion) Kennedy is to deliver live on Friday night after the hearing. Kennedy also insists that the speech be broadcast from his father's home, vetoing suggestions of Ethel's or Jacqueline's residence. (He felt that using either of those homes would make it seem that he was playing on past tragedies.) Hookups to his own Squaw Island home would be too difficult with 1969 technology.

Ted Sorensen severely scolds Markham and Gargan for failing to report the accident.

The members of the press feel hurt and betrayed. They are being treated like the enemy, even though they had always adulated and protected the Kennedy family.

# THURSDAY, JULY 24

*Martha's Vineyard Airport*
Steele and Arena meet with the Clarks to confirm the deal. Kennedy will plead guilty to leaving the scene of an accident, but no other charges will be filed against him.

*Pacific Ocean*

**12:20 P.M. (approximately)**
*Apollo 11* splashes down.

# FRIDAY, JULY 25

**8:00** A.M.

*Oak Bluffs, Martha's Vineyard*
Senator and Mrs. Kennedy and Stephen Smith arrive aboard the *Marlin*. They enter an unmarked police car and are driven to Edgartown.

**8:35** A.M.

*Edgartown*
The police car pulls up in front of the courthouse.

**9:00** A.M.

Judge Boyle enters the courtroom, greets Kennedy. Arena hands Kennedy his summons and disappears. (He will be called as a witness.)

Walter Steele arrives to prosecute the case. Kennedy pleads guilty to leaving the scene of an accident. Steele calls Arena as a witness. Several eyewitnesses later say Kennedy looks vaguely around the courtroom as if he doesn't really know what's going on. The Clarks, Kennedy's lawyers, have no questions.

The judge questions Arena as to whether there was a deliberate attempt to conceal the defendant's identity. (See appendix G on Massachusetts law.) Arena says no, there was no attempt to conceal Kennedy's identity.

The judge asks for disposition. Richard McCarron, a Martha's Vineyard attorney also representing Kennedy, starts a plea saying Kennedy has legal defenses. The judge says that is not proper unless Kennedy wishes to change his plea to "not guilty."

"I am concerned now with the question of disposition," says Judge Boyle. "Mitigating circumstances, aggravated circumstances."

McCarron tries his speech again. He pleads that Kennedy's character is well known to the world and asks for a suspended sentence.

Steele asks for two months, agrees to a suspension of the sentence.

Judge Boyle queries the probation officer. She reports that Kennedy has no criminal record.

Judge Boyle says, "Considering the unblemished record of the defendant, and the Commonwealth represents that this is not a case where he was really trying to conceal his identity . . ." "No, Sir [Steele] . . . Where it is my understanding he has already been and will continue to be punished far beyond anything this court can impose, the ends of justice would be satisfied by the imposition of the minimum jail sentence, and the suspension of that sentence, assuming the defendant accepts the suspension."

Some writers have implied that Judge Boyle was deferring to a Kennedy by asking whether he would accept the suspension of the sentence. In fact, however, note: The question of acceptance must be asked. The question is posed because all defendants have the right to accept their sentence. If a defendant accepts a sentence, he or she can appeal it. Once a defendant accepts probation, he or she cannot appeal.

McCarron agrees to accept. The clerk, as is the custom in Massachusetts, announces the finding of guilt and the sentence of two months in the House of Correction at Barnstable; sentence suspended.


**7:30 P.M.**

*Hyannis Port*
Kennedy appears on live television to tell his story. He speaks for about ten minutes, addressing the people of Massachusetts.

# SATURDAY, JULY 26

*New Bedford*
Dinis considers asking for an inquest. He also contacts Pennsylvania to see if he can get the body back to do an autopsy.

# TUESDAY, JULY 29

*Boston*
Killen accompanies a suspected accomplice in the Tony Costa case to police headquarters to undergo polygraph testing.

# WEDNESDAY, JULY 30

*Washington, D.C.*
Kennedy announces that he will continue to serve as senator and will run for reelection in 1970.

# THURSDAY, JULY 31

Kennedy returns to the Senate. He is subdued and has lost considerable weight. His voice is tremulous.

He announces that he will not be a candidate for president in the 1972 election.

*New Bedford*
District Attorney Dinis, his suspicions and political survival hackles aroused by Kennedy's speech, requests an inquest into the death of Mary Jo Kopechne.

# MONDAY, AUGUST 4

*Edgartown*
Lieutenant Killen and Bernie Flynn open an official investigation of the accident on Chappaquiddick preparatory to the inquest.

# FRIDAY, AUGUST 8

*Edgartown*
Judge Boyle, the only justice of the District Court of Dukes County, sets September 3 as the date for the inquest and announces his intention to allow legitimate and accredited members of the press to attend. He orders subpoenas issued for fifteen witnesses.

# WEDNESDAY, AUGUST 27

Kennedy, Crimmins, and Gargan petition for the right to be represented by counsel, have counsel present during the entire inquest proceeding, have counsel permitted to examine and cross-examine all witnesses and seek rulings with respect to relevancy of evidence, present evidence, and have the power of subpoena.

On the mainland, Robert A. Beaudreau, presiding Justice, Barnstable Superior Court, in the case of Tony Costa, orders impoundment of defendant statements, bill of particulars, autopsy and pathological reports, and defense request to inspect evidence, because of pretrial publicity. This action was partly the result of inflamatory statements given to the press by District Attorney Dinis at the time of Costa's arrest.

# THURSDAY, AUGUST 28

*Edgartown*
Judge Boyle rules that the due process clause has never been read into the Massachusetts inquest procedure. Witnesses will come singly into the courtroom, may be represented by counsel only to advise them against self-incrimination or on privileged communication and for no other purpose, and counsel should then leave the courtroom when the witness leaves.

# TUESDAY, SEPTEMBER 2

*Boston*
A justice of the Supreme Judicial Court of Massachusetts issues an injunction stopping the inquest until there can be a full hearing on Kennedy's, Gargan's, and Crimmins's petitions asking for a review of Judge Boyle's order setting forth the procedures for the inquest.

*Hyannis Port*
Joan Kennedy suffers a miscarriage.

# WEDNESDAY, SEPTEMBER 3

Originally scheduled date for inquest.

# THURSDAY, SEPTEMBER 18

*Wilkes-Barre, Pennsylvania*
Edmond Dinis, district attorney for the Southern District of
Massachusetts, and Robert W. Nevin, M.D., medical examiner for
Dukes County, Massachusetts, petition in Luzerne County, Penn-
sylvania, for the exhumation of the body of Mary Jo Kopechne.
The petition is ruled insufficient, and twenty days is allowed for
filing an amended petition.

# UNSPECIFIED DATE AFTER EXHUMATION REQUEST AND BEFORE INQUEST

*Washington, D.C.*
Lieutenant Bernie Flynn meets a Kennedy lawyer, Herbert J.
(Jack) Miller, Jr., at National Airport and orally tells him everything the prosecution has for the inquest. Flynn's information
can't be much more than Arena has already given the Clarks, but
no lawyer was ever hanged for being redundant.

# WEDNESDAY, SEPTEMBER 24

*Wilkes-Barre, Pennsylvania*
The Kopechne family files an opposition to the petition for
exhumation.

# WEDNESDAY, OCTOBER 8

*Boston*
Argument on the petition of Kennedy's lawyers that the inquest law of Massachusetts be enforced. (The law provides for a closed hearing.) The lawyers also asked that all witnesses be accorded the rights and protections of an accused in a criminal trial. [*Kennedy v. Justice*][1]

# MONDAY AND TUESDAY, OCTOBER 20 AND 21

*Wilkes-Barre, Pennsylvania*
The third petition for exhumation filed by Dinis actually goes to hearing.

# THURSDAY, OCTOBER 30

*Boston*
The Massachusetts Supreme Judicial Court issues the decision in *Kennedy* v. *Justice* ordering a closed inquest but denying inquest participants the rights of defendants in a criminal trial.

# TUESDAY, NOVEMBER 18

*Hyannis Port*
Joseph Patrick Kennedy, eighty-one, dies at his home.

[1]See Appendix E.

# MONDAY, DECEMBER 8

*Wilkes-Barre, Pennsylvania*
Bernard Brominski, judge of the Court of Common Pleas, Luzerne County, Pennsylvania, denies the petition for exhumation.

# THURSDAY, DECEMBER 11

*Edgartown*
Judge Boyle sets a new inquest date of January 5, 1970.

# BEFORE CHRISTMAS

*Boston*
Stephen Smith and Jack Miller are told by Lieutenant Bernie Flynn that there will be no surprises at the inquest.

# MONDAY, JANUARY 5, 1970

*Edgartown*
An inquest is convened at the Dukes County Courthouse to inquire into the death of Mary Jo Kopechne. Dinis and Killen are still in case preparation for the trial of serial killer Tony Costa and have to take valuable time from that case to deal with Kennedy.

# WEDNESDAY, FEBRUARY 18

Judge Boyle issues his report on the inquest.


# TUESDAY, MARCH 17

*Edgartown*
Leslie M. Leland, grand jury foreman in Edgartown, sends a registered letter, requesting permission to hold a special session for the purpose of investigating the death of Mary Jo Kopechne, to the chief justice of the Massachusetts Supreme Court, who denies having received it.


# THURSDAY, MARCH 26

Leland publicly displays the chief justice's signature on the postal receipt, at which time the chief justice immediately grants permission for a special session of the grand jury on April 6.


# MONDAY, APRIL 6

The grand jury convenes at Edgartown.
Judge Wilfred J. Pacquet addresses the grand jury for ninety minutes. During this extraordinary address he informs them that they are only an appendage of his court, they may not have access to the inquest testimony, they may question no witnesses who appeared at the inquest, and they have no recourse to appeal to any higher court or authority. (We will go into this at greater length later.)

# TUESDAY, APRIL 7

*Edgartown*
The grand jury adjourns after calling only four witnesses. They have no findings and bring in no bill.

# MONDAY-FRIDAY, MAY 11-22

*Truro, Massachusetts*
Tony Costa is tried in the cases of two of the four victims found dismembered. He is found guilty of two counts of murder in the first degree. The jury recommends against the death penalty.

# MAY 18

*Boston*
A "Hearing on a Fatal Accident" is held by the Registry of Motor Vehicles. The hearing examiner agrees with Judge Boyle that Kennedy was going too fast.

# MAY 27

A letter to Edward M. Kennedy from the Registry of Motor Vehicles revokes his license to operate a motor vehicle. A revocation is permanent, but application can be made to reinstate after one year.

This concludes the official acts that had a direct bearing on the Chappaquiddick affair.

# CONTINUING EVENTS

There were some loose ends yet to tie up. On April 29, 1970, the inquest proceeding was unsealed, and the court sold 111 copies of the transcript. One went to Henry A. Zeigler, who published an abridged and edited version under the title *Inquest*.

Court reporter Sidney R. Lipman brought suit demanding the money charged for transcripts. Based on custom and usage in the state, court reporters had the right to the monies charged for transcripts.

The case went to hearing at the Federal District Court with summary judgment (dismissal).

That dismissal was appealed to the U.S. Court of Appeals for the First Circuit and remanded for trial.

After trial the case was dismissed.

Dismissal was again appealed to the First Circuit, which finally decided the issue in favor of the plaintiff, Mr. Lipman, the court reporter, in 1973.

In May of 1974 Tony Costa, having lost his bids for appeal, hanged himself in his cell at the Massachusetts Correctional Institution at Walpole.

## 5

*Seven Little Theories*
*and How They Grew*

The authors of *Teddy Bare,
Death at Chappaquiddick,* and even such favorable works as
*Camelot Legacy* continually bring up the question, "What was
Senator Kennedy doing wandering around in the dark with a
woman who was not his wife?" For purposes of our analysis, we
don't particularly care.

Though we grant that Senator Kennedy was a married man and
that adultery was a moral, though not a criminal, offense in the
Commonwealth of Massachusetts in 1969, we don't think it
would have justified a cover-up. Kennedy had already acquired a
reputation as a womanizer and been linked with several women,
so why should anyone have bothered? Only the senator knows
what did or did not take place between eleven fifteen and twelve
forty-five that night, and he may not remember.

Several more hours of that night are in question, however.
What was Kennedy doing in the hours between 12:45 A.M. when
Look saw him, until an hour and a half later, when Russ Peachy
gave him the time?

From the time of the conversation with Russ Peachy that night
until nearly eight o'clock in the morning, what was he doing? Why

did Kennedy neglect to report the accident to the authorities immediately and fail to get help for Mary Jo?

Several people have tried to guess why and what happened. Most of them have chosen to overlook some evidence in their attempts to prove every level of responsibility for Ted Kennedy, from innocent victim to evil villain.

Let's take a look at those theories and accusations and at the evidence that supports or disproves each one. Which ones are supported by the evidence? Which ones do the evidence prove incorrect?

# THEORY 1:

*The accident was engineered to keep Ted out of the White House.*

According to James McGregor Burns in *Edward Kennedy and the Camelot Legacy*, radicals speculated that the Central Intelligence Agency or some other sinister government agency (at that time working for the Nixon administration) somehow drugged Kennedy and set up the whole thing.

R. B. Cutler, in his self-published *You, the Jury*, theorizes a complex scheme involving an A squad, a B squad, and a C squad of some sort of intelligence or espionage operatives and even a fake Teddy Kennedy running around to be spotted. If the fake Teddy Kennedy reminds anyone in the audience of the fake Oswald that peoples some JFK assassination theories, Mr. Cutler has worked that ground too. He accuses some person or persons unspecified who did not wish Kennedy to be elected president.

Cutler uses a plethora of official documents and photographs to "prove" the case. Yet he includes a confusing list of photographic credits.

The same photographs were used as a basis for a new theory (at least with clear photo credits) in Kenneth Kappel's *Chappaquiddick Revealed.*

If a frame was constructed, it was put together with chewing gum. It would seem much easier to drug the senator and photograph him in compromising positions with a live Mary Jo or someone else, or just film him in one of the many extramarital liaisons he was widely believed to indulge in.

But would so simple an exposé have worked?

In the pre-Watergate era, such explicit photographs might not have gotten printed. To the press, sex and booze were minor infractions, and should neither count against a candidate nor be revealed about a politician. Most members of the press could be counted on to ignore these little foibles, especially by the Kennedys, who hand-fed them and kept them as pets.

A scandal can be manufactured out of almost anything. For example, if a story with photos is placed in an Italian Communist or anti-American Arab newspaper, that very fact becomes a story that the American press can't ignore. Soviet disinformation specialists used this technique for years. It was a favorite method, and they got very good at it. By 1969, even the CIA must have figured out how it was done.

If you are a politician and being framed for political reasons, why not scream political frame-up? Doing so will not only raise a defense, it will obscure the issues and change the story's framework. Kennedy not only neglected to scream frame-up, he originated the story. Kennedy himself made the first statement, that he was driving the car. Even if he had been in a befuddled state of mind due to forcible drugging, he couldn't have made such clear statements about what he did remember. A week later, when the hypothetical drugs would have worn off, he made even clearer statements about the night's events. In all his statements, publicly and to the police, he admitted that he was the person who drove the car off the bridge.

Finally, the Watergate tapes reveal that Nixon sent his plumbers to investigate the incident at Chappaquiddick. Why send secret agents to investigate a frame designed by your own people? Open, official agents, yes. Then you appear not to be involved. In this case, no one was supposed to know that Nixon had a cadre of investigators. They did not exist publicly. Why send them to investigate?

The frame-up theory does not square with the known facts.

Even the title of *You, the Jury* is misleading. Every jury in this country gets to hear both sides of a story. Both sides present evidence to the jury. Each side has an opportunity to cross-examine witnesses. No cross examiners or witnesses for the defense are presented to "you, the jury."

In 1971 Frederick Forsyth published a work of fiction called *Day of the Jackal*. This best-selling work dealt with a plot to assassinate French president Charles de Gaulle. Forsyth used many real incidents and characters, but the work is filed exactly where it belongs: on the fiction shelves.

Mr. Cutler's work, which contains many photographs and excerpts from official documents, can be found on the nonfiction shelves.

Who is making these determinations?

# THEORY 2:

*Ted wasn't in the car.*

This favorite theme was the first theory to see light and has been repeated often in different guises.

**SUBTHEORY 1:** *Mary Jo herself drove the car off the bridge while the senator stood helplessly by.*

Jack Olsen, in *The Bridge at Chappaquiddick*, says Kennedy left the car after encountering Deputy Look and that he had

Kopechne drive on so that he would not be caught in the car with her. Olsen theorizes that Kennedy panicked when he encountered Look. The senator then requested that Kopechne drive on, circle around, and come back for him. Confused by the unfamiliar car and slightly under the influence of alcohol, she drove the car off the bridge.

Olsen apparently assumes that Kennedy is right about the time of the accident, because he bases part of his theory on the tidal conditions at about 11:30 P.M. (slack tide). He says Kennedy wasn't in the water because the tidal conditions at 11:30 P.M. were not as Kennedy described them. He also claims that, had tidal conditions been as Kennedy described them, he could not possibly have escaped from the car.

Then, because Kennedy said he saw no lights in the roadside houses on his walk back to the cottage, Olsen assumes he didn't walk back. Miss Malm turned her light off at about midnight. The night-lights in both the Malm house and another house on Dyke Road may not have been particularly bright or noticeable to a man on foot, who had to keep his head down and watch his feet to avoid tripping in the dark.

Olsen further argues that Kennedy could not have been drunk enough to drive off the bridge because, had he been, he would have lost control of the car long before he got to the bridge.

This argument is not necessarily valid. There was no other traffic on the island but Deputy Look. According to Look's testimony, the senator drove partway into a dirt road, backed out, and then went down the Dyke Road about 12:45 A.M. As far as we can determine, the senator lost control at the first dangerous place he came to. The island is flat and sandy. He may well have driven off the pavement or dirt road several times before he ever got to the turn. Unless he had run into a parked car or a tree, there was no way for him to have an accident. Since no one walked the roads of Chappaquiddick looking for Oldsmobile tire tracks, we'll never know where he drove in that hour and a half.

Olsen also bases his assumption that Kennedy wasn't drunk partially on the fact that he appeared clear-eyed to Russ Peachy. When Peachy saw him it was dark, the lighting was poor, and

Kennedy was standing on a balcony above him. By the next morning, he appeared to be less than alert but still clear-eyed. By many accounts, Kennedy had had considerable experience with alcohol. He would have known how to prevent a hangover: large doses of vitamin $B_{12}$, lots of aspirin, eye drops, and lots of water.

Another piece of Olsen's evidence is the tidal conditions. Olsen says that the tide at eleven thirty or so was not as Kennedy said it was. At that time, the tide was indeed low and slack.

At 1:00 A.M., however, the tide was running in fast and hard. We know that by the conditions that prevailed when Police Chief Arena dived on the wreck the next morning. If we look at a tide graph, we can determine how high the tide was at 1:00 A.M. We also know by the physical evidence what happened to the car when it went in the water. The car went off the bridge, and as it did so, it started to roll. The car struck the water passenger side down, smashing out all the windows on that side and bending in the unreinforced steel of the doors. The car kept rolling and landed on its roof, bending the roof frame, pushing in the roof, and cracking the windshield. The current had to be running in fast, because the car was turned. The weight of the engine acted as a sea anchor, with the lighter, buoyant trunk end being pushed "upstream." Had the tide been slack, the car should have come to rest at a different angle. Once it had settled on the bottom, the current would not have been enough to turn it. The scratches on the hood may have been caused as the car "touched down" on the bottom, with the current still forcing it along.

The pressure of the water acted on Kennedy, next to the open driver's side window, like pressure of carbon dioxide on the cork of a champagne bottle, forcing him through the window. In December of 1986, a physician from northern Virginia was caught in flood conditions. His car was washed off a bridge, and he was washed out the window of the car. His body was found in April of 1987.

Kennedy's physical injuries, combined with the action of being washed out of the car, explain why he maintained he didn't know how he got out.

On July 19 Dr. Robert Watt, trauma specialist at Cape Cod Medical Center and Kennedy's personal physician since he broke his back in the airplane crash, examined Kennedy at the Hyannis Port compound.

The medical findings were that Kennedy had suffered "a half-inch abrasion and hematoma over the right mastoid, a contusion of the vertex, spasm of the posterior cervical musculature, tenderness of the lumbar area, a big spongy swelling at the top of his head." Partly on the basis of the memory lapse reported by the patient, Dr. Watt diagnosed concussion.

On July 21 Kennedy was taken to Cape Cod Hospital and Dr. Brougham joined Dr. Watt. Kennedy underwent an X-ray examination, which showed no fracture or depression, but a straightening of the cervical vertebrae. Dr. Brougham diagnosed acute muscular spasm, confirming cervical strain. An electroencephalogram was negative.

Dr. Brougham attempted to do a lumbar puncture, but Senator Kennedy's previous back injury made it impossible. This would indicate nothing except the seriousness with which the doctors took the injury. The procedure was attempted to look for bleeding into the cerebrospinal fluid, which would have indicated a bleeding injury to the brain. A lumbar puncture, sometimes known as a spinal tap, is a serious invasive procedure carrying minor risks of death and paralysis and frequently causes persistent, severe headaches. It is not like an X-ray or an electroencephalogram, which doctors order just to make sure of their diagnoses. It is now rarely used for any reason other than to diagnose meningitis.

It was the opinion of the doctors that his mental confusion had a definite physiological component.

Watt again prescribed a muscle relaxant, heat and rest, and this time fitted Kennedy with a cervical collar.

It is a shame that today's positron emission tomography (PET) scan, magnetic resonance imaging (MRI), and thermogram technology were not available at the time. These imaging techniques are used to examine brain function as well as soft-tissue damage in a way that simply was not possible in 1969.

The follow-up examination indicates not that the Damage Control team was covering its ass but that Dr. Watt was very worried about his patient. Doctors do not perform these procedures for political reasons.

The trip to Cape Cod Hospital was made in secrecy and Kennedy never used his injuries as a defense. Had the examination been done for political purposes it would have been a media event, with reporters invited along to cover it. If not that, the results at least would have been released to the press. Instead, Damage Control attempted to keep Senator Kennedy's medical condition from the press and would not allow his hospitalization.

During both medical examinations Kennedy was surrounded by the political advisors who kept getting in the doctors' way.

Retrograde amnesia *always* occurs with a concussion. The patient forgets the blow itself and often a period of time before the injury. The length of time affected varies, from an instant (the actual blow) to as long as a lifetime. Usually the amnesia is not total, but it is always present to some degree. The blow interferes with the brain's ability to store memories, so that from a few seconds before the blow through the blow itself, the neuron changes that make memories do not occur. In addition, posttraumatic amnesia, a period of forgetfulness and confusion commencing at the time of the trauma and persisting for up to several weeks after, usually occurs also. Posttraumatic amnesia isn't amnesia in the usual sense of the term; rather, it is an inability to form new memories. Like trauma amnesia, it occurs because the brain has not yet recovered enough to store memories.

Ordinarily, posttraumatic amnesia is diagnosed by observing a hospitalized patient and questioning him or her about events of the day. Physicians can then determine when the posttraumatic amnesia ends. The length of time it persists is often directly proportional to how long the retrograde amnesia lasts.

The tide level and action at about twelve fifty to one o'clock match Kennedy's description perfectly. Before he made his statement, he had no opportunity to study tidal conditions to formulate a credible "lie." He had not been on the island long enough to be able to predict the times of the tides and make up a description. Had he studied them, he would have described conditions as they had been at eleven thirty, the time he *thought* he went in. He could not have received his injuries by getting out of the car and letting Mary Jo drive on alone. In fact, Kennedy seems to have been in Poucha Pond at close to one o'clock in the morning.

Kennedy could well have been drunk enough or concussed enough to forget the encounter with Deputy Look. The amnesia could have covered all the events from the time he got into the car until it went off the bridge. In his initial statement, actually written by Markham, not by Kennedy, Kennedy seems to remember none of it. Even if he was very drunk, the stress of the cold water and the shock of the event could have been powerful enough to sober him up in a hurry. Therefore, his lack of memory must be due to some other cause.

The most telling argument that Kennedy was in the car is that he didn't say he wasn't there. This may seem simplistic, but why would he get himself into so much trouble when the truth would have been so much better? Why would he say he had driven a car off a bridge and left someone in it when he could have said that he got out of the car and didn't know what had become of Mary Jo until the next morning; that his friends had looked for her and been unable to find her?

Mr. Olsen wrote his book hurriedly—it was finished December 15, 1969, well before the February inquest. Although he denies it, it appears that the theory that Ted was not in the car was fed to him whole by Lieutenant Bernie Flynn. While Olsen is now the dean of American true crime writers, he got taken on this one.

Olsen apparently did not notice his inconsistency. He has accepted both Look's statement of the sighting at twelve forty-five and Kennedy's statement that he went off the bridge around eleven thirty. The tide conditions were right at around twelve forty-five, when Look sighted a black car, to coincide exactly with Kennedy's description of tides and his walk back to the cottage.

If you take Kennedy's time as the time of the accident, the tide was slack, and Olsen uses slack tide conditions to back up his theory. Yet Olsen also accepts the fact that Look saw Kennedy.

We find it difficult to accept a theory that has an accident occurring at two different times simultaneously: 11:30 P.M. and 12:50 A.M.

Malcolm Reybold, in a fictionalized version of theorizing entitled *The Inspector's Opinion*, also maintains that the senator was not in the car. He puts forward a different motive for Kennedy to leave the car.

According to the "Inspector," there was liquor in the car. After Look saw the car, Kennedy hurried along Dyke Road, stopped at the end of the bridge, and got out to dispose of the liquor and glasses. He then saw the headlights of the Valiant containing Markham and Gargan coming down Dyke Road. Reybold has invented this drive to fit his theory, because no one else mentions it at any time. He continues to theorize that Kennedy thought the headlights were those of Deputy Look, whom he had just seen, and panicked. He had Mary Jo drive on, and the rest of the scenario follows Olsen.

The arguments for unreasonable jeopardy apply to this theory as well as they do to Olsen's. Reybold does go a step further and make mincemeat out of Kennedy's statement that Markham and Gargan dived on the wreck. We think they did try to get to the car, but we don't feel they tried nearly as hard as Kennedy says they did.

Reybold feels Kennedy couldn't have been in the car because he assumes the car's occupants would have slammed down against the windows and been cut up on the glass. When objects fall together, they move at the same speed. When the car reached the water, the water broke the glass in and began rushing through the car before anyone had time to slam down against any windows.

We know that water came in explosively from the evidence of glass scattered throughout the car. With the windows blown in, the car is, in effect, traveling downward through the water, and the water isn't coming in from all sides, it is a current moving through the car.

The senator was probably washed out before the car completed its roll and came to rest, but Mary Jo, on the down side at the time of the impact, was not. The currents through the car had to change as the car rolled, before she reached the driver's side window, and may have forced her into the backseat. The senator could have blocked her from being washed out.

Reybold may be partially right about Markham and Gargan's dives on the wreck. They may have swum out and looked at the wreck—probably after they took Kennedy to the ferry landing—but it seems unlikely that they spent as much time and effort on the search as Kennedy claims. There wasn't time enough between the accident and the encounter with Russ Peachy.

Gargan was supposed to have been hurt, scraped all the way up his side and his arm, while he was looking for Mary Jo. Chief of Police Arena specifically did not observe any injuries on July 19, when Gargan was wearing a short-sleeved shirt. (However, he also didn't observe the skid marks on the bridge, so we can't depend on his powers of observation.) Another trained observer, Inspector George Kennedy of the Motor Vehicle Administration, also failed to see Gargan's injuries. (He did see the skid marks.) In the report Senator Kennedy filed on Saturday, July 19, he didn't mention Gargan's dive. The only corroborating statement is from Rita Dallas, nurse to Joseph Kennedy. She noticed Gargan wearing a long-sleeved shirt and moving stiffly. When she asked about it, he told her that he had hurt his arm looking for Mary Jo. That was on Sunday, July 20. Except for the observed stiffness, the statement is hearsay.

The story of the Markham and Gargan dive didn't really surface until Kennedy's television statement, after the Hyannis Conference.

If the car went off the bridge some time between twelve forty-five and one o'clock, there was no time for a forty-five-minute diving session to have taken place and have the senator appear at 2:25 A.M. in dry clothes on the balcony of the Shiretown Inn asking Russ Peachy the time. It would, however, conveniently fill the missing hour and a half in the timetable Kennedy puts forth. Unfortunately for Markham and Gargan, it fills it in the wrong time gap. Because of the physical evidence, we know Kennedy went into the pond around one o'clock. Had he gone in at eleven thirty, as he thought, the diving would fill up the time quite nicely. As it is, it adds time after one o'clock that should not be added.

All in all, we fault *The Inspector's Opinion* for taking Kennedy out of the car and partially agree with Reybold on the activities or lack of activities of Gargan and Markham.


**SUBTHEORY 2:** *Someone else was up front, Mary Jo was asleep in the back, and the senator didn't know about her until morning.*


This is the theory put forth by the never-published Ladislas Farago book, *Worse Than a Crime*. The Republican National Committee liked this one too. It was also popular with the Edgartown Fire Department in the early 1970s. We don't know why. Farago refines the original theory by having Ted get out near the bridge and Rosemary Keough drive into the pond with the unfortunate Mary Jo in the backseat.

This theory is based the paired facts that Keough's lunchbox-style purse was found in the submerged car and that Miss Kopechne's is reported to have been back at the Lawrence Cottage. The idea is that Mary Jo, not used to so much strong drink, had crawled into the back of the Oldsmobile for peace and rest. Teddy and Rosemary Keough had gone off joyriding for whatever purpose and both escaped the car when it went into Poucha Pond. No one realized until the next morning that Mary Jo was also missing. This theory is also supported by Deputy Sheriff Look's testimony that there were two, possibly three people in the Oldsmobile with the sevens in its license tag which he saw at twelve forty-five on the fatal morning. He described the possible third person as just a shadow.

Mary Jo's mother still believed this theory twenty years later. She is apparently trying to protect Mary Jo's reputation and doesn't see any other innocent reason for her daughter to have been in that car. Yet Mary Jo's character should speak for itself.

Obviously the shadow was Miss Keough's lunchbox purse on the rear shelf of the Oldsmobile. Had Mary Jo been asleep, she would not have been visible as a shadow in the back. Once again, Kennedy's injuries and Rosemary Keough's lack of injuries tend to support the senator's version of events.

In addition, Rosemary Keough was walking around the island with Charles Tretter at the time of the accident.

It is also rather obvious that if you have left a partially inebriated sleeping person in your car through innocence or ignorance, you say so. You do not open yourself to possible charges of manslaughter. You do not somehow silence the one witness who could confirm your innocence. You do not construct a complex falsehood that is so full of holes and loose ends that more than twenty years later people are still trying to solve it. You express horror, shock, and grief over the terrible workings of fate.

**SUBTHEORY 3:** *Joe, the senator's nephew, did it and Ted took the rap to protect him.*

The Prep School Theory, which made a brief appearance in a newspaper article or two, is mentioned in the Burns biography but died quickly. It doesn't take long to dispose of.

Joe was in the presence of witnesses all evening. At dinnertime, he and friends made dates with some waitresses. They killed some time having a drink until the girls' quitting time, when they collected them and went off to the yacht club party. They stayed there until midnight, when the party ended, then wandered around, "borrowed" a rowboat, and rowed around the harbor awhile, returned the boat, and then went swimming in the pool at Harbor View Hotel. The guys took the girls home, and after the group split up, Joe was spotted around 3:00 A.M. walking alone in Edgartown.

The Tedrows, father and son, dismiss this theory in *Death at Chappaquiddick* for, they said, another reason: They don't think Kennedy was a good enough guy. We think that insult is another glowing example of yellow journalism. The Tedrows knew why the theory was invalid. They read Olsen's book too. They simply chose to be snide.

# THEORY 3:

*The party was a booze-up and Mary Jo and Ted were smashed.*

Burns and Hersh, in their favorable biographies, refer to the fact that many people believe theory 3.

Robert Sherrill, in *The Last Kennedy*, goes so far as to attempt to analyze every drink that was taken that evening. He uses the testimony at the inquest of how much liquor was bought and who drank what and what was left over. He maintains that this leads to the inescapable opinion that, if everyone is to be believed, Miss Kopechne drank gallons.

This theory has been used to explain why everyone waited until the next morning to report the accident. It has been said that Kennedy's friends needed the time to sober him up, that they dared not have him seen by police and friends in the drunken state he was in.

Kennedy probably was drunk according to today's standards. We know now that *any* alcohol interferes with the efficient operation of a motor vehicle. Yet in Massachusetts in 1969, a blood alcohol level of .15 percent was considered intoxicated. Even though at about eleven o'clock the Silvas, in their neighboring cottage, were hearing chants and singing, by one o'clock things had quieted down. Mary Jo's alcohol level was .09 percent, and it's hard to conceive of Ted Kennedy drinking less than his female companions, at least in those days. Yet he still might not have been legally drunk. Kennedy outweighed Mary Jo by a great deal. He was male and therefore metabolized alcohol faster than a woman. Even if he had had two healthy drinks, or four or five bar-size drinks, his blood alcohol level would probably not have been as high at one o'clock as Mary Jo's was.

We fail to see the significance of the alcohol intake, except to explain why Kennedy drove off the bridge. Possible, and even likely, as already stated, it could explain the lost hour and a half between the time they left the party and the time Look spotted the car. Perhaps Kennedy was holding Mary Jo's head, or Mary Jo was holding Ted's head, or they were trying to sober each other up before going back to town.

The problem is that there is no evidence whatsoever to back this theory up. No one took a breath, blood, or urine reading on the senator or the party guests, and there are no witnesses to drunken behavior. It is all conjecture.

# THEORY 4:

*Ted drove the car but attempted to get Gargan and Markham to lie and say he wasn't driving.*

It has been alleged by Jack Anderson, in one of his syndicated columns, and Leo Damore, in *Senatorial Privilege*, that Kennedy asked Gargan to say that Gargan was driving the car or to report the accident as a solo affair with Mary Jo driving herself off the bridge.

Jack Anderson's column sat around for years without anyone taking much notice. His idea was that Kennedy wanted Gargan to claim responsibility for the accident.

Damore's theory of ruthless cover-up came out in 1988, based on statements by Joe Gargan. Gargan claimed that on the drive from the wreck to the ferry slip, Kennedy asked two members of the Massachusetts bar to lie and say Mary Jo had been driving the car. Even Gargan does not say that Kennedy ever repeated this request.

According to Damore's version of "key witness" Gargan's

"revelation," he and Markham believed that Kennedy was going to report the accident, but Kennedy believed that they were going to report his suggested version. As a result, by the next morning no report at all had been made.

No one has alleged that Gargan or Markham ever agreed to say that someone other than Kennedy was driving the car. With Kennedy suffering from shock, exposure, and a head injury, they were the only rational persons on the scene. If Gargan's story is correct, it provides a reason why he and Markham did not report the accident.

Gargan's story is one that any lawyer would know is not actionable, either against Kennedy or against himself; yet it managed to make Kennedy a villain and poor Joe Gargan that trendy modern character, a "victim."

This is the heart of Damore's allegation. He adds 436 pages of tedious detail and mispronounces Pennsylvania law. (See chapter 8.)

The lie was never told. Kennedy said from the beginning that he himself drove the car off the bridge. Other people theorized that Mary Jo was driving, but Kennedy never said that. No one except Jack Anderson ever said, in theory or as testimony, that Gargan drove Mary Jo off the bridge.

As we've said earlier, there is no reason to tell a lie that makes you look worse than the truth would make you look, when the truth is easier to prove. The lie creates unreasonable jeopardy. If you lie and the truth is found out, you have become a liar in the minds of the public. Even in 1969, when the press dealt with adulterers and drunks more easily than it does now, the press and public would not tolerate blatant lying. That is probably why Kennedy never said Mary Jo was alone or Gargan was driving.

# THEORY 5:

*Kennedy failed to call for help in time to rescue Mary Jo. She then lingered three or four hours and died of suffocation.*

Thomas L. And Richard L. Tedrow offer this theory in their book, *Death at Chappaquiddick*. This theory relies on the testimony of Farrar, the scuba diver who pulled Mary Jo's body out of the car; on the theories of Frieh and Guay, the undertakers who prepared the body for burial; and on several anecdotal cases they quote of rescues after long immersion under overturned boats.

Leo Damore, in *Senatorial Privilege*, gives a great deal of weight to Farrar's statements about air pockets and how long someone might have survived in the car. He also discusses Farrar's "potentially damaging testimony" and maintains that the testimony was "elided" at the Pennsylvania hearing on exhumation.

Farrar was an expert scuba diver. His views on tides and rescues certainly carry weight, but part of his theory is based on the buoyancy of the body when he removed it from the car. He thought that large amounts of air would have been trapped in the car because of its position, forgetting about the car's blown-in windows and how it had passed through the water. The trunk was remarkably dry, but air trapped in a trunk is not necessarily accessible to a person in the passenger compartment. Farrar then went on to mention several rescues: A half-dozen men were rescued off Barcelona, Spain, after two hours under an overturned launch; in the Gulf of Mexico, two men were rescued after fifteen hours under an overturned small craft; at Fort Hood, Texas, a soldier was rescued after eleven hours in an overturned submerged personnel carrier. Note that all of these cases were warm-water rescues.

The fact that victims in warm-water accidents have survived in air pockets in submerged vehicles and under capsized small boats for long periods of time does not imply, let alone prove, that Mary Jo could have survived for hours in Poucha Pond.

Farrar should have known better. He himself wore a wet suit to dive on that wreck. A wet suit is worn to prevent hypothermia, which is the cooling of the human body to a temperature below which it cannot survive, even given an adequate supply of air.

Taking our time of 1:00 A.M. local time as the time the car hit the water, the outside limit of survivability is set by hypothermia.

While the accident occurred in July, it happened in a tidal pond off New England. As mentioned, the Labrador current keeps water temperatures low there even during the summer. It helps make the coast frequently foggy, and moderates summer temperatures to make this a very desirable place to spend July and August.

In water below 65 degrees Fahrenheit, hypothermia is the greatest threat to life.

In water under 50 degrees Fahrenheit, average survival time for young and healthy men, most of whom outweigh Mary Jo considerably, is less than three hours. Mary Jo was a thin young woman. (These statistics were gathered by the United States Coast Guard and can be found in its *Search and Rescue Manual.*) Modifying factors are alcohol and exercise. During the hour and a half that it takes blood alcohol to reach maximum levels after ingestion, the body heats up. After that, the alcohol depresses body temperature. People who have exercised will cool off more quickly in cold water. These facts bring us to an estimate of the time of death.

When Mary Jo's body was brought up, her limbs were rigid in *rigor mortis.* The flesh was rock-hard when Farrar first touched it, at about eight forty-five that morning.

*Rigor mortis* is the result of a chemical process, a lactic acid reaction in the muscles. Like all chemical reactions, it is hastened by heat and slowed by cold. (This may not be what you've read in mystery stories, but it is true.) The process is also hastened by vigorous activity before death.

*Rigor mortis* begins about two to four hours after death and is complete after twelve hours. It persists for a variable period. We have no testimony or hearsay about when *rigor mortis* passed off in Mary Jo's case. While *rigor* can't prove the time of death, it can help us. Balancing cold water and the short spurt of vigorous activity we have evidence of (from her position in the car), we can estimate that Mary Jo Kopechne had been dead for six to eight hours. All her joints were stiff: Farrar had difficulty extracting her from the car, and Dr. Mills noticed that her arms were in an awkward position. However, Dr. Mills could palpate the abdomen, so her central trunk was not yet totally rigid. That puts us over halfway between onset and completion of *rigor mortis* if the body had been at room temperature of seventy-two degrees.

This means that Mary Jo Kopechne had been dead at least six hours and, because of the cold, probably closer to eight. Her body was first touched eight hours after Look had seen the black car on the road.

Ah, you say, but an analysis of her stomach contents would have shown how long before death she had had her last meal, and the time of death could have been calculated from that. Wrong again. You see, under severe stress, the stomach simply ceases digestion. All an analysis would have shown was that she began to experience severe stress a certain length of time after eating. Anyone trapped in a car underwater is experiencing severe stress.

Metabolization of alcohol is one process that does not stop under stress. It does, however, stop at death.

Mary Jo Kopechne had a blood alcohol content of .09 percent. In the Commonwealth of Massachusetts in 1969, this was not legally drunk. It isn't even legally drunk there now. In men, on which all the charts are based, blood alcohol level rises quickly to a peak about an hour and a half after ingestion, then decreases at a generally standard rate (except in chronic alcoholics, which Mary Jo was not) of about .015 percent per hour, ceasing at death. Blood alcohol level then remains static until putrefaction begins. In women, factors are somewhat different. Women absorb alcohol more quickly and metabolize it more slowly, and their rates vary according to the menses.

Mary Jo was pretty drunk when she died. We know that some time during the evening, she consumed enough alcohol to bring her blood alcohol level to .09 percent at death. Inquest testimony stated that she had to have had four or five drinks (bar drinks, which are a standard ounce and a half). In 1969 and until recently, all the alcohol absorption rate charts were based on tests on men. When women were tested, the results were confusing. Modern research has enlightened us. Women lack a stomach enzyme that, in men, breaks down half of the alcohol consumed. It takes only half as much alcohol to body weight to bring a woman's blood alcohol up to the same level as a man's. To further confuse the issue, women metabolize alcohol at different rates depending on their menstrual cycle. She could have had one healthy house drink poured by someone with a heavy hand, metabolized the alcohol very slowly, and died an hour and a half after she stopped drinking. Even if she was metabolizing slowly, she would have had to be drunk when she left the cottage.

Alcohol also affects women differently. Many women who drink infrequently get ill when they drink too much. If they drink enough so that their blood alcohol level is still .09 percent after four and a half hours (the missing hour and a half plus the hypothetical three hours of lingering death), they would have been so sick they couldn't leave the bathroom in the cottage. They might even have been passed out cold on a sofa. Mary Jo was not a heavy drinker.

Remember that the car went off the bridge about an hour and a half after it left Lawrence Cottage. There was no evidence in the car or anywhere else that drinking continued on the road.

Mary Jo reportedly told Senator Kennedy she didn't feel well and wanted to go back to her hotel.

This level of drinking does give us a script for the hour and a half: Ted could have been holding Mary Jo's head while she was throwing up on the beach.

Farrar maintained (to all comers while he held court in the

back room of his bait and tackle shop) that the body should have sunk, that it was too buoyant for a drowning victim.

The way Mary Jo was wedged in that car, her body had no way to sink and no place to sink to.

The buoyancy Farrar noticed is different. Not all drowning victims sink. This has been established since the case of Spencer Cowper, in July 1699, when in order to prove or disprove that Sarah Stout (whose body floated) had drowned, investigators experimentally drowned far too many dogs. Many of them sank, but many floated too. To this day, there is no rule. Rumors persist of men floating facedown and women floating faceup after regaining buoyancy (putrid gases and such), but this is usually after having first sunk.

Ten to 12 percent of drowning deaths are from asphyxia caused by a closure of the larynx as a protective reflex rather than by the actual inhalation of water. These cases are still classified as drownings because the reflex is triggered by the water initially inhaled. They are not cases of simple asphyxia caused by the oxygen in the lungs being depleted. The official death certificate, recognizing this fact, states "asphyxiation by immersion."

Undertaker Frieh contended that not enough water was expressed from the victim's lungs by the "barrel," which is used specifically to remove the water from a drowning victim's lungs. Frieh testified at the inquest that only about a cup of water came out. Frieh and Guay, the other undertaker, thought that was proof that Mary Jo didn't drown.

However, Dr. Mills noticed considerable water flowing from Mary Jo's mouth and nose when he expressed her chest at the site. More flowed out when he turned her body over to check the back for abrasions. Thus very little was probably left for Frieh to extract.

Either of the theories takes care of Frieh. Either she had suffered reflexive asphyxia or Mills had already drained the body.

The Tedrows mention several other tests for drowning that could have been done had an autopsy been performed. Every one is suspect. By the authors' own admission, hemorrhages of the inner ear are found in only 70 percent of cases. Edema in the lungs is usually present in freshwater drownings, not necessarily in saltwater drownings because the high salinity of ocean water reverses osmosis. Diatoms and algae are frequently found in lungs from breathing them in with air. (Mary Jo had been on the beach that very day, breathing in salt spray complete with diatoms.) Foreign matter deep in the lungs is found only when there is a lot of foreign matter in the water inhaled. Water in the stomach means only that the victim swallowed it. Above-average chloride content in the left ventricle of the heart may be found—or it may not.

In truth, forensic pathologists rely as much on the scene of the death as they do on physical evidence in the body. Farrar's own description of the body in the car has Mary Jo's head completely submerged, her hair floating in the current.

It is theoretically possible that had expert emergency assistance been summoned very shortly after the car hit the water and had help arrived, searched, and rescued her within an hour, Mary Jo Kopechne might have been saved. But the only way we can see this happening is if a U.S. Coast Guard rescue unit were scrambled.

That could have been done. Kennedy was a U.S. Senator. Had those around him had the presence of mind to find a telephone and call a rescue helicopter to lift the car, Mary Jo might possibly have been saved. We think this is the only way she could have been saved.

Let's look at the time elapsed.

Kennedy, Kopechne, and the car go into the water at about 12:50 A.M. The current forces Kennedy out of the car, and he makes his way to the bank. He gets himself together and swims/wades back to the car to see what he can do. He can accomplish nothing because of the dark and the tidal current. Ten minutes have elapsed so far. Leaving out his attempt at rescue, we add another fifteen minutes to stumble/run/walk back to the cottage. Even if he hit the emergency bell on the firehouse across the street immediately, about twenty-five minutes have elapsed. We believe it would have been impossible for Kennedy to meet even this schedule. (See chapter 6.) According to telephone company records, the only phone at the cottage was in a locked studio out back. The tenants were not even aware of its presence.

The next morning, it took a fully awake and dressed Farrar twenty-five minutes to make it from his bait and tackle shop to the firehouse for his gear and over an operating ferry (a three- or four-minute trip) to the site. That adds up to fifty minutes *under ideal conditions*; Farrar himself said it would have taken him forty-five minutes to get there at night—obviously his estimate was much too low. It then took him another fifteen minutes in the daylight, when visibility was as good as it ever gets, to get Kopechne's body out of the car.

That adds up to one hour and five minutes at the very minimum, and under much better conditions than were present at one in the morning. We haven't counted the time Kennedy spent trying, against current and darkness, to get to her. Nor have we counted the time it would have taken Farrar to get dressed and get started from his bed at 1:30 A.M.

If someone on the island had been fool enough to try to rescue Mary Jo without first calling for trained reinforcements, that would have added even more time.

We are coming very close to the maximum hour and a half we believe was the limit of survivability in the cold water of the North Atlantic. Why the Tedrows insist on five or six hours is beyond us. The position of her body and her death grip on the back of the seat leaves little question that Mary Jo was alive for some moments after the car submerged and that she was trying to use what air there was. Her actions during that time—whether she lived those moments in painful and anguished fear of death, whether as a novena Catholic she used them to make a good Act of Contrition and make her peace with God, or whether she was so busy working at survival she didn't have time to think of anything else—don't matter.

There is a reason to think that Mary Jo did not survive more than just a few minutes. Had she had time to collect herself and think clearly, she would have tried to get out of the car. She was an educated woman accustomed to making executive decisions.

She was a swimmer and reasonably athletic. She would not have waited around ten minutes, let alone an hour and a half or six hours to be rescued; she would have set about rescuing herself. Only one window was closed. The other three were open or broken out. She would have attempted to find an open window and would more than likely have been successful. Once she had escaped from the car, natural buoyancy would have taken over and she would have popped to the surface of the water.

The bare facts are bad enough if you wish to use them as a club to beat Senator Kennedy and his associates. Stretching credulity by saying Miss Kopechne spent three or four agonizing hours waiting to be rescued is simply overkill.

Not content with accusing the senator of allowing a woman to die because of his failure to attempt to rescue her, the Tedrows try to smear his character even more.

They discuss at length a series of seventeen mysterious telephone calls made "in the middle of the night," supposedly to find out what to do. They used them to prove that the senator was not in shock, that he was in full possession of his senses and he was not trying to get some sleep.

We have put in long hours on those telephone calls. In those days there was only one telephone company, which makes searching the records easier.

We have developed this chain of events: James T. Gilmartin, a lawyer and real estate agent from the Bronx, New York, claims to have seen the records, "leaked" by a telephone company employee whom he refused to identify. He supplied that information to Arthur C. Egan of the *Manchester Union Leader*, a violently anti-Kennedy newspaper. The calls were reported to have begun just after midnight, almost an hour before the car was seen by a reliable witness still on dry land. There was not yet an accident to report and everyone was still on the island.

Anthony Ulasewicz, a former New York City police detective and White House plumber, reportedly saw the same records. We believed him until we read his book, *The President's Private Eye*. Not only is he still hipped on the Kennedy-wasn't-in-the-car theory, but on page 216 he describes his memory of the phone records. He isn't very good about the specifics of the times, but he states that the codes on some of the records indicated the "Chesapeake and Potomac telephone companies respectively." He indicates that they were coded with two different codes, "Ch" and "Pot." This is impossible. Two of the credit cards reported on, those for Kennedy's office and his Virginia home, would both have been issued by the single "Chesapeake & Potomac" telephone company. It was then and has always been coded "C&P." Telephone bills never stated the local company, anyway. This raises three possibilities: that the records he was shown were out and out fakes; that his memory is very, very bad; or that he just plain lied.

Gilmartin, the original source, in 1980 claimed to have destroyed those records.

Jack Anderson reported the calls in *The Washington Post* immediately after the publication of Egan's article in the *Union Leader*. The Tedrows then picked up Anderson's report for their book.

Evidence shows that calls were made on four different credit cards. Senator Kennedy's personal credit card actually carried the name of the Park Agency in New York. The Park Agency was the successor in interest to Joseph P. Kennedy, Inc., the custodian of the family fortune, and at that time was run by Stephen Smith. Kennedy's staff also used cards on the senator's Boston office; the Washington, D.C., Senate office; and the senator's northern Virginia home. Only the record from the Boston office was put in evidence at the inquest.

The first call on the list admitted in evidence was made at 10:57 A.M. In sworn testimony, Senator Kennedy stated that he made his first call some time after 8:00 A.M. when he tried to reach David Burke to get Stephen Smith's telephone number. Information uncovered by the *New York Times* in 1980 showed that the first call on the Park Agency card was made at 7:52 A.M., not far off the time the senator stated. The fact that no calls were made before 7:52 A.M., about an hour before Kennedy first contacted the police, indicates that no hurried conferencing in the middle of the night took place.

The telephone calls made "in the middle of the night" were allegedly made to a whole list of Kennedy intimates. Even though other credit cards were used, and other lists of telephone calls were not admitted into evidence at the inquest, the list of parties called on the Boston office credit card beginning at about 10:00 A.M. correlates exactly with the list given by Egan in the *Union Leader* as having been made in the middle of the night. The calls were made in the same order to the same people. We must conclude that the after-10:00 A.M. list is really the one all these people kept referring to. Therefore, no calls were made in the middle of the night.

Ulasewicz was sent to Chappaquiddick specifically to investigate the Kennedy accident. If as experienced and partisan an investigator as Ulasewicz couldn't make any more dirt out of the phone calls than he did, we doubt anyone could. If he had, the Republican Party would have used it long before now.

After the 1980 disclosure of these matters in the *New York Times*, Kennedy again characteristically whined that the news media were invading his and his family's privacy. This attitude has done as much as anything else to keep alive speculation about Chappaquiddick.

# THEORY 6:

*There was an earlier accident that stunned Mary Jo, and Kennedy and several friends tried to hide the car, thereby drowning her.*

Kenneth Kappel in *Chappaquiddick Revealed*, working from the same stories as the Tedrows, has Kennedy and two friends push the car into the pond to cover up an earlier accident. Mary

Jo is not dead as they believe but alive. After that he follows the Tedrows.

Kappel read the theory in Olsen that Ted was too drunk to have driven all over the island without having an earlier accident. Kappel decided that Kennedy was drunk. He used Olsen's idea to look at some "new" twenty-year-old photographs and deduced that Kennedy had had an earlier rollover accident.

He claims that the rollover accident caused the damage to the side, hood, and roof of the Oldsmobile and that the scratches on the hood could have been caused only by contact with dry ground.

He further maintains that the accident stunned Mary Jo. Kennedy panicked and ran to get his friends, who then righted the car and pushed it into the water. They did this to buy time to cover Kennedy's drunkenness. They had assumed Mary Jo was already dead, but she revived and then drowned.

This theory drags in a person not reported to be on the island. David Hackett played an important role in the earlier get-togethers with the boiler room personnel. Because of that, Kappel makes a leap of faith that Hackett may have been on Chappaquiddick the night of the accident. He claims that a mysterious airplane took Hackett off the island. Kappel based his extra-man theory on an anonymous unconfirmed report that Ted Kennedy was seen near the airport in Hyannis Port, not Martha's Vineyard, at about two o'clock in the morning. His theory was that Hackett joined Ted, Gargan, and Markham by flying in, and then the senator flew out with them. This does not explain the sighting by Russ Peachy at two twenty-five, sworn and testified to.

Not only has Kappel theorized an extra person, but he has failed to think through his physical evidence.

Kappel does not understand what happens when thin unreinforced steel meets water. What he takes to be "rollover accident" damage is, on close inspection, just what you would expect from the flimsy steel of a 1960s vintage American car hitting water. Why do you think Ralph Nader and Japanese cars have been so successful? We drove death traps in those days.

The photographs of the Oldsmobile show the doors and fenders buckled inward, leaving strong frame supports in their original position. In a rollover accident, the body sheet metal does not dent in farther than the frame members. The photos also show that the edges of the doors protrude beyond the frame members. This is absolutely impossible in a land rollover accident.

Kappel also claims the scratches on the hood could not have been made in the water, but must have been made when the car rolled over on land. The explanation for the scratches is quite simple. When the accident team originally attempted, at 11:00 A.M., to pull the car in, the tide was still running. The car was partly lifted, and it started to swing toward the bridge. Close inspection of photos of the area shows rocks, not a pure-sand bottom. The rocks and sand on the bottom are the logical abrasive agents.

Just as possible is the theory that the current dragged the car along the bottom before it finally came to rest.

Either of these theories will do to destroy the idea that the scratches are "proof" of a land rollover accident.

Another argument against a rollover accident on land and later "dumping" the car in the water is that the left side, the driver's side, is not damaged. For a rollover accident to cause damage to the right side and roof of the car and leave the left untouched, the car would have had to come to rest on the roof and not completed the rollover, yet he claims damage to the left side was caused by rollover.

Yes, the driver's side mirror was hanging loose. But the glass in it was unbroken, and Kennedy could have kicked the mirror loose trying to get out and away from the car. There was no other damage to the driver's side.

Not only that, a rollover accident in a 1967 automobile would have crushed the roof down to the top of the doors. Modern cars have roll bars built in to prevent this, but in 1969 there was no such reinforcement.

If the car came to rest on its dented-in top, how did Kennedy and his "three friends" get a two-ton car back on its wheels and into the water? They would have required a crane.

And let's discuss skid marks. With or without a prior accident, if the car had been pushed into the water it would not have left the clear, dark, measurable skid marks described by accident inspector George Kennedy. The only way a heavy American car could be pushed and leave skid marks is for the pushers to lock the brakes and push the car with a bulldozer. Those skid marks absolutely preclude anything but hard braking at excessive speed.

Kappel thinks that he has made out a case for manslaughter. In reality, he has made out a case for felony murder. Conspiring to conceal an accident rises well above the misdemeanor of leaving the scene and reaches a felony conspiracy level. Any death that occurs during the commission of a felony, whether intended by the participants or not, is felony murder. This is one more case of a man who has very little idea of what the law actually is attempting to discuss a legal case.

# THEORY 7:

*Mary Jo was already dead when Kennedy drove the car off the bridge to hide the fact.*

Zad Rust, in the suggestively titled *Teddy Bare*, bounces manual strangulation around like water on a hot griddle. He never actually comes out and says "Senator Kennedy strangled Mary Jo Kopechne then drove the car off the bridge to hide the crime," but he certainly does hint around a lot. He does, all through his book, keep mentioning a vague Dark Secret. He says that an autopsy would have ruled out manual strangulation, which is one way of postulating strangulation without accusing a person in print. However, Dr. Mills would have found the external marks of strangulation, since he caught a small bruise on Mary Jo's arm. He did a thorough examination on the beach.

The motive bandied about for this implied strangulation is that Mary Jo was pregnant.

If she were pregnant, she was less than eight weeks along. Mills palpated her uterus and found no enlargement at all.

Assuming she was pregnant and had been pregnant long enough to be sure of it, several other solutions to a problem like this are much cleaner and easier if you have the resources of a Kennedy.

One: *Abortion was legal in New York, Puerto Rico, and various other jurisdictions, but Mary Jo was a good Catholic, and perhaps that was out of the question.*

Two: *She could have taken an extended holiday and given the baby up for adoption.*

Three: *She could have been married off to a minor minion. (This solution is not unheard of, by the way. Lyndon Johnson allegedly impregnated a secretary and married her off to an aide. Johnson didn't have half the resources of the Kennedys.)*

Four: *She could be sent on assignment somewhere, gotten "married" out of the country, and returned a sad widow with child. A work of fiction with exactly this plot was a "shocking" best-seller in the late 1950s. Some of you may remember, and some of you may have heard of, Peyton Place.*

A lot of this stuff sounds like sensational fiction.

More telling against Ted's impregnation of Mary Jo is her work schedule. She was not in Washington during the week but in New Jersey. When she went home to Washington on weekends, it was to be with her fiancé. There was simply no time for her to play around with a Washington-based senator.

Of course, the best evidence against a preaccident murder is the position of the body when it was found. It is obvious that Mary

Jo was alive when the car hit the water. Dead bodies do not get themselves washed into positions like that.

If it is postulated that Mary Jo was murdered by the car being driven into the water with her in it, our suspect would not be a U.S. Senator who hardly ever drove, but the dean of Hollywood stunt drivers.

Rust also recounts some cases of cars going into the water. In one a car rolled off a sea wall with a girl inside. Help was summoned immediately, the water was reasonably calm and clear, there was a rope tied to the door handle for the rescue worker to follow down, it was daylight, and she was rescued.

Rust also discusses his own experience. It seems he was driving a car that went off a bridge into a shallow creek. Yet in this case, the car stayed upright and the creek had only a couple of feet of water. So how can he compare this accident with Kennedy's?

Through all of this, Zad Rust continues to harp on the Evil Commie Plot. He even goes so far as to say that John Kennedy was in Spain during the civil war working for the Communists. In truth, it was his big brother Joe Kennedy who was in Spain, on a civilian passport to avoid embarrassing his father. Joe sympathized with Franco and the church and sent letters back expressing this sentiment. While his brother Joe was in Spain, John was taking six credits at Harvard so he could take a spring vacation. While he was on that vacation, he visited several eastern European countries that would turn Communist after the war, visited Russia, and wrote some very unflattering things about communism.

The garbage Rust feeds to the loyal Birchites strains credulity.

# THEORY GROWTH

Authors favorable to Kennedy have mentioned "a nation of Perry Masons" ready to pick apart every statement and every fact. The problem has been not so much the Perry Masons but the Quincys who, with little or no knowledge of forensic medicine, rush into print with their theories of causes of death and times of death. Mssrs. Rust, Tedrow, Reybold, and Kappel come quickly to mind. These people read one article about a warm-water rescue in the *Reader's Digest* or confuse the standard of review for ordering an autopsy with that for ordering an exhumation, or construct theories based on elaborate timetables worthy of Dorothy L. Sayers' *Five Red Herrings* and have solved the case.

Ladislas Farago, a man of experience and ability in writing about historical and intelligence matters, gets carried away by his "inside intelligence sources." Those inside sources are, in all probability, speculations that someone wrote up and filed. They are probably not facts but some agent's fantasies. Inside sources aren't much use in this case anyway unless you accept Theory 1: The CIA framed Kennedy. That isn't Mr. Farago's theory.

Taking *all* the known facts, adding scientific and medical knowledge, and reexamining theories shows us that the Seven Little Theories are all, or almost all, wrong, and the drunkenness theory is really unimportant.

Legitimate journalists of good reputation, such as Jack Olsen and Leo Damore, start out merely reporting events. Yet even they feel compelled to come up with "A Theory."

We now believe that Mr. Olsen's theory was fed to him by Lieutenant Bernie Flynn, who by his own admission was playing as many ends as he could find against his fear of transfer or dismissal.

Mr. Damore also believed Flynn, who now had a new story. Flynn must be an excellent raconteur. Damore chose, too, to believe Joe Gargan when he broke his fourteen-year "silence."

Even we have a theory. It has the advantages of not being based on any witness's "new" story and of being free of politics. Everyone assumes that since the accident happened to a political person, and since his response to it was a political response, it was somehow a political accident. This is a natural association but not necessarily a correct one.

# 6

*One More Theory*

A theory that has received no exposition in any published work and has been denied, ignored even by favorable biographers, and ridiculed by those who would seem to have wished to use it against Kennedy is that the senator was largely telling the truth. This theory might be called "Purloined Letter," *Naked Is the Best Disguise*, or *Hide in Plain Sight*.

Knocking out the Seven Little Theories still leaves us with two major questions: Why did Kennedy insist that he drove directly from the Lawrence Cottage to the bridge and into the water? And why did Kennedy fail to report the accident until almost 9:00 A.M. the following morning?

The answer to the second question can be found if you read the statements and testimony available to almost anyone who cares to look.

Let's take a look at what some journalists and writers reported were "different" versions of the same story; on close examination, however, these versions are progressively more informative rather than conflicting.

The original statement, made to Police Chief Arena, written by Markham in longhand, typed by Chief Arena, and okayed orally by Kennedy, follows:

*On July 18, 1969, at approximately 11:15 P.M., on Chappaquiddick Island, Martha's Vineyard, I was driving my car on Main Street on my way to get the ferry back to Edgartown. I was unfamiliar with the road and turned onto Dike Road instead of bearing left on Main Street. After proceeding for approximately a half mile on Dyke Road I descended the bridge. There was one passenger in the car with me, Miss [name left out because Kennedy didn't know how to spell Kopechne], a former secretary of my brother Robert Kennedy. The car turned over and sank into the water and landed with the roof resting on the bottom.*

*I attempted to open the door and window of the car but have no recollection of how I got out of the car. I came to the surface and then repeatedly dove down to the car in an attempt to see if the passenger was still in the car. I was unsuccessful in the attempt.*

*I was exhausted and in a state of shock. I recall walking back to where my friends were eating. There was a car parked in front of the cottage and I climbed into the back seat. I then asked for someone to bring me back to Edgartown. I remember walking around for a period of time and then going back to my hotel room. When I fully realized what happened this morning, I immediately contacted the police.*

The statement is very sketchy. We believe it is true because Kennedy (or Markham) described the position of the car before either had had a chance to see it that morning. The barking dogs mentioned in the chronology testify to the fact that someone walked along Schoolhouse Road (frequently called Main Street) toward the Lawrence Cottage at about 1:30 A.M. The statement doesn't include the Gargan-Markham dive or Kennedy's swim back to Edgartown.

No one who had not actually felt what had happened could have known how the car came to rest. Kennedy had no opportunity to see the wreck the next morning before he went to Arena's office.

There are reports of two persons speaking to Kennedy on Chappaquiddick the next morning and telling him about the accident. Neither mentioned the position of the car.

The conventional theories for the time discrepancy are that Kennedy was:

*A.* Deliberately lying about the time to cover up sexual activities with Mary Jo Kopechne between eleven-fifteen and twelve-forty-five.

*B.* Deliberately lying to prevent anyone from inferring that any sexual activity (which did not actually take place) might have taken place.

*C.* Either of the above plus the fact that the ferry usually stopped running at midnight and such timing was required by the story about attempting to catch it.

*D.* The first two of the above presuppose that Kennedy and Kopechne actually left at eleven-fifteen and that Kennedy thought enough witnesses saw him that he was stuck with the time.

Our theory does not make any of these ideas impossible, but it will suggest another possibility that is consistent with the statement and the known evidence.

On July 25, one week after the accident and only hours after his conviction on a charge of failure to report an accident, Kennedy went on television. There he told the story again (here edited to the facts, leaving out the bathos):

On the weekend of July 18, I was on Martha's Vineyard Island participating with my nephew, Joe Kennedy—as for thirty years my family has participated—in the annual Edgartown sailing regatta. Only reasons of health prevented my wife from accompanying me.

On Chappaquiddick Island, off Martha's Vineyard, I attended on Friday evening, July 18, a cookout I had encouraged and helped sponsor for a devoted group of Kennedy campaign secretaries. When I left the party, around 11:15 P.M., I was accompanied by one of these girls, Miss Mary Jo Kopechne. Mary Jo was one of the most devoted members of the staff of Senator Robert Kennedy. She worked for him for four years and was broken up over his death. For this reason, and because she was such a gentle, kind and idealistic person, all of us tried to help her feel that she still had a home with the Kennedy family. . . .

Nor was I driving under the influence of liquor. Little over one mile away, the car that I was driving on an unlit road went off a narrow bridge which had no guard rails and was built on a left angle to the road. The car overturned in a deep pond and immediately filled with water. I remember thinking as the cold water rushed in around my head that I was for certain drowning. Then the water entered my lungs and I actually felt the sensation of drowning. But somehow, I struggled to the surface alive. I made immediate and repeated efforts to save Mary Jo by diving into the strong and murky current but succeeded only in increasing my state of utter exhaustion and alarm.

My conduct and conversations during the next several hours, to the extent that I can remember them, make no sense to me at all. Although my doctors informed me that I suffered a cerebral concussion as well as shock, I do not seek to escape responsibility for my actions by placing the blame either on the physical, emotional trauma brought on by the accident, or on anyone else. I regard as indefensible the fact that I did not report the accident to the police immediately.

Instead of looking directly for a telephone after lying exhausted in the grass for an undetermined time, I walked back to the cottage where the party was being held and requested the help of two friends, my cousin Joseph Gargan and Paul Markham, and directed them to return in order to undertake a new effort to dive down and locate Miss Kopechne. Their strenuous efforts, undertaken at some risk to their own lives, also proved futile. . . .

Instructing Gargan and Markham not to alarm Mary Jo's friends that night, I had them take me to the ferry crossing. The ferry having shut down for the night, I suddenly jumped into the water and impulsively swam across nearly drowning once again in the effort, and returned to my hotel about 2:00 A.M. and collapsed in my room. I remember going out at one point and saying something to the room clerk.

As we see, this is the same statement, just with more information. Kennedy did not change what happened, he spoke a script written by the P.R. or Damage Control conference at Hyannis.

Then came the inquest. There the senator told the story over again, in small bits, under questioning from District Attorney Dinis and Judge Boyle.

As in all courtroom testimony, much of Kennedy's testimony provides answers to questions that were asked out of curiosity, or much that is irrelevant to this discussion. Here we have edited the transcript for continuity and brevity. The entire text appears in appendix B, so that those who are interested may peruse it.

Questioning first establishes identity, time, and location. We pick up where the questioning gets to details.

*Q.* Now, you were familiar with the island of Chappaquiddick: Had you ever been there before?

*A.* Never been on Chappaquiddick Island before that day.

*THE COURT.* You said you took a swim on Chappaquiddick Island Friday afternoon?

*THE WITNESS.* Yes, I did. If your Honor would permit me, at this time of the afternoon upon arrival on Chappaquiddick Island as at the time I was met at Martha's Vineyard Airport, I was driven by Mr. Crimmins to the cottage and to the beach, returned to the cottage subsequent to the point of rendezvous with the *Victoria* [*sic*].

*Q.* What automobile was being used at that time?

*A.*   A four-door Oldsmobile 88.

*THE COURT.*   Who drove you to the beach?

*THE WITNESS.*   Mr. Crimmins.

*THE COURT.*   Was the car operated over the Dyke Bridge or was it left on the side?

*THE WITNESS.*   No, it was operated over the Dyke Bridge.

*Q.*   What transpired after you arrived at the cottage after your arrival at 7:30 P.M.?

*A.*   Well, after my arrival I took a bath in the tub that was available at the cottage, which was not available at the Shiretown Inn, and soaked my back. I later was joined by Mr. Markham, who arrived some time about eight o'clock, engaged in conversations with Mr. Markham until about eight-thirty, and the rest of the group arrived at eight-thirty or shortly thereafter. During this period of time Mr. Crimmins made me a drink of rum and Coca-Cola.

*Q.*   When you left the party at eleven-fifteen with Miss Kopechne, had you had any prior conversation with her?

*A.*   At eleven-fifteen, I was talking with Miss Kopechne perhaps for some minutes before that period of time. I noticed the time, desired to leave and return to the Shiretown Inn and indicated to her that I was leaving and returning to town. She indicated to me that she was desirous of leaving, if I would be kind enough to drop her back at her hotel. I said, well, I'm leaving immediately; spoke with Mr. Crimmins, requested the keys for the car and left at that time.

*Q.*   Does Mr. Crimmins usually drive your car or drive you?

*A.*   On practically every occasion.

*Q.*   Was there anything in particular that changed those circumstances at this particular time?

*A.*   Only to the extent that Mr. Crimmins, as well as some of the other fellows that were attending the cookout, were concluding their meal, enjoying the fellowship, and it didn't appear to me to be necessary to require him to bring me back to Edgartown.

*Q.*   Do you know how Miss Kopechne was dressed, do you recall that?

*A.* Only from what I have read in the—I understand, slacks and a blouse, sandals, perhaps a sweater; I'm not completely—

[Kennedy is saying he does not remember.]

*Q.* And where was Miss Kopechne seated?

*A.* In the front seat.

*Q.* Was there any other person in the car at that time?

*A.* No.

*Q.* And on leaving the cottage, Senator—Mr. Kennedy, where did you go?

*A.* Well, I traveled down, I believe it is Main Street, took a right on Dyke Road and drove off the bridge at Dyke Bridge.

*Q.* Did you at any time drive into Cemetery Road?

*A.* At no time did I drive into Cemetery Road.

*Q.* Did you back that car up at that time?

*A.* At no time did I back that car up.

*Q.* Did you see anyone on the road between the cottage and the bridge that night?

*A.* I saw no one on the road between the cottage and the bridge.

*THE COURT.* Did you stop the car at any time?

*THE WITNESS.* I did not stop the car at any time. I passed no other vehicle and I saw no other person and I did not stop the car at any time between the time I left the cottage and went off the bridge.

[Yet Deputy Sheriff Huck Look directly contradicts this statement in testimony. Kennedy is so positive in his belief that it is clear he does not remember. If he remembered, he would try to add this incident to his story.]

*A.* Now, would you describe your automobile to the Court?

*A.* Well, it is a four-door black sedan, Oldsmobile.

*Q.* Do you recall how fast you were driving when you made the right on Dyke Road?

*A.* No, I would say approximately seven or eight miles an hour.

*Q.* How fast were you driving on Dyke Road?

*A.* Approximately twenty miles an hour.

*Q.* At what point, Mr. Kennedy, did you realize that you were driving on a dirt road?

*A.* Just sometime when I was—I don't remember any specific time when I knew I was driving on an unpaved road. I was generally aware sometime going down that road that it was unpaved, like many of the other roads here in Martha's Vineyard and Nantucket and Cape Cod.

*THE COURT.* I'm going to ask one question. At any time after you got on the unpaved road, the so-called Dyke Road, did you have a realization that you were on the wrong road?

*THE WITNESS.* No.

[Does he remember?]

*Q.* Well, what happened after that, Senator?

[Until now, Kennedy's statements have been vague and suddenly the description becomes clear and lucid. The question was "What happened?" and he answers with what he remembers.]

*A.* Well, I remembered the vehicle itself just beginning to go off the Dyke Bridge and the next thing I recall is the movement of Mary Jo next to me perhaps hitting or kicking me and I, at this time, opened my eyes and realized I was upside down, that water was crashing in on me, that it was pitch black. I knew that and I was able to get a half a gulp, I would say, of air before I became completely immersed in the water. I realized that Mary Jo and I had to get out of the car.

I can remember reaching what I thought was down to try to get the doorknob of the car and lifting the doorhandle and pressing against the door and it was not moving. I can remember reaching what I thought was down, which was really up, to where I thought the window was and feeling along the side to see if the window was closed, and I can remember the last sensation of being completely out of air and inhaling a lung full of water and assuming that I was going to drown and the full realization that no one was going to be looking for us that night until the next morning and that I wasn't going to get out of the car alive and then somehow I can remember coming up to the last energy of just pushing, pressing, and coming up to the surface.

*Q.* Senator, how did you realize that you were upside down in the car?

*A.* Because—that was a feeling that I had as soon as I became aware that—the water rushing in and the blackness, I knew that I was upside down. I really wasn't sure of anything, but I thought I was upside down.

*Q.* Were you aware that there was any water rushing in on the passenger's side?

*A.* There was complete blackness. Water seemed to rush in from every point, from the windshield, from underneath me, above me. It almost seemed like you couldn't hold the water back even with your hands. What I was conscious of was the rushing of the water, the blackness, the fact that it was impossible to even hold it back.

*Q.* And you say at that time you had a thought to the effect that you may not be found until morning?

*A.* I was sure that I was going to drown.

*Q.* And did you go through the window to get out of the car?

*A.* I have no idea in the world how I got out of that car.

*Q.* Do you have any recollection as to how the automobile left the bridge and went over into the water?

*A.* How it left the bridge?

*Q.* Yes. What particular path did it take?

*A.* No.

[Once again, Kennedy's memory is at best vague of events before impact.]

*Q.* Did it turn over?

*A.* I have no idea.

*Q.* Senator Kennedy, what did you do immediately following your release from the automobile?

*A.* I was swept away by the tide that was flowing at an extraordinary rate through that narrow cut there and was swept along by the tide and called Mary Jo's name until I was able to make my way to what would be the east [nearer the ocean] side of that cut, waded up to about my waist and started back to the car, at this time I was gasping and belching and coughing. I went back just in front of the car.

Now the headlights of that car were still on and I was able to get what I thought was the front of the car, although it was difficult—and I was able to identify the front of the car from the rear of the car by the lights themselves. Otherwise I don't think I would be able to tell.

*Q.* Did you pass under the bridge?

*A.* The vehicle went over the bridge on the south side and rested on the south side, and that was the direction the water was flowing, and I was swept I would think to the south or probably east, which would be the eastern shore.

*Q.* Now, in order to get back to the car was it necessary for you to swim?

*A.* By the time I came up I was, the best estimate would be somewhere over here, which would be probably eight to ten feet, it is difficult for me to estimate specifically, and I think by the time I was able at least to regain my strength, I would say it is about thirty feet after which time I swam in this direction until I was able to wade, and wade back up here to this point here, and went over to where the front of the car was, and crawled over to here, dove here, and the tide would sweep out this way there, and then I dove repeatedly from this side until, I would say, the end, and then I was swept away the first couple of times, again back over to this side, I would come back again and again to this point here, or try perhaps the third or fourth time to gain entrance to some area here until at the very end when I couldn't hold my breath any longer. I was breathing so heavily it was just a matter of seconds. I was just able to hold on to the metal undercarriage here, and the water itself came right out to where I was breathing, and I could hold on, I knew that I just could not get under water any more.

*Q.* And you were fully aware at that time of what was transpiring?

*A.* Well, I was fully aware that I was trying to get the girl out of that car and I was fully aware that I was doing everything I possibly could to get her out of the car and I was fully aware at that time that my head was throbbing and my neck was aching and I was breathless, and at that time, the last time, hopelessly exhausted.

**THE COURT.** You were not able to stand up at any point around any portion of that car?

**THE WITNESS.** No, it was not possible to stand. The highest level of the car to the surface were the wheels and undercarriage itself. When I held on to the undercarriage and the tide would take me down, it was up to this point (indicating).

*Q.* Mr. Kennedy, how many times if you recall did you make an effort to submerge and get into the car?

*A.* I would say seven or eight times. At the last point, the seventh or eighth attempts were barely more than five- or eight-second submersions below the surface. I just couldn't hold my breath any longer. I didn't have the strength even to come down even close to the window or the door.

*Q.* And did you then remove yourself from the water?

*A.* I did.

*A.* Well, in the last dive, I lost contact with the vehicle again and I started to come down this way here and I let myself float and came over to this shore and I came onto this shore here, and I sort of crawled and staggered up some place in here and was very exhausted and spent on the grass.

*Q.* On the west bank of the river?

*A.* Yes.

*Q.* Now, following your rest period, Senator, what did you do after that?

*A.* All right, after I was able to regain my breath, I went back to the road and I started down the road and it was extremely dark and I could make out no forms, or shapes or figures, and the only way I could even see the path of the road was looking down the silhouettes of the trees on the two sides and I started going down that road, walking, trotting, jogging, stumbling as fast as I possibly could.

*Q.* Did you pass any houses with lights on?

*A.* Not to my knowledge; never saw a cottage with a light on.

*Q.* What did you do? Did you sit in the automobile at that time?

*A.* Well, I came up to the cottage, there was a car parked there, a white vehicle, and as I came up to the back of the vehicle, I saw Ray LaRosa at the door and I said Ray get me Joe, and he mentioned something like right away, and as he was going in to get Joe, I got in the back of the car.

*Q.* What happened after that?

*A.* Well, Paul came out, got in the car. I said, there has been a terrible accident, we have got to go, and we took off down the road, the main road.

*Q.* Now, before you drove down the road, did you make any further explanations to Mr. Gargan or Mr. Markham?

*A.* Before driving? No, sir. I said there has been a terrible accident, let's go, and we took off—

*Q.* And where did you stop the white automobile that you were riding in?

*A.* Mr. Gargan drove the vehicle across the bridge to some location here (indicating) and turned it so that its headlights shown [sic] over the water and over the submerged vehicle (indicating on blackboard).

*Q.* And what happened after the three of you arrived there?

*A.* Mr. Gargan and Mr. Markham took off all their clothes, dove into the water, and proceeded to dive repeatedly to try to save Mary Jo.

*Q.* Now, do you recall what particular time this is now when the three of you were at the . . .

*A.* I think it was twelve-twenty, Mr. Dinis, I believe that I looked at the Valiant's clock and believe that it was twelve-twenty.

[There was no clock in the Valiant. There was no clock offered as factory installed, and *Time* magazine examined the actual car and found no drill holes or dashboard scratches indicating a clock was ever there. Kennedy is not so positive about this. He repeats "think" a lot.]

[There is considerable conversation here, and the upshot of it is that Kennedy gets to tell about the dive in his own words.]

*THE WITNESS.* —at some time, I believe it was about forty-five minutes after Gargan and Markham dove they likewise became exhausted and no further diving efforts appeared to be of any avail and they so indicated to me and I agreed. So they came out of the water and came back into the car and said to me, Mr. Markham and Mr. Gargan at different times as we drove down the road towards the ferry, that it was necessary to report this accident.

. . .

As we drove down that road I was almost looking out the front window and windows trying to see her walking down that road. I related this to Gargan and Markham and they said they understood this feeling, but it was necessary to report it. And about this time we came to the ferry crossing and I got out of the car and we talked there just a few minutes.

I just wondered how all of this could possibly have happened. I also had some sort of a thought and the wish and desire and the hope that suddenly this whole accident would disappear, and they reiterated that this had to be reported and I understood at the time I left that ferry boat, left the slip where the ferry boat was, that it had to be reported and I had full intention of reporting it, and I mentioned to Gargan and Markham something like, "You take care of the girls, I will take care of the accident" —that is what I said and I dove into the water.

Now, I started to swim out into that tide and the tide suddenly became, felt an extraordinary shove and almost pulling me down again, the water pulling me down and suddenly I realized at that time even as I failed to realize before I dove into the water—that I was in a weakened condition, although as I had looked over that distance between the ferry slip and the other side, it seemed to me an inconsequential swim; but the water got colder, the tide began to draw me out and for the second time that evening, I knew I was going to drown and the strength continued to leave me. By this time I was probably fifty yards off the shore and I remembered being swept down toward the direction of the Edgartown Light and well out into darkness, and I continued to attempt to swim, tried to swim at a slower pace and be able to regain whatever kind of strength that was left in me.

And some time after, I think it was about the middle of the

channel, a little further than that, the tide was much calmer, gentler, and I began to get my—make some progress, and finally was able to reach the other shore, and all the nightmares and all the tragedy and all the loss of Mary Jo's death was right before me again. And when I was able to gain this shore, this Edgartown side, I pulled myself on the beach and then attempted to gain some strength . . . walking through the parking lot, trying to really gather some idea as to what happened . . .

*Q.* Do you have any idea what time you arrived at the Shiretown Inn?

*A.* I would say some time before two.

*Q.* When you arrived at the Shiretown Inn, did you talk to anyone at that time?

*A.* I went to my room and I was shaking with chill. I took off all my clothes and collapsed on the bed, and at this time, I was very conscious of a throbbing headache, of pains in my neck, of strain on my back, but what I was even more conscious of is the tragedy and loss of a very devoted friend.

*Q.* Now, did you change your clothes?

*A.* I was unable really to determine, detect the amount of lapse of time and I could hear noise that was taking place. It seemed around me, on top of me almost in the room, and after a period of time I wasn't sure whether it was morning or afternoon or nighttime, and I put on—and I wanted to find out and I put on some dry clothes that were there, a pants and a shirt, and I opened the door and I saw what I believed to be a tourist, someone standing under the light off the balcony and asked what time it was. He mentioned to me it was, I think, two-thirty, and went back into the room.

The only inconsistencies we find between Kennedy's various statements and the other evidence are in the early part of the timetable and the time and effort of the Gargan-Markham dive on the car.

At 12:45 A.M., Huck Look spotted a car matching the description and having a license plate close to that of Senator Kennedy's. It pulled into Cemetery Road, backed out, and sped down Dyke

Road. At the inquest, there was some attempt to cast doubt on this being Kennedy's car, but the judge apparently decided that this was irrelevant. The odds were unthinkable that another car so close in appearance and license number should have been on the small, sparsely inhabited Chappaquiddick at that hour on that night.

At midnight, [Miss] Malm turned off her light. She had heard no splash, and in a later test, a mere rock thrown into Poucha Pond was clearly audible at the house.

Kennedy saw no lights on his walk back.

At eleven-fifteen to eleven-thirty, there was not enough current to turn the car. Closer to one, the tide was strong enough to slew the rear end "downstream."

At one-thirty, John Silva's dogs barked. Since they barked only at pedestrians, and we can't find anyone else walking at one-thirty, the person seems to have been the senator. One-thirty is about the right time for the dogs to bark at Kennedy if he went off the bridge at twelve-fifty. The dogs did *not* bark between twelve-fifteen and twelve-thirty, when Kennedy claims he walked back.

Those five pieces of evidence and testimony pretty well refute Kennedy's statement that he went directly from the cottage to the bridge and then into the water. We must conclude that he was wrong about the time or he would have included Look's car and the lights at the Malm cottage, especially after learning of them.

An elaborate workup in the *Reader's Digest* attempted to prove Kennedy was lying throughout. In it John Barron used the times of the tides to prove that conditions had to be wrong when Kennedy said he performed various acts. The author states that low tide in Poucha Pond was 10:30 P.M. July 18, that the tidal differential was two feet, and that low tide in Edgartown Channel was at 1:30 A.M. July 19. The fact that the "expert" based his reconstruction on November 9, 1979, and admitted that the bottom had probably changed in the years since the accident calls the article's credibility into question. Since several witnesses on the scene described a difference of several feet of tide within two hours, the two-foot tide is also wrong. We based our chart on the eyewitness accounts from July 19, 1969, and an almanac citation of average mean tide time differential. An outgoing tide sweeps toward Edgartown Light; an incoming tide sweeps toward Katama Bay.

First, *eyewitness statements* indicate that low tide occurred at the Dyke Bridge the next morning at 11:30 A.M. The tidal interval on that day at that latitude was twelve hours, which puts the previous low tide at 11:30 P.M. If we assume that the expert who did the testing on November 9, 1979, expressed his report in standard time, and the author forgot that on July 18, all the times reported were in what was formerly called Daylight Time, we find a reason for such a gross error.

If, indeed, the author is an hour off on the Poucha Pond tides, then he is an hour off on the Edgartown Channel tides, where he stated low tide occurred at 1:30 A.M. If the tide in fact turns an hour later, at 2:30 A.M. to correlate with the low tide in Poucha Pond and have the same time difference, then the current, though weak, would indeed be running toward Edgartown Light, as Kennedy said it was, and not toward Katama Bay.

Kennedy, Markham, and Gargan all say that Kennedy jumped from the dock unexpectedly and without warning and began his swim. He was a strong swimmer but he failed to consider that he had already been exhausted by his experience in Poucha Pond. Gargan and Markham weren't as worried as they should have been. Gargan testified at the inquest that Kennedy could swim four or five times the five-hundred-foot distance (when the senator was rested and healthy).

Kennedy's description of the swim to Edgartown is correct once you realize that the *Reader's Digest* article made a simple mistake. Once more, we have the senator telling the truth, and now his times coincide with witnesses. He said he made the swim somewhat before 2:00 A.M. He was seen, after having changed clothes, at two-twenty-five at the Shiretown Inn. It would have taken that long after an eight-minute swim to rest, walk back to the inn, rest a few minutes more, change clothes, and be seen on the balcony.

Our other problem is Gargan and Markham's supposed diving.

We discussed this earlier in the Reybold theory, but it's worth going over again.

Statements regarding the diving episode did not surface until after the Hyannis conference. As we mentioned, we think Gargan and Markham did look the wreck over, but we don't think they made as hard a rescue attempt as they and Kennedy claim. Two trained observers and the rest of the party in the cottage failed to notice any injury to Joe Gargan. Nurse Rita Dallas noticed stiffness but never actually saw an injury.

Gargan and Markham may well have waded out and surveyed the car and decided they hadn't a chance to do anything. They may have done some diving after they let Kennedy out at the ferry slip.

The only reason we can find for them to exaggerate their efforts is to attempt to fill the time allowed by Kennedy and make his reported times more credible.

They failed in this attempt because there is too much other evidence that the accident occurred minutes after twelve-forty-five, and no corroboration that it was earlier.

Kennedy mentions in his inquest testimony that the clock in the Valiant read twelve-twenty. As we noted, there was no clock in the Valiant. The Olds, a luxury model, undoubtedly did have a clock. It was probably that clock that read 12:20, *before* the car entered the water. Moving the memory of the clock from one car to another would have been consistent with Kennedy's amnesia; the clock was transferred not intentionally, but because of his befuddled state.

Yet this still leaves us with some questions.

Why is Kennedy so adamant about the time, which has been disproved? Why did Gargan and Markham apparently embellish their story to fill up that time? And why, as Mary Jo's father asked, did Markham and Gargan fail to do the right thing? Why did neither man take action to help both Kennedy and Mary Jo?

Why did three members of the Massachusetts bar fail to report an accident until nine o'clock the following morning?

Let's look at some more of the testimony and statements—all regarding occurrences *after* the accident.

Kennedy testified that he, Gargan, and Markham intended to call the police but then neglected to do so. At the time the police were mentioned, it was an hour after the accident.

Kennedy, without warning Gargan and Markham, jumped in and swam across the channel, back to Edgartown, and walked back to the Shiretown Inn, where he changed into dry clothes and collapsed onto the bed. He rested fitfully but was disturbed by a noise "all around." He got up, went out onto the balcony, and asked Russ Peachy the time.

The next morning Markham and Gargan picked him up and spirited him away to the telephone booth on Chappaquiddick where he finally contacted his lawyer, Burke Marshall.

Marshall convinced him he should report the accident, and Kennedy finally realized the gravity of his position.

In his appeal to the voters of Massachusetts, Kennedy describes his actions and feelings after the accident:

My conduct and conversation during the next several hours make no sense to me at all. . . . All kinds of scrambled thoughts—all of them confused, some of them irrational, many of them which I cannot recall and some of which I would not have seriously entertained under normal circumstances—went through my mind during this period. They were reflected in the various inexplicable, inconsistent and inconclusive things I said and did, including such questions as whether the girl might still be alive somewhere out of that immediate area, whether some awful curse did actually hang over all the Kennedys, whether there was some justifiable reason for me to doubt what happened and delay my report, whether somehow the awful weight of this incredible incident might in some ways pass from my shoulders. I was overcome, I'm frank to say, by a jumble of emotion—grief, fear, doubt, exhaustion, panic, confusion and shock.

Then, later in the speech, he says, "In the morning, with my mind somewhat more lucid . . ."

At the inquest Paul Markham testified that Kennedy said, on the way to the ferry, "I just can't believe this happened." Markham also testified that Kennedy was ". . . very emotional. He was sobbing and almost on the verge of actually breaking down and crying."

At the police station, when Kennedy's statement was completed, Inspector Kennedy of Motor Vehicles drove the senator, Gargan, Markham, and the pilot to the Shiretown Airport. Ted kept repeating "Oh, my God, what's happened?" on the drive. This was reported by Bobby Carroll, the pilot, who at the time had only a sketchy idea what the problem was.

In the police station, Chief of Police Arena barely spoke to Kennedy. Only Markham had much contact with him.

Even as late as November 1979—ten years later—in an interview with reporter Roger Mudd, Kennedy was hardly coherent about the accident:

> Oh, there's—the problem is—from that night—I found the conduct, the er, ah, er the behavior almost beyond belief myself. I mean that's why it has been—but I think that's—that's the way it was. That—that happens to be the way it was. Now I find it as I have stated that I have that the conduct that—that evening in—in this as a result of the impact of the accident of the—and the sense of loss, the sense of hope and the and the sense of tragedy and the whole set of—circumstances, that the er—ah—behavior was inexplicable . . .

These are the words of a man who was an experienced United States senator for seventeen years; a man who was known for his oratory (colleagues claimed that was the only way he ever won a case), blithering about an event that had occurred ten years before.

All of this testimony, including Kennedy's own, paints a picture of a man who was at least temporarily *non compos mentis*. This picture illustrates the best reason we can find that three members of the Massachusetts bar failed to report an accident. They wanted, at all cost and whatever the other consequences, to keep anyone else from seeing The Candidate in that condition.

They hid him from the other guests at the party (who, presumably, were friendly).

They hid him from the police and possible press attention. There was some attempt to hide his condition from his wife, his mother, and his father's nurse once they got back to Hyannis Port. Joan Kennedy was told, in fact, to stay upstairs in her bedroom.

Why potentially violate the law to keep one man's mental condition from witnesses? Let's look at a few recent cases.

Reacting to his wife's response to a piece in a Canadian publication (later proved libelous), Senator Edmund Muskie broke down in front of reporters and wept away his chances at the presidency.

The vice presidential candidacy of Senator Thomas Eagleton of Missouri died when a mental hospital record was revealed in July 1972.

Ted Kennedy's own brother, John, denied to his death that he had Addison's disease. Addison's disease, a deficiency of cortisone, reduces the ability to handle stress. Later theorists have supposed that the cortisone he took to control the condition may have contributed to his hypersexuality. The cortisone would help but not completely remedy the stress-reaction problems.

A bit farther back, Franklin Roosevelt went to great lengths to conceal from the public the fact that he was paralyzed from the waist down, despite the fact that no one, then or later, ever so much as hinted that the paralysis affected his mental ability.

Any hint of mental instability marks the end of a political career. Since 1949, when the Soviets first tested an atomic weapon, it has been important that the President of the United States be alert and sane.

Before that time, several presidents were less than stable. Abraham Lincoln was melancholic. Ulysses S. Grant was a serious alcoholic who regularly drank himself into a stupor in the Round Robin Bar of the Willard Hotel. Woodrow Wilson was unable to function for a month at a time, and Mrs. Wilson and Colonel House ran the White House for him.

Today, when the President is followed around by a warrant

officer with a briefcase containing codes that can start or stop a world conflagration, mental instability is not the best quality in a candidate.

We all know it too. Every citizen (and voter) knows the President should be mentally stable or we may all be doomed.

Gargan and Markham were well aware of the political realities of this public knowledge. They would not allow Kennedy to be seen in that condition. They wouldn't even seek medical attention for him on the spot, for fear he needed psychiatric attention. But what Kennedy really needed was a neurological examination, and his friends' fear and ignorance kept him away from hospital. They were not medically literate enough to recognize the symptoms of physical trauma.

Why, then, go ahead and report Kennedy's confusion later?

There is a great deal of difference between hearing about something and seeing it. A good analogy is the difference between a philosophical discussion of the merits of capital punishment and finding a friend brutally murdered. The impact of finding the body is immediate and emotional. The impact of seeing the senator sobbing and incoherent would have been immediate and emotional.

The sight of Kennedy crying, tearful, hysterical, and out of control might have ruined more than his presidential hopes. It could have destroyed his senatorial career as well.

The dilemma facing Markham and Gargan was "Do we obey the law and report the accident by calling in the rescue parties for a woman we are sure is already is dead, thereby turning two hundred pounds of quivering gelatin over to the tender ministrations of the police and press?" Of course they couldn't. They didn't recognize that the senator himself might have needed medical attention. After all, he was moving.

Kennedy himself said in his televised speech, "Although my doctors informed me that I suffered a cerebral concussion as well as shock, I do not seek to escape responsibility for my actions by placing the blame either on the physical, emotional trauma brought on by the accident . . ."

Why doesn't he seek to escape responsibility? A woman is

dead. A car is destroyed. An inexplicable delay in reporting has taken place. We would grab any excuse we could find lying around loose. So, probably, would you. Especially one that could be certified by independent professionals.

The decision "not to seek to escape responsibility" was a political decision. To escape responsibility and make it stick, Kennedy would have to admit that he was actually out of touch with reality for ten hours or longer.

Burton Hersh says it best in *The Education of Edward Kennedy*: "Better guilty than crazy, better demonic than helpless."

Kennedy's behavior over the next days, weeks, and months is entirely consistent with some kind of mental breakdown, whether caused by stress or injury.

The next morning, at the Shiretown Inn, when he appeared "calm but distracted," he more than likely could not or would not face what had happened. At his hearing on the charge of leaving the scene of an accident, he spoke only one word, "Guilty," and appeared to be alternately wool-gathering and paying rapt attention. He went (or was taken) into seclusion, and no one dared even call a psychiatrist. During the Hyannis conference the political advisors gave up even talking to him because, according to Hersh, Burns, David, and Lerner, he would wander off in the middle of a conversation. Drs. Watt and Brougham, a trauma specialist and a neurosurgeon, examined the senator and reported that he had suffered from retrograde amnesia, which is perfectly consistent with his other symptoms.

Traumatic amnesia—amnesia caused by a blow to the head—has two aspects: retrograde and posttraumatic amnesia. Both are nearly always, if not always, present in head injuries.

Retrograde amnesia covers the period *before* the trauma and the trauma itself. It can be complete and continuous, or there can be isolated, vivid memories that the patient attempts to put into some kind of logical framework, which is not always the correct one. Sometimes memories from other events are added to make a whole. Retrograde amnesia varies in length. It lasts for a much shorter time than posttraumatic amnesia, but the two types are closely correlated. In other words, a posttraumatic amnesiac period of about twenty minutes would usually be found with a retrograde amnesiac period of a few seconds. A posttraumatic period of several days' amnesia could be found with a retrograde period of several hours' amnesia.

Retrograde amnesia can seem to be of a longer period than it actually is in a patient experiencing posttraumatic amnesia. The patient may not really be certain of what he or she does remember because of the confused state of mind. This lack of *confidence* in memory can seem to be a lack of actual memory.

Posttraumatic amnesia is a period of confusion and memory loss following the trauma. It lasts from minutes to weeks, and can be difficult to diagnose because the patient may go "in and out." This period is characterized by befuddlement. There is usually a loss of cognitive ability, sometimes a substitution of memories of similar events for the causative and even "current" ones. The patient may seem rational and not be able to remember events that happened in the hospital only a short time before the questioning. When the patient is hospitalized, an estimate of the period of post-traumatic amnesia can be made by checking against the hospital records of events. Without this clinical check, it is impossible to tell how long the posttraumatic amnesia period lasted. After continuous memory returns, the memories of the posttraumatic period begin to come back, and eventually all the gaps except the actual blow may fill in. The memory of the actual injury never does return. In rare cases the entire retrograde memory loss is permanent.

In spite of the assertions of "medical experts" consulted by the *Boston Globe* in 1974, an electroencephalograph (EEG) will not show any signs of the confusion and memory loss of posttraumatic amnesia. The then "experts" knew too little about what the tracings meant. In 1969, you were lucky if you could diagnose petit mal epilepsy, much less the constant background mutterings of an epileptic brain between seizures. It certainly would not have shown something as subtle as the brain's inability to form new memories and the confusion that results from that condition.

Even emergency workers who have previously dealt with posttraumatic amnesiacs are totally confused when they themselves suffer from this loss of memory. Occurring in a lawyer with little or no knowledge of amnesia, it must have added trauma to the trauma.

No one did a proper medical assessment of Kennedy. No one did the clinical observation and testing that would have shown the severity and duration of posttraumatic amnesia, the duration of retrograde amnesia, and, thereby, the real severity of the head injury.

What we have to go by are symptoms reported by Joe Gargan, Paul Markham, Rita Dallas (Joseph Kennedy's nurse), and several other observers from the Hyannis conference, and a finding of retrograde amnesia from two physicians.

If the senator was, indeed, suffering from retrograde amnesia, it would be likely that he would lack memory of the time between eleven-fifteen, when people may have told him he left the cottage, and twelve-fifty or thereabouts, when he went into the water. He could have forgotten everything that happened between the time he got into that car and the time the car hit the water.

Even today he may not remember all of it. While memory usually returns after the posttraumatic amnesia ends, the medical literature reports numerous cases of permanent memory loss.

Kennedy may have stated the time he left the cottage as eleven-fifteen. Markham, who prepared the first statement, simply accepted Kennedy's statement that he had driven straight from the cottage and off the bridge. Remember, Markham hadn't seen Kennedy again until about one-thirty and didn't know when the car went into the water.

Later, when Kennedy's advisors filled out the timetable as well as they could, they tried to avoid the lawyer's nightmare of prior inconsistent statement; in other words, they tried not to let it appear that Kennedy was lying about or could not remember his original statement.

Dissociative behavior is another, though less likely, reason for Kennedy's inconsistency or forgetfulness. Some people simply cannot face something that is a proven fact. Their minds shut off on the subject and they will not think about it.

Amnesia and dissociative behavior, separately or together, can well explain much of Kennedy's behavior starting the next morning, including his calm behavior before Markham and Gargan picked him up from the Shiretown Inn.

Nurse Dallas describes Kennedy as being "in a stupor from the day after the accident until the end of the week." She thought he should have been hospitalized, that he was suffering from "deep emotional shock." He could have been suffering from the effects of the injury *and* emotional shock.

One of the most interesting things to turn up in Dallas's book, *The Kennedy Case*, is her description of Gargan's change in behavior. He had been a diffident person up until then, waiting for permission to enter a room, always deferring to Ted or any other Kennedy. After the accident, Dallas was amazed to witness Gargan enter a room, mix himself a drink, and sprawl over an easy chair.

Had Kennedy been in charge that night at Chappaquiddick, Gargan would have had no reason to change. If, however, Joe had taken charge of a Kennedy and done what he thought was the best possible thing under the circumstances, Gargan would have gained the self-confidence he had always lacked. He could have decided that he was at least as good as a Kennedy.

In summary, all indications are that Senator Kennedy suffered a serious trauma and breakdown that night. Gargan and Markham dared not let him be seen because his clinical symptoms strongly resembled mental incompetence.

If we are correct, and from 1:30 A.M. on Saturday, July 19, 1969, until at least Friday, July 25, Senator Edward Moore Kennedy of Massachusetts was not in control of himself, everything is explained.

The advisors had to create a story using everything that Gargan, Markham, and Kennedy remembered: Kennedy may have remembered leaving the cottage, driving down the road, turning right, driving to the bridge, hitting the water, and being out of the water. He remembers diving on the wreck, walking back to the cottage, being driven back to the bridge and then to the ferry slip, and swimming the channel. Gargan and Markham remember Kennedy's appearance at the cottage, driving him back to the bridge, going to the ferry slip, and, perhaps, returning to the Olds and attempting to dive on it. Those writing the speech were bound only by the outside time limits and Kennedy's apparent few moments of lucidity when he made his statement to Chief Arena.

We say apparent because it is well established that Markham actually wrote the statement that everyone was stuck with later.

We think charges of cover-up leveled at Kennedy are mistaken. From 1:30 A.M. on, he is blameless.

Fourteen years later Gargan claimed that Kennedy thought of a cover-up that said Mary Jo was in the car alone. This is partly the same theory newspaper columnist Jack Anderson proposed, discussed in Chapter 5, except that in Gargan's account Mary Jo supposedly left the party alone.

Gargan claimed that when Kennedy jumped into the water to swim to Edgartown, Gargan believed that the senator wasn't going to take the blame. Gargan believed that he and Markham were expected to claim that Mary Jo had been driving. Gargan also claimed that in response to this request by Kennedy, he and Markham had pointed out that no one knew whether Mary Jo had a driver's license and that too many people at the party had seen Kennedy and Kopechne leaving together. Gargan further states that neither he nor Markham had agreed to lie. Worrying about witnesses seems to prove that there was no serious intention to coordinate all the stories. Even by Gargan's own account, he seems to have tried to reason with a man who was irrational. Kennedy was in no condition for anyone to take his ideas seriously, and none of the Kennedy people ever presented to the public the Mary Jo–was–driving theory.

Kennedy says he left Gargan and Markham with the impression that he would report the accident. Clearly he was incapable of any such act; their error was in not recognizing that fact.

Gargan reported his version of the story to Leo Damore in a self-serving account in *Senatorial Privilege*. In interviews with Damore, Gargan complained that he had worked for the

Kennedys for thirty years and been made a laughingstock to his family because of Chappaquiddick, and that it wasn't his fault. Certainly neither Kennedy nor Markham ever claimed publicly that Mary Jo was driving.

Gargan's coming forward over fourteen years later brings to mind the famous legal question, Were you lying then or are you lying now? This question is especially apt since his revelations came after his public estrangement from the Kennedy forces. Did he read that theory somewhere and decide to capitalize on it?

Charges of cover-up leveled against Kennedy's advisors are based on misunderstanding. Those advisors had to deal with a man who could remember nothing before the accident, not much of what happened after it, and could not face any of it. They were not attempting to cover up the senator's wrongful behavior and incriminating facts, they were attempting to cover up his condition and the lack of any facts whatsoever. They were not, in fact, trying to cover up guilt. They were trying to cover up innocence: the innocence of someone with no memory of what had really happened.

They had to walk a tightrope. They had to reveal enough of the truth to avoid most criminal liability and conceal enough to protect Kennedy's chances to be President of the United States. They could allude to his condition on the morning of July 19 but could not describe it graphically. The magic and exculpatory phrase "temporary insanity" could never pass anyone's lips. Since the temporary insanity occurred after the accident, it would not really answer the question of causation, only that of delay in reporting.

Actually, temporary insanity, while understandable by the public, would not have been the proper defense. The proper defense plea would have been "impossibility." Kennedy would not be required to perform a legal duty, such as reporting an accident, if he were unconscious, physically restrained in some way, or if he did not remember enough of the accident to be able to report it.

It is impossible to prove such a diagnosis at this time. Our theory matches the known evidence much better than theories requiring us to accept Machiavellian plots, sinister forces, concealed pregnancies, people bouncing in and out of the Oldsmobile, and the other trappings of popular fiction with which many are replete.

Another problem with the amnesia-incompetence theory is that it is emotionally unsatisfying. It gives us no heroes and almost no villains, no hot sex or drunken orgies. It is the simple human tragedy and stupidity that most of us have experienced. It makes a Kennedy a simple human being just like the rest of us, and those who prefer to think him a giant of evil or good cannot accept that. Of course, its very mundanity makes it that much more probable.

The tragedy is for Miss Kopechne and her family. There is also tragedy and bad judgment for the senator, and bad judgment for Messrs. Markham and Gargan and many of the investigators and theorists involved. Bad conduct may have raised its head in the persons of Lieutenant George Killen, Judge Wilfred J. Pacquet, and Lieutenant Bernie Flynn (see chapter 7), but they are minor actors after the fact.


Senator Kennedy's stupidity was in roaring around the unfamiliar, unlighted dirt roads of Chappaquiddick with an unmarried young woman when he was impaired, practically if not legally, by drink. It is hardly a wise position if you consider yourself a presidential candidate. Consider the recent misfortune of Gary Hart and Donna Rice, or that of Ted's grandfather Honey Fitz and Toodles the cigarette girl.

The stupidity of Messrs. Markham and Gargan was in failing the senator. Even if he was their boss, no matter how sacred he was, when he started acting in an irrational manner, they should have sought some form of medical help, which they neglected to do.

If we are correct, a good deal of Senator Kennedy's stumbling and inaccuracy can be traced to the fact that he had to rely on Markham and Gargan for accounts of his own behavior that night.

We have, by believing Mr. Kennedy on most points, and believing he thought he was truthful throughout, found a way to explain most of the evidence. No one could verify this theory save Paul Markham and Joe Gargan because, if it is correct, even Kennedy himself couldn't verify it.

## Justice Observed

Since July 25, 1969, when Edward Kennedy pled guilty to leaving the scene of an accident and received a two months' suspended sentence, various segments of society have been hollering that he "got off" for the accident at Chappaquiddick. The complainers were not just political opponents, Kennedy haters, jealous-of-the-rich types, and conspiracy theorists. Even journalists and lawyers who should know better have joined in.

Before claiming that someone "got off," it is necessary to understand what a person is guilty of. In this society, under our legal system, people are guilty of what can be proved in court, beyond a reasonable doubt. If a person says that anyone, other than a public figure, is guilty of a crime and has no proof, that person will be sued for libel per se and *the plaintiff will collect*.

To decide what Ted Kennedy was guilty of, we have to know what evidence was available within the applicable statute of limitations and what crimes he could be accused of under what laws.

Kennedy has been accused of (in alphabetical order) adultery, bribery, conspiracy, driving under the influence, leaving the scene of an accident, manslaughter, murder, perjury, reckless driving, subornation of perjury, and wrongful death (civil).

Let's take them in the same order.

# ADULTERY

Even if Kennedy had had sexual relations with Miss Kopechne, in 1969 in Massachusetts the act would not have been adultery. Massachusetts law then defined adultery as sexual relations between any man, even an unmarried one, and a married woman. Kennedy and Kopechne would have been a married man and an unmarried woman.

The proper offense would have been fornication: two persons, not married to each other, indulging in sex. In Massachusetts at that time, fornication was a misdemeanor carrying a fine of thirty dollars or three months in jail, and was very seldom prosecuted.

The Tedrows lay out the best case for adultery or fornication. Their evidence combined the lost hour and a half; Kennedy's reputation; the party of married men and younger, unmarried women; the specifics of Mary Jo's clothing (her body was wearing no panties); and the much-touted "blood stain" on her shirt (on the back and the backs of the neck and arms). The Tedrows imply that the stain was not blood but grass.

Let us take the last "evidence" first and dispose of it.

The benzidine test used to discover this "bloodstain" is crude and unreliable. It reacts to not only grass and blood but to some paints, many fruits and vegetables including all citruses and some others, some chemicals and oxidants, including iodine salts, and all green leaves. The reaction is primarily to the iron and iodine salts found in many organic materials, including the iron in human hemaglobin. By 1958 the Ouchterlony test, which could definitely distinguish between human blood and other protein products, replaced the benzidine and various other tests as the forensic standard. However, John J. McHugh, a State Police chemist working as a forensic scientist for the Department of Public Safety in Boston, presented the results of only the outdated benzidine test.

While a little educated cross-examination at the inquest should have cleared up this problem, the Kennedy lawyers were not allowed to cross-examine. At the exhumation hearing, the lawyer who examined the witness knew no forensic medicine and let the "expert" bully him.

There are a number of possible sources for the stain. Mary Jo could have leaned against a wall with reactive paint on it. Also, she had been in the ocean for at least eight hours. A floating piece of seaweed, rubbing against her back, could have caused a stain that would react in the benzidine test.

According to rumor, other tests were attempted but were inconclusive. The real problem is that the press repeatedly referred to a positive benzidine test result as a positive "blood" test result. This left a gaping hole in the evidence through which the Tedrows drove a truckload of ignorant implication.

Another problem is that the alleged bloodstain on Mary Jo's blouse was "discovered" some time after the main investigation. If the stain was, indeed, blood, the logical explanation is that it occurred when the body was lying on its back on the stretcher and Dr. Mills expressed the slightly bloody froth from the mouth and nose. The stain pattern is exactly what one would expect when bloody foam spreads out from the neck into a soaking wet shirt. Pathologists at the exhumation hearing in Pennsylvania testified that the pattern was entirely consistent with bloody froth from a drowning victim who was examined while on her back.

The lost hour and a half is more suggestive and admissible than an inconclusive test of a very, very faint stain. The gap precludes an "alibi." If a person is unable to say where he was at a specific time, then the prosecution is free to fill that time however the evidence indicates. Yet in truth, the prosecution has no physical or circumstantial evidence with which to fill the disputed time.

Kennedy's reputation is not admissible in a criminal case. The fact that someone has done something before can never be admitted as evidence to prove he has done it again. It might be admissible in order to prove that he knew how, but the law presumes that every person knows how to commit adultery or fornication.

The circumstances of the party, whereas admissible, are not particularly evidentiary. Even if you could show that all the other people at the party paired off into couples *and had sex*, you still would have proved nothing against Ted and Mary Jo.

The specifics of Mary Jo's clothing might be suggestive of a sexual encounter. She was wearing a neatly buttoned up white blouse, black slacks with a gold chain belt, a light blue bra, no underpants, and sandals. These facts are admissible, but not probitive. That a young woman, away for a weekend at a summer resort, leaves off a bit of clothing is not remarkable. Perhaps she didn't pack enough. Perhaps it was not her habit to wear panties—no one has collected any evidence on this subject.

Tests available in 1969 might have found sperm, but results would yield only the man's blood group, Rh factor, and whether he was a secretor. Even the most sophisticated procedure available at the time could not have proved more than a sexual encounter with a person or persons unknown.

A lot of the evidence that might have been collected during an autopsy had already been destroyed before the body was embalmed. While Frieh was waiting to find out about any autopsy, he washed the body with germicidal soap and, according to Damore, "cleaned all body orifices with an astringent." Most information of interest to sexual voyeurs was then almost impossible to obtain.

Had the body been exhumed and an autopsy performed, it is unlikely that any evidence of sexual congress would have remained. Since Mary Jo was an accident victim and not a strangulation or stabbing victim, the requisite tests might not even have been ordered.

An autopsy is usually performed to find a cause of death and, when that cause of death is suggestive, to secure the evidence the police might need to conduct an investigation and convict a killer. If the cause of death is strangulation or stabbing, vaginal swabs are usually taken. If the cause of death is drowning or poisoning, there is usually no reason to look for sexual congress. If the victim died in an accident, there is even less reason to check.

As we can see, the case against Kennedy for adultery or fornication is very weak. There is little reason to imagine any tests would have been done to prove or disprove sexual intercourse unless the pathologist is a voyeur. Not only is the verdict "not guilty," a grand jury will not issue an indictment.

# BRIBERY

Bribery is defined as the giving of anything of value to influence the action of a *public official*.

Three public officials involved in this case not only acted in ways extremely favorable to Kennedy (or to what they might have perceived as his interests); their actions are also apparently irrational and susceptible to few other explanations than that these three wished to help Kennedy.

Lieutenant George Killen, his assistant Bernie Flynn, and Judge Wilfred J. Pacquet of the Massachusetts Superior Court should have explained why they acted as they did.

Lieutenant Killen is the man directly responsible for the fact that Mary Jo Kopechne's body was not autopsied. It is he who told Dr. Mills not to do one. It is he who, after District Attorney Dinis ordered an autopsy, called the doctor back and said *not* to do one. It is also he who, after promising investigatory help, sat back and did nothing until August 4, when the upcoming inquest required him to make some sort of effort. Martha's Vineyard prosecutor Steele wanted him to go to Hyannis Port and interview the principals. Yet Killen never appeared at the compound. He never interviewed the party guests. Interestingly, but perhaps irrelevant, both Killen and Crimmins, Kennedy's chauffeur and general factotum, had served as investigators with the state police. We have no evidence that they ever met. We do know that Killen had a really serious case on his hands—that of Tony Costa, the serial killer. To put this into proper perspective, if you were a cop with four dismembered bodies in one case and a victim drowned in an auto accident in another, on which one would you spend more time?

Bernie Flynn may be subject to discipline, depending on the rules in Massachusetts. He claims he leaked the prosecution's lack of case to the Kennedy people. Yet there is no supporting evidence that he did so.

He claims to have met Andy Tunney, assistant to F. Lee Bailey (neither associated with the case), and told him the theory he had told writer Jack Olsen: that Kennedy wasn't in the car and that he was getting a raw deal. Tunney, who confirms that conversation, then asked Bailey's advice (leaving out the fact that Flynn was a cop). Bailey told Tunney to urge Flynn to contact the Kennedy people. Tunney then put Flynn in touch with Stephen Smith, Ted Kennedy's brother-in-law and head of the Park Agency. Smith set up the meeting with lawyer Miller at Washington National Airport, and Flynn told all.

At a second meeting, in December, after Kennedy was sentenced but before the inquest, Flynn told Miller and Smith that they didn't need to worry about anything new. Then he told them that for doing what he had done, he could be charged with conspiracy to obstruct justice or be fired from the state police, and that at the least he could draw a punitive assignment to western Massachusetts, as he put it, "riding a camel in Pittsfield." He said that if that happened, he wanted help to get back.

He neglected to mention the real reason, according to Leo Damore, he might have gotten transferred: his dalliance with a doctor's wife. The woman's husband was a political power with a line straight to then-governor John Volpe. The affair had been discovered, and Flynn feared for his job. Because he thought the Kennedy people could help him, he manipulated them into indebtedness to him and actually asked for help if he were transferred.

In Leo Damore's book, *Senatorial Privilege*, Flynn states, "Ted Kennedy cheated at Harvard and he cheated at the inquest."

In truth, District Attorney Dinis had already given Kennedy's lawyers, the Clarks, the full statement that he planned to read into the record at Kennedy's trial for leaving the scene of an accident. So Flynn's little subterfuge before the inquest was redundant. He managed to con everybody in sight.

Bernie Flynn has to be admired. He managed to con Jack Olsen, an experienced journalist. He managed to con the Kennedy forces into thinking he had given them something that, in truth, they already had. He managed to con Leo Damore into thinking he had "hot" inside information. He did all this without ever learning the ways of the Dromedary or the highways of Western Massachusetts.

The last of the three who acted unprofessionally was Judge Wilfred Pacquet. Leslie Leland, foreman of the grand jury then in session in Dukes County, forced Pacquet to allow presentation of evidence in the Kennedy case. But before so doing, Pacquet swore the grand jurors to secrecy, telling them "forever, your lips are sealed." Yet *all* grand jury deliberations are secret, and all grand jurors sworn to secrecy. Why Judge Pacquet felt it necessary for them to swear again is best known only to him.

The judge then placed a Roman Catholic priest *on the bench with him*. The priest offered a few prayers that mercy and charity replace prejudice in the hearts of the grand jurors. Lack of prejudice is a fine quality in grand jurors, but we don't hire them for mercy and charity. We hire them to accuse the guilty and bring in true bills against them.

The judge then made a ruling based on *Kennedy* v. *Justice of the District Court* that barred the grand jury access to the inquest testimony. The decision specifically gave access to the transcript to an appropriate district attorney. Usually the district

*Left:* Mary Jo Kopechne shown here in her college graduation photograph, one of the few photos extant. (UPI/Bettmann)

*Below:* Lawrence Cottage where the party was held on July 18, 1969. (UPI/Bettmann)

Dyke Bridge at Chappaquiddick one day after the accident. The skid marks and marks on the rub rail show the path of the Oldsmobile and application of the brakes. (Courtesy of *The Boston Globe*)

The bumper of the Oldsmobile emerges as the tide drops in Poucha Pond. (Jack Hubbard/Black Star)

John Farrar, the volunteer fire-department scuba diver who recovered the body of Mary Jo Kopechne, entering the partially emerged Oldsmobile. Note the wet suit worn by Farrar and the impact pattern on the windshield. (UPI/Bettmann)

The Kennedy Oldsmobile showing the license plate and the windshield damage. (UPI/Bettmann)

Senator Kennedy's Oldsmobile after the accident. Here, note the rounded damage to the passenger side doors with sheet metal buckled out beyond the frame members, the dented-in but not crushed roof, and blown-in passenger side windows. (UPI/Bettmann)

Joseph Kopechne escorts his wife, Gwen, down the steps of St. Vincent's Church following the funeral mass of their daughter, accompanied by Mrs. Frances Kopen, sister-in-law to Mrs. Kopechne. (UPI/Bettmann)

Senator Kennedy wearing an orthopedic collar walks with his wife, Joan, as they are surrounded by newsmen upon their return from the funeral. (UPI/Bettmann)

Senator Kennedy looks depressed as he attends a Senate subcommittee hearing August 8, 1969 for the first time since the July 18 accident. He lost twenty pounds in the months immediately following the accident. (UPI/Bettmann)

Joseph F. Gargon, Cousin of Senator Kennedy, entering the courthouse in Edgartown on the first day of the inquest. (UPI/Bettmann)

Paul F. Markham, friend and political associate of Ted Kennedy,
faces the press on January 6, 1970. (UPI/Bettmann)

The five women who attended the party on Chappaquiddick Island reurn to testify on January 8, 1970, the fourth and final day of the inquest. Left to right: Rosemary Keough, Maryellen Lyons, Nance Lyons, Susan Tannenbaum, and Esther Newburgh. (UPI/Bettmann)

John Farrar, leaning on the belatedly-placed higher guard rails on Dyke Bridge, points to the place where he retrieved Mary Jo Kopechne's body. (UPI/Bettmann)

The tiny ferry travels from the Chappaquiddick slip to the Edgartown dock, showing the distance that Kennedy swam following the accident. Note the wake of the ferry demonstrating the strong tidal current even in this channel. (UPI/Bettmann)

Senator Kennedy and his new wife, Victoria Reggie Kennedy, in New York in July 1992. (UPI/Bettmann)

attorney's confidentiality can be coupled with that of the grand jury, thereby allowing the jurors access. Furthermore, the basic point of *Kennedy* v. *Justice* was following Massachusetts inquest law: preventing premature disclosures to the press and public. The intent was not to deny access to organs of the court itself, such as the grand jury.

Judge Pacquet then ruled that the grand jury could not even question any of the witnesses who had testified at the inquest proceeding.

District Attorney Dinis could have, if he had wished, appealed these rulings and probably won, but he did not do so. This left the grand jury with few subjects to interview save the 1967 Oldsmobile, and it wasn't talking. After forty-five minutes of sheer frustration, the grand jury took no action.

Because of these facts, we believe that Judge Pacquet should have been a subject for the Massachusetts commission on judicial competence or its equivalent. Or if not susceptible to that, he be awarded with the old American custom of tar, feathers, and a ride out of town on a rail attended by the irate citizenry. Judge Pacquet suborned a grand jury process (our heritage since the Magna Carta), mixed church and state, and clearly subverted justice.

Despite all this, not one iota of evidence has ever been brought forth that either Killen or Pacquet received one cent or any other favors from Kennedy. Both men were actually at the ends of their careers, so political favors could hardly have been the price. Flynn let it be known that he was hoping for a favor in return if he needed it, but there is no evidence the Kennedy forces agreed or that he ever needed it.

Killen may have been guilty of paying more attention to a capital murder case than to a traffic accident, but that's no crime. To prove bribery you need a public official who violates his duty—which we have—but you also need money or favors. Much later Leo Damore quoted Killen as saying "Senator Kennedy killed that girl the same as if he put a gun to her head and pulled the trigger." Considering Killen's performance during the case, this may be the height of hypocrisy, but it is certainly no indication that the Kennedys bought and paid for him.

Flynn probably can't be tried for any crime, since the information he provided was already "discovered," and hypocritical self-righteousness has not been legislated against. He could be disciplined for short-circuiting the legal process, though.

# CRIMINAL CONSPIRACY

Criminal conspiracy is an agreement to achieve an unlawful end by lawful or unlawful means, or to achieve a lawful end by unlawful means. It is a common-law crime in Massachusetts; in other words, the legislature never passed a law but the offense has been established by custom in the American courts since 1789, based on Anglo-Saxon judge-made law spanning six hundred years.

R. B. Cutler, in *You, the Jury*, claims that "outside forces" conspired against Kennedy to frame him for the accident. Since we are considering charges against Kennedy, the outside forces must remain unknown and unindictable.

Kenneth Kappel specifically accuses four people in *Chappaquiddick Revealed*. He says that Kennedy, Paul Markham, Joe Gargan, and David Hackett conspired to change a rollover accident that had stunned and, they thought, killed Mary Jo into an into-the-drink accident that had actually killed her. This manipulation was performed to conceal the fact that Kennedy was drunk and could possibly be charged with manslaughter if the accident were reported as it had actually happened. Kappel uses photographs of the damage to the car as evidence. We have already disposed of this alleged evidence. (See chapter 5.)

Kappel claims that Kennedy's knowledge of Mary Jo's location in the car is proof that she was unconscious in the back when the car went in. At the inquest Kennedy stated that ". . . even though I knew that Mary Jo Kopechne was dead and believed firmly that she was in the back of that car, I willed that she remained alive." What we have here, of course, is the normal pattern of a person adding what he finds out later to what he knew then and testifying to it. This is one of the reasons eyewitness testimony, in general, is so unreliable. In this particular case, if we are correct, Kennedy needed all the information he could get because his memory function was impaired.

We have already discussed at length the greatest problem with Kappel's theory—skid marks. Pushed cars do not leave skid marks unless the brake in the car is on, and then a very large force is required to push the car up the slight grade.

The most common conspiracy theory, found originally in Jack Anderson's column and later in the exhaustively (thought not always correctly) researched *Senatorial Privilege* by Leo Damore, has Kennedy attempting to conspire with Gargan and Markham either to put the blame on Mary Jo as the driver and sole occupant of the car, or to put the blame on Joe Gargan as the driver of the car.

Most states require an act in furtherance of the conspiracy to be present before there can be a criminal charge. In other words, a conspirator must do something besides talk. All require that, for a conspiracy to exist at all, there must be an agreement among the conspirators. Massachusetts does not require an act, but it does require an agreement. Even if you believe Gargan as quoted by Damore 100 percent, there never was an agreement. Therefore, there was no crime. The possibility of phonying the evidence in a motor vehicle accident that has led to death may have been discussed. Talking about it would have been stupid, even reprehensible. But talking about it is not a crime. The First Amendment to the Constitution protects free speech.

There is no evidence that anyone agreed to a cover-up. Even if Gargan's statements somehow are construed to allege an agreement, and even if the allegation was made soon enough to make a difference in the outcome of the case, there is no corroborative evidence. An accused cannot be convicted of conspiracy on the unsupported testimony of a co-conspirator. No one has ever found any corroborative evidence.

# DRIVING UNDER THE INFLUENCE

The statutory standard for driving under the influence of alcohol in Massachusetts in 1969 was a blood alcohol level of .15 percent. To convict, a prosecutor must prove that an individual drove a motor vehicle with that blood level by testing breath, blood, or urine; or by observing behavior that tends to show that the driver was drunk.

We have a great deal of evidence of strange behavior, all of which occurred after the accident, when it might be explained by mental or physical shock. Almost all of the evidence comes from Senator Kennedy himself in his own statements.

We also have inference. In deciding a case, a tryer of fact is permitted logically to infer from the evidence on hand. The evidence shows that on a calm, dry night the senator drove off a bridge that no one had driven off in its previous twenty-two years of existence. The evidence showed that the senator had been drinking; according to his own claim, two rum and Cokes. A great deal of alcohol was available at the party. No witness ever testified as to exactly how much Kennedy had to drink. Analysis of Mary Jo's blood showed an alcohol level of .09 percent, which was not legally drunk in Massachusetts. Depending on how long she lived after the car went into the water, and how long before the car went into the water she had stopped drinking, she could have been quite drunk at eleven thirty, when they left the party. The best argument to believe Kennedy was intoxicated is the presumed likelihood that he would have drunk more than an infrequent drinker like Mary Jo. He had a reputation for drinking quite a lot.

But remember, evidence of reputation isn't admissible in court. Like many people, we think there is a high probability that Kennedy was drunk, but no tests were performed at the time, and no conviction of drunk driving could ever have been secured on the evidence available the next morning.

# LEAVING THE SCENE OF AN ACCIDENT

Kennedy himself confessed to leaving the scene of an accident and pled guilty to it, which should close the issue. However, we're examining the entire case, so let's open it up again.

This is the charge brought by the prosecution. The only evidence with which to prove it was Kennedy's own statement and the fact that the senator had managed to call some other people before calling the police. All citizens have the right to call an attorney before turning themselves over to law enforcement. Kennedy claimed the calls he made, beginning at about eight o'clock that morning, were to chase down his attorneys, as was his right as a citizen.

The offense in Massachusetts is and was going away after knowingly colliding or causing injury to any person, without stopping and making known name, residence, and registration number of the vehicle. According to the testimony at the inquest, within an hour or so of the accident—as soon as he was physically able to do so—Kennedy did in fact make known those details to two people: Paul Markham and Joe Gargan.

The law does not specify to whom you have to make known this information, although presumably it means the authorities. Exactly how high do you have to go? Markham and Gargan could be considered guilty of the offense by not passing the information on to the appropriate local authorities. However, the traffic law puts the duty only on the person causing the injury.

Robert Clark, Jr., and Robert Clark III, Kennedy's defense attorneys, did indeed want to defend him by explaining that, by telling someone, Kennedy was not guilty of concealment. Yet this defense was rejected on political grounds.

Another defense, which the Clarks may or may not have raised but which was undoubtedly vetoed by Kennedy's political advisors, was temporary insanity or impossibility. The sworn testimony of two physicians that during part of the time, certainly, Kennedy had been suffering from retrograde amnesia (forgetfulness of events before the accident) and posttraumatic amnesia (which made it impossible for him to act responsibly after the accident) could easily have been worked into a defense against the charge of leaving the scene of an accident.

If Kennedy had raised the amnesia or injury issue, a prosecutor could never have won the case before a jury.

Almost all authors complain that when Kennedy was sentenced for this offense, the probation officer stated that he had no prior record. The following offenses did appear on his record in the state of Virginia, where Kennedy had attended the University of Virginia law school:

March 1957:   Speeding, fine $15

June 1958:   Speeding, fine $15, racing, fine $35

December 1959:   Failure to obey a traffic control, red light, fine $10

Yet Virginia, like many other states, operates under what is called the "point system." Points are assigned to each violation. The accumulation of a number of points over a limited time leads to the suspension or revocation of the driver's license. In Virginia in the 1950s, the points, and the record, disappeared after three years. Even if Kennedy had been charged with a violation in Virginia any time after December 1962, he or his counsel could quite cheerfully announce that he had no points—in other words, a clean driving record. If the points had fallen off by 1962, they were still gone in 1969. No one has ever found any violations on

Kennedy's driving record beyond 1962. Another reason that these old charges were not mentioned is that the law of Massachusetts[1] in these cases requires the prosecution to inquire into and present only the record of the previous six years.

# MANSLAUGHTER (ALSO NEGLIGENT HOMICIDE)

In some states, manslaughter is called vehicular manslaughter. This charge is almost never applied when the victim is one of your own party or in your own car. It is usually applied to the driver, drunk or sober, who roars down the road bowling over pedestrians, shopping carts, and cars. Since there was obviously no intention to kill in this case, the prosecution would have to show "reckless disregard" (of human life). The best evidence shows that Kennedy approached the Dyke Bridge at approximately twenty-two miles per hour. Senator Kennedy testified he had been going twenty miles per hour. Motor Vehicle Inspector Kennedy estimated the speed at between twenty and twenty-two miles per hour on the basis of the skid marks. The Arthur D. Little study, admitted as evidence but not backed up with testimony, said about thirty. The study commissioned by the *Reader's Digest* in 1980 estimated thirty to thirty-eight.

Even twenty is obviously too fast, but a speed of at least fifty-five or sixty would have to be demonstrated to prove reckless disregard. The Arthur D. Little study has often been mentioned in works on Chappaquiddick. The judge accepted the report but refused testimony on the grounds that the report was speculative, some of the experiments sounded like a grade-school physics experiment, and was biased since it had been prepared at the expense of Senator Kennedy.

[1] See Appendix G.

According to one theory, anyone who operates a car when he or she might be impaired by alcohol is indulging in reckless disregard. In 1969, getting into a car on an isolated island with little or no traffic with a few drinks under your belt would hardly qualify.

The Kennedy lawyers themselves were worried about a precedent that they thought might apply. *Commonwealth* v. *Welansky*[2] is a 1944 case dealing with a business owner who was under what is called a "duty of care" to the business invitees or visitors who come into his establishment. In this case an owner of the New Coconut Grove nightclub was held responsible for deaths resulting from a fire. The exit doors were locked or blocked. Even though the man had been hospitalized for months before the incident and had not been running the club, as the owner he was held responsible.

The Kennedy lawyers feared that Ted Kennedy could have been held criminally responsible for Mary Jo's death even though there is no "duty to rescue" under Massachusetts law. They should not have worried. *Welansky* concerned itself with commercial patrons invited in to spend their money. The party on Chappaquiddick was social. Mary Jo was not even employed in any way by any Kennedy at the time. She was a social guest at the party and in the car. Kennedy testified that he had attempted to dive and rescue her. But Kennedy was under no affirmative duty, as that of business owner to customer, to rescue her. Anglo-Saxon law allows you to observe a drowning man, count the number of his screams, check whether he stays down after the third time, and go merrily on your way, having violated no statute and having incurred no civil liability. Legally you do not in any way have to put yourself at risk for any other human being to whom you do not owe a legal duty. Legal duty attaches parent to child, guardian to ward, businessman to customer. It does not attach host to guest unless gross negligence can be demonstrated.

[2]296 Mass. 239, 55, N.E. 2d 902 (1944).

Kenneth Kappel thinks he makes a case for manslaughter in *Chappquiddick Revealed*, but his scenario would call for a charge of felony murder, which we will describe in the next section.

Skillful presentation of the prosecution might get an indictment from a grand jury of teetotalers and reformed drunks but this was not the normal application of the charge in 1969.

Kennedy's lawyers and political advisors feared manslaugher more than any other charge. Manslaughter is a felony, and since 1951 the Massachusetts code has provided specifically that an individual convicted of a felony vacates any office he holds under the constitution or laws of the commonwealth.

# MURDER

Except for idle gossip, absolutely no shred of evidence has ever been brought forward to show any motive for murder. Opportunity, there obviously was. But the means—taking someone with you as you drive off a bridge and hoping you can escape—belongs to the realm of fiction, and not to any practical reality. If this had happened your suspect would be a Hollywood stuntman, not a U.S. senator who very seldom drove.

Kopechne's position in the car is proof that she was alive when the car hit the water. If so, she could not have been murdered and the car sent off the bridge to cover up the fact. Manual strangulation is not an option, since the evidence shows that she was alive when the car went into the pond.

Felony murder, another form of the charge, is the death of someone as a result of the commission of a felony. That person's death may not be intended, but as long as she died as a result of the commission of the crime, felony murder has been committed. In New York this could go as far as the death of your own accomplice if shot by the police.

Kenneth Kappel in *Chappaquiddick Revealed* accuses Kennedy of felony murder by the presentation of his theory but calls it manslaughter.

He theorized that Kennedy, after having an accident that seriously injured Mary Jo and damaged the Olds, persuaded three friends (one of whom seems to be a fantasy) to help push the car into the pond. The problem here is the lack of any positive evidence except the damage to the car, which can be accounted for by the admitted accident. There is also the negative evidence of the skid marks, carefully measured by Inspector Kennedy of the Motor Vehicle Bureau. You don't get skid marks by pushing a car over the side. You need to approach at speed and then brake. Only a stuntman would drive off intentionally.

Kappel's charge is that an alive but stunned Mary Jo, whom the conspirators believed to be already dead, died as a result of the attempted cover-up of the previous accident. Under Massachusetts law this is not negligent manslaughter. This would be a weird Massachusetts anomaly called second-degree felony murder. In Massachusetts, first-degree felony murder is a death occurring in the commission of a crime that is punishable by death or life imprisonment. A death occurring during the commission of a lesser crime is second-degree felony murder. The crime being committed here would be conspiracy, which would be a felony even if it were only a conspiracy to conceal the misdemeanor of reckless driving.

The law tends to pyramid charges. That is one reason we are pretty sure three Massachusetts lawyers did not commit any more crimes than they absolutely had to.

Since we have proved with physical evidence that there was never a land accident to cover up with a conspiracy, then a felony murder as a result of that cover-up cannot have happened.

# PERJURY

Even the most fawning and favorable sycophantic biographers accept the fact that Kennedy perjured himself during the inquest (the only time he made a sworn statement). Many statements Kennedy made at the inquest were contradicted under oath by others or outside at a later date. Outside statements not made under oath can be dismissed for evidentiary purposes.

People are almost never charged with and convicted of perjury when the perjury consists of lying to protect themselves in a legal proceeding where they are the focus. Being found guilty or culpable of the initial charge is considered sufficient punishment. In this case, Senator Kennedy had pled guilty.

To prove perjury you must show that Kennedy was not merely wrong, forgetful, or ignorant, but that he *knowingly* gave false testimony under oath.

According to our theory, that would be almost impossible. However, let us consider the favorite targets of the critics.

## KENNEDY'S STATEMENT OF THE TIME HE LEFT THE PARTY

Kennedy and all the other witnesses testified that he left the party between 11:15 and 11:30 P.M. No contradiction of this testimony appears in the record. As a matter of fact, the disparity between this time and the time when most evidence, including Kennedy's own account of tide conditions when the car went into the water, has given rise to all the adultery speculation. Kennedy and Kopechne probably left between eleven-fifteen and eleven-thirty. This is truth, not perjury.

## KENNEDY'S STATEMENT THAT HE WAS
## HEADED FOR THE FERRY

Justice Boyle didn't buy this one. Nor did anyone else. Kennedy would have had to be extremely drunk, confused, or unfamiliar with the island to think that the unpaved road to the Dyke Bridge was the paved road to the ferry.

## KENNEDY'S STATEMENT THAT HE DROVE
## DIRECTLY TO THE BRIDGE

This is contradicted by Look, who spotted the car at twelve-forty-five, and by Kennedy's own description of the tidal conditions. (See below.)

## KENNEDY'S STATEMENT THAT HE WAS
## DRIVING THE CAR WHEN IT WENT OFF
## THE BRIDGE

It would have been against Kennedy's interests to say he was driving if he was not. Perjuring himself to make himself look worse than the truth would would have served no purpose. Kennedy's description of the car and the water are too vivid to have been fiction. He was in that car, in the water.

# KENNEDY'S STATEMENT THAT HE DIVED ON
# THE WRECK

First, you have to realize that to an experienced swimmer, any time you are completely submerged you have dived. Kennedy describes holding onto the undercarriage of the car, trying to duck down far enough to reach into the car, and failing because of the swift tidal current. His description of the position of the car, the depth of the water, and the current are all too accurate to have been invented later. What it does is place him and the car in the water at about 1:00 A.M., rather than at 11:45 P.M. Were he going to concoct an elaborate story of submersion and risky maneuvering at a certain time, he would have gotten his tide conditions correct for the time he was trying to establish. As it is, his own testimony puts his time off by an hour and a half.

# KENNEDY'S STATEMENT THAT GARGAN AND
# MARKHAM DIVED ON THE WRECK

Their diving wasn't mentioned in Kennedy's original statement to the police. In testimony, he says Gargan and Markham "dived repeatedly" to look for Mary Jo. He claims they spent about forty-five minutes at it and that Gargan was hurt in the process. But two trained observers, Police Chief Arena and Inspector Kennedy of the Motor Vehicle Administration, failed to see any injury to Gargan the next day. Since Kennedy and the car were seen out of the water at 12:45 A.M., and Kennedy had to go into the water, dive on the wreck, get back to the cottage, be driven around the island, swim the channel, and be in the hotel and seen at 2:25 A.M., there simply wasn't time for all that fooling around. We think the activity was expanded to fill that missing hour and a half, that Gargan and Markham expanded it, and that they convinced a mentally less-than-alert Kennedy that it was so. They probably drove to the bridge and looked at the scene. They may even have made a feeble attempt to dive. We don't think they spent forty-five minutes at it unless they did so after Kennedy left for Edgartown.

## KENNEDY'S STATEMENT THAT HE SWAM THE EDGARTOWN CHANNEL

The *Reader's Digest*, with all its elaborate time charts that are off by an hour, proved that Kennedy's description of the swim *was* correct. They thought they had proved him lying. If you turn the tide in the hour that they miscalculated, Kennedy is absolutely correct.

## KENNEDY'S MENTAL STATE

Finally, many people have said that Kennedy was lying about his mental state. The only lying he did on this account was to *minimize* the extent of his problem.

Considering that people are almost never charged with perjury for defending themselves, and that the only real evidence conflicts with out-of-court (hearsay) statements, there isn't enough evidence to indict.

# RECKLESS DRIVING

The best evidence of reckless driving is Judge Boyle's finding at the inquest that Kennedy operated his motor vehicle negligently, and that such negligence contributed to the death of Mary Jo Kopechne. This, from a judge who was the only one to hear all the evidence and who has been roundly and widely accused of pro-Kennedy bias, is highly persuasive. It was the judge's finding (and remember, he lived there) that an approach to the Dyke Bridge, even at twenty miles an hour, which was Kennedy's testimony, was negligence in itself, so the judge convicted Kennedy using Kennedy's own words.

The registry hearing also found Kennedy culpable and suspended his license for an extra six months.

But there is an anomaly in Massachusetts law. Reckless driving is found in the same subsection of the law as leaving the scene.[3] Leaving the scene is punishable by imprisonment for not less than two months. Negligent driving carries the lesser penalty of a fine from twenty to two hundred dollars or imprisonment for not less than two weeks. That makes it a "lesser included offense." Under common-law merger, you bring the highest charge possible, and that contains the lesser charge. Since the charge is considered to be the same one for purposes of jeopardy, a later prosecution on the lesser charge constitutes double jeopardy.

Say a man is accused of murder and acquitted, but manslaughter is a "lesser included charge." If double jeopardy were allowed, the prosecution could then bring a charge of manslaughter and try the defendant all over again. That is forbidden in the Constitution of the United States.

The Massachusetts legislature can be blamed for the wording of the law. There was no reason to include reckless driving in the same offense as leaving the scene of an accident and then make it the lesser charge by making its penalty smaller. The statute has not been modified to this day. Interestingly, Burke Marshall called an expert in Massachusetts motor vehicle law twice during the Damage Control conference. Could he have found this one as hard to believe as we do?

[3]Massachusetts General Laws, Ann., Chapter 90, Section 24 (2)(a).

# SUBORNATION OF PERJURY

Subornation of perjury means to get another person to commit perjury by bribe or threat.

Markham and Gargan were the only two people whose testimony Kennedy could have suborned. They were the only ones who knew anything. Any favors Kennedy might have done for them could just as easily have arisen from their mutual friendship going back many years, and not been an attempt to influence their testimony. Besides, they had an independent motive for perjury—their own asses to cover. They, too, had failed to report the accident for nine hours. Yet that is not a crime in Massachusetts—only the driver of the car causing the accident is charged with reporting it.

Markham and Gargan, as attorneys, were officers of the Court of Massachusetts. As such they were under some duty to follow established procedures. They also may have considered themselves Kennedy's attorneys, in which case they had an affirmative duty not to disclose anything harmful or dangerous to their client. Perjury would not have been necessary. Invoking attorney-client privilege may have been sufficient. Judge Boyle himself recognized this when, in his original ruling, he stated that witnesses might have their attorneys present to instruct on "questions of privilege."

There is no evidence available, even through inference, that Kennedy suborned perjury from Markham and Gargan. Anything that might have been discussed in the car on the way to the ferry landing was never claimed in court.

There is ample evidence that Gargan and Markham exaggerated their actions, especially on the issue of rescue efforts. However, our concern here is *Kennedy's* possible criminal exposure. Markham and Gargan were never the targets of anyone's investigation.

# Wrongful death (civil)

In most of the country, wrongful death is a statutory tort growing out of Lord Campbell's Act of 1846. Massachusetts is different. In *Gaudette* v. *Webb*,[4] the Massachusetts Supreme Court deemed wrongful death to be so established that it is a common-law action. The plaintiff in a death action is the decedent's estate, spouse, or children. What must be proved is that the defendant wrongfully caused the death of plaintiff's decedent, and the remedy is money damages.

There is no question that Edward Kennedy was guilty of the wrongful death of Mary Jo Kopechne. His insurance company admitted it. It settled the claim for $50,000, the limit of his policy. Kennedy himself added $90,000. In sworn testimony, Kennedy admitted driving the car and offered no other reason for the accident than his own poor driving. This would be almost sufficient to make the wrongful death case in court.

Kennedy and his insurance company did the correct thing. They recognized his exposure and settled out of court.

While the findings in a criminal case (beyond a reasonable doubt) are admissible in a civil suit, the findings in a civil action, to the lower standard of proof (a preponderance of evidence), are *not* admissible in a criminal proceeding.

Kennedy was charged with and pled guilty to the only crime of which there was sufficient evidence (his own admission) to convict him.

It was probably not the proper crime. The proper crime would have been the lesser offense of reckless driving, but Kennedy couldn't have been charged with that because he had pled guilty to leaving the scene of an accident.

[4]362 Mass. 60, 284 N.E. 2nd 222 (1972).

The differences between wrongful death and negligent manslaughter are the standard of proof required (much lower for wrongful death) and the aggravating circumstances: Was the conduct extremely reckless? Was the conduct repeated (was there more than one victim)?

Another standard is whether the victim (in this case the decedent's relatives) was fairly compensated. If the relatives have been, there is a feeling that their (and society's) desire for vengeance may be slaked.

Please remember that our word "murder" grows out of the Old English "murdrum," which was the fine or blood money paid by the killer of one individual to the family of the dead individual or to the king. This fine was invoked to prevent private vengeance and the commencement of a blood feud that would further breach the King's Peace.

An eye for an eye has never been the standard for Anglo-Saxon justice. Keeping order has been a higher and more common standard. Even those who maintain that the Kennedys "bought off" the Kopechnes can't say what it is that was bought.

If the Kopechnes were bought off a civil suit, that merely means that they reached a settlement without costing citizens the tax money of courtroom space and a judge's time. Should the Kopechnes have sought blood vengeance? That is, after all, the only alternative to a money settlement.

Were they bought off pressing a criminal charge? They had no evidence to present in criminal proceedings. They had no standing in the criminal justice system since they were not victims of battery who needed to sign a complaint. The state could have brought any charges against Kennedy without needing the Kopechnes to do anything.

Were the Kopechnes bought off to prevent an exhumation and autopsy? No one can say for sure. However, Catholics do not like exhumations.

This is why we can safely say that Kennedy was guilty of wrongful death, but the proper remedy was applied, and it is highly unlikely that he could have been prosecuted successfully for manslaughter.

# MISCELLANEOUS CRIMES AND ALLEGATIONS

Why can't we prove more? Why was there so little evidence? Why didn't Chief of Police Arena comb the island to find possible tire tracks, crushed grass, footprints, or any other evidence? Why did no one question all the persons present at the party, before they left town, to find out what they knew? All these theories arose after any physical evidence either way would have weathered away.

Today we are engaged in a vendetta to rid the highways of drunken drivers. Rightfully so. In 1969 we were not. In 1969 no one investigated a traffic accident in depth. Arena had a car, a driver, a body, and an admission of guilt. He didn't think he needed much more.

Why was there no autopsy?

Lieutenant Killen was an obstructionist. He talked Dinis out of ordering an autopsy, then told Dinis the body had left Martha's Vineyard when it hadn't. That effectively stopped an autopsy.

Killen also did not question the prime witnesses, as he had promised Arena he would do. He had agreed to go to Hyannis Port and talk to people, but he didn't go, and didn't talk, and didn't question.

Killen had four possible motives: He may have been a gung-ho Kennedy loyalist and didn't want anything that could "hurt" the senator; he may have been a Southern District of Massachusetts chauvinist and didn't want anything that could "hurt" the area; he may have been a goof-off and a time-server: retirement wasn't that far away and he may not have wanted to get involved in a messy case that might force him to work; or he had a bigger killer to fry in the person of serial murderer Tony Costa and he didn't have time for a traffic accident. Or it could have been any combination of the above.

Dr. Mills did his part. According to the medical examiner statute of Massachusetts, he followed the book. In Massachusetts the prosecutor had the authority to order an autopsy. The statute said that the medical examiner was to notify the district attorney, who had the authority to direct and control the criminal investigation of the death. In section 6 of the medical examiner statute, it *appears* that the ME has the authority to order an autopsy. But in reading section 7, we see that this authority is limited to those circumstances in which the ME can certify (swear) that he cannot ascertain the cause of death without an autopsy. Mills could not so swear. He was morally certain it was a drowning. Mills called the district attorney's office. Arena called the DA's office. Lieutenant Killen, acting for District Attorney Dinis, told them no autopsy, no district investigation. It was just a traffic accident, and they were to handle it as such.

In practice, the procedure by which a medical examiner ordered an autopsy was elaborate. The local medical examiner had to send written certification that he could not determine cause of death to the state medical examiners in Boston. The local medical examiner would not perform the autopsy, but would send the body to Woods Hole, where one of the medical examiners from Boston would meet it and perform the procedure.

In 1978 the statute was changed. The medical examiner is now empowered to order an autopsy for any reason.

Why did a judge in Pennsylvania deny the exhumation? Why couldn't the body be exhumed and an autopsy be performed even after Mary Jo was buried?

To explain that, we have to explain the difference between standards for performing an autopsy and exhuming a body.

The standard for performing an autopsy had long before 1969 become probably the second lowest in the law. (The lowest is that for worker's compensation, which is *any possibility* that the claim or injury is work related.)

The courts will allow an autopsy, even in the face of religious or practical objections by immediate family members, should any treating or examining physician or any medical examiner or coroner express a desire for one.

After a person dies and the body has been released by the state (if it ever held it), the next of kin own the remains. No one but the next of kin has any say over the disposition of the body, within the health and safety codes of the state. In this case, an autopsy was not ordered, and the Kopechnes buried their daughter.

The "standard" for exhumation does not vary from state to state.

There is no Pennsylvania case law before 1969, so we have to look to neighboring states. Rhode Island case law in 1949 stated that, except where necessary, "the sanctity of the grave should be maintained" and a body would not be ordered disinterred "unless there is a strong showing that it is necessary and interests of justice require it."[5]

New Jersey law in 1960 stated that a body should not be disinterred "unless it be clearly shown that good cause and urgent necessity for such action exists."[6]

Judge Brominski was consistent with these decisions when he said, in his decision, "Disinterment for the purpose of examination or autopsy should not be ordered unless it is clearly established that good cause and urgent necessity for such action exist. An order should not be made except on a strong showing that the facts sought will be established by an examination or autopsy."

After Chappaquiddick and the Kopechne decision, the sentiments and legal principles were upheld in Maryland in 1978: "Any right of wife to remove body of husband after it is interred is conditioned upon her having a sound reason."[7]

And in Maryland a year later: "While the disposition of each case involving potential disinterment is dependent on its own peculiar facts and circumstances, courts, exercising a benevolent discre-

[5] *Sylvia* v. *Helger* 67 A2d 27 75 R.I. 397 (1949).

[6] *Regna* v. *Spadone*, 159 A2d 142 60 N.J. Super. 353 (1960).

[7] *Doughterty* v. *Mercantile-Safe Deposit & Trust Co.*, 387 A2d 244 282 Md. 617 (1978).

tion, will be sensitive to all those promptings and emotions which men and women hold for sacred in disposition of their dead."[8]

The courts had not changed their minds in New Jersey in 1985 in a case even closer to the Kopechne case where the father had no right to his son's body after its interment, and could not even obtain an order for disinterment of the body "except by clear and convincing showing that autopsy sought would, in all probability, disclose the information sought."[9]

Obviously, disturbing the dead is considered a very serious matter in American society.

With all this in mind, it is much easier to understand Judge Brominski's decision. The standard for exhumation, even if the next of kin desire it, has been held to be *clear and convincing evidence*, a standard higher than preponderance but below beyond a reasonable doubt, that a useful or necessary purpose will be served.

Leo Damore, in *Senatorial Privilege*, states that Judge Brominski challenged a 1956 Pennsylvania Supreme Court ruling. Damore quotes *Frick* v. *McClelland*[10] as ruling "It is the duty of the court to have the body exhumed and an autopsy performed." The Tedrows cite that case as well. However, that language does not appear in the case. The case concerns the rights of coroners to do autopsies on fresh, not exhumed, bodies. Damore has admitted to us that he got the quote wrong.

No clear and convincing evidence could be offered to show cause for exhumation of Mary Jo Kopechne's remains.

The purpose of an autopsy is to determine a cause of death, not to satisfy the morbid curiosity of press and public about who had sex with whom how recently before the event or how long Mary Jo survived in the water. These details might be useful to know for political reasons, but legally they are of no significance.

The only claim Dinis could bring to court was that after he heard Kennedy's television speech, which he considered a con-

---

[8]*Gallaher* v. *Cherry Hill, Inc.*, 399 A2d 936 42 Md. App. 186 (1979).
[9]*Acevedo* v. *Essex County*, 504 A2d 813 207 N. J. Super. 579 (1985).
[10]384 Pa. 597, 122 A2d 43 (1956).

trived load of self-serving garbage, his suspicions and political survival hackles were raised, and he wanted more information. He could offer no probable theory for an alternate cause of death, nor could he claim that an autopsy would probably uncover evidence of a crime. Dinis could not even say that the Commonwealth of Massachusetts lacked sufficient evidence to prosecute any of the following charges: reckless driving, leaving the scene of an accident, driving while intoxicated, or vehicular manslaughter.

Mary Jo's death by drowning in the car was sufficient for Kennedy to be charged with any of these crimes except driving while intoxicated, and no amount of postmortem work on Mary Jo could prove that Senator Kennedy was intoxicated.

Experts in forensic medicine could not testify that an autopsy would provide "clear and convincing" evidence that a crime had been committed. No physician could testify to a reasonable medical certainty that another cause of death would be found. No law enforcement official could testify that there was probable cause that evidence of a crime would be found. See also chapter 5.

The Tedrows claim that the judge in this case ignored two hundred years of legal precedent. Brominski actually upheld it. Despite the fact that Thomas L. Tedrow has legal qualifications, both men do not seem to understand the difference between the standard for autopsy and the standard for exhumation. They quote several sources to "prove" that the exhumation should have been granted, but every one of those deals with autopsy, not exhumation. Even their statement that the Massachusetts law required an autopsy is wrong. The Massachusetts autopsy law[11] *allowed* an autopsy but did not require it.

Many authors have also condemned the Kennedy lawyers for asking that the inquest be closed.

Why was the inquest closed? Massachusetts law[12] allowed it

[11]See Appendix VII, Chapter 38, section 6.
[12]See Appendix VII, Chapter 38, section 8.

to be closed, and inquests usually were closed. It was Judge Boyle who first tried to stretch law and custom by allowing the press in. Kennedy and other prospective witnesses challenged this in their suit against him. They carried this further by asking for, in effect, the rights and privileges that would accrue to a criminal defendant for all witnesses, whether charged or not.

The Tedrows and Zad Rust go on about the secrecy of the inquest, as if a secret inquest is unusual. Inquests have always been more investigative than judicial proceedings. An inquest, like a grand jury proceeding, determines if there really was a crime in the first place. Its purpose is to inquire into the allegations and evidence and determine which of those allegations might be supported by enough evidence to show that a crime was committed and, sometimes, if there is enough evidence to try a defendant—and sometimes which defendant.

Investigations are usually confidential. An inquest may find that there was no irregularity at all in the death. Irrelevancies might be uncovered that are embarrassing to the subject of the investigation. Evidence might be found that would exonerate him or her, or too little evidence might be presented to bring a charge.

Not until charges are actually brought in court does the public have a right to know what evidence has been found to support what charges. Until recently the United States Supreme Court felt that the defendant was the only party interested in a public trial and that the openness of the trial was solely to protect the accused's rights to a fair trial.

In an inquest it is presumed that, because no charges have been brought, no legal defense is necessary.

The decision of the Supreme Court of Massachusetts granted some of the relief Kennedy asked for, but not all. The most controversial ruling was the impounding (not "sealing," as the Tedrows called it) of the inquest until all possibility of any criminal charges had passed. This impoundment applied only to the news media and the general public, not to the district attorney investigating the case. The problem with this decision surfaced later when Judge Pacquet decided that the "general public" included a duly constituted grand jury. This, of course, was nonsense, which we discussed earlier. Basically, the inquest was closed because inquests always had been in Massachusetts and *the statute allowed that they be closed.*

According to Kenneth Kappel, on January 25, 1982, an article in the *New York Times* claimed that the U.S. Supreme Court "reversed the Kennedy decision." There is no such article.

Kappel might have been referring to an article that appeared on page D21 on Thursday, June 24, 1982. This article is a straightforward account of *Globe Newspaper* v. *Superior Court for the County of Norfolk*,[13] a case that was not decided until June 23, 1982. This case actually dealt with the application of Massachusetts law, Chapter 278, section 16A. The article never mentions the words "Kennedy decision" or Kennedy.

This statute required that at a trial "for a crime involving sex where a minor under eighteen years of age is the complaining witness the judge shall exclude the general public from the courtroom during the testimony of such minor." In a 6–3 decision with four opinions filed (this was not a clear case), the court found that any such general rule for trials (not *pre*trial proceedings or inquests) violated the First Amendment, and should be applied only on a case-by-case basis when a compelling governmental interest makes it necessary. The court did not even say that a trial could never be closed; it said that each case must be decided on its own merits.

There is, indeed, a Supreme Court decision that upholds and would seem to affirm *Kennedy* v. *Justice.* That decision is *Gannet Co.* v. *DePasquale, County Court Judge of Seneca County, New York*, et al.[14] It states: "To safeguard the due process rights of the accused, a trial judge has an affirmative constitutional duty to minimize the effects of prejudicial pretrial publicity. . . . Publicity concerning pretrial suppression hearings poses special risks of unfairness . . . it may influence public opinion against a defendant. . . ."

[13]457 U.S. 596 (1982).
[14]443 U.S. 368 (1979).

The kindest thing we can say about Mr. Kappel is that he is very wrong.

Practically every book we've mentioned confuses or misrepresents facts and the law. The elder Tedrow is a lawyer, but he got the law on inquests and the law on exhumation wrong. Leo Damore interviewed a group of lawyers and believed them apparently without checking their statements against the applicable cases and statutes. All of these authors argue that the law is what they think it should be or what would achieve their ends.

No one without full medical training would offer opinions on the fine points of an appendectomy, even though it's the simplest of major surgery. Since the law is written in English, everyone thinks that he knows what it is. In a democracy, everyone has a right to say what the law *should* be. Courts and legislatures find themselves in continual disagreement over what it is.

Now that we have cleared up the misimpressions of over twenty years of yellow journalism, we come to the real question: Did Kennedy, because of his position, power, and money, get away with it (whatever *it* is)?

In order to answer that question, we need to understand what the punishment and penalty would be in a similar case for the normal, ordinary Joe off the street. Had this happened to Joe Street, a reasonably well-to-do citizen who could afford to vacation in Edgartown and could afford competent counsel, there would probably have been no inquest, no autopsy, and the sentence might have been even lighter.

Had Joe Street wandered into Chief Arena's office, counsel in tow, ten hours after an accident and announced that he'd driven his car off the Dyke Bridge, wandered around half the night, tried to get some sleep, and had a crack on his head, Arena, the competent professional, would have taken his statement and asked him if he needed medical attention, which would have been a good idea in Kennedy's case. Medical Examiner Mills would have had the same findings. If Mr. Street could afford to have the body transported to its relatives, he might well have done so. Lieutenant Killen probably would not have been so obstructive but there would have been no urgency about an autopsy since the cause of death appeared obvious and the press wouldn't have been breathing down anybody's neck. Mr. Street's counsel could well have arranged a plea bargain for reckless driving or leaving the scene of an accident, and no one would have thought much more about it, especially if the girl's parents, as in this case, were out of state and didn't stir up any fuss.

Things like this happen every day. Like most other people, few law enforcement officers go looking for extra work. Make it easy on them and they'll make it easy on you.

There has been much criticism of the plea bargain between DA Dinis and Kennedy's lawyers. Such plea bargains are an everyday fact of life in every court in the country. No prosecutor and no court could try all the cases that are brought. Nearly 90 percent are bargained out. Almost all of the evidence that Dinis had in this case came from Kennedy's own statements. This is not a strong position from which to try a case. Prosecutors don't like to lose. They'd rather nail the defendant for something than let him go.

In plea bargains, each side must rely on the other's word. In some courts, formal written plea agreements are filed, but in most the word of the attorneys involved must be relied on. The only sanction you have to enforce the prosecutor's word is that if he lies to you, you will: A, report him to his superiors; B, blackguard his name around the local bar association to such an extent that no one will trust him, and he will have to try or dismiss every one of those cases that he now plea bargains. Every day lawyers take each other's word over telephones for millions of dollars and for the liberty of their clients. If they couldn't, the whole judicial system would collapse. Dinis had, in effect, promised Kennedy's lawyers that the only charge against Kennedy would be leaving the scene of an accident. If he had brought another one, his reputation in the Massachusetts bar might have been destroyed.

Why, then, did Dinis reverse himself and try to force an exhumation in Pennsylvania? That's easy. He wasn't going after Kennedy, he was going after a cause of death. He probably fully expected the cause of death to be drowning and the record to be cleared. If the cause of death had been something else, it would have meant that Kennedy, through his lawyers, had lied to Dinis, and all bets would be off. Dinis could quite rightly have it both ways. By the time of the grand jury, it was evident there would be no autopsy, and Dinis was stuck with his original bargain.

For over twenty years jealous citizens, vindictive political rivals, and sensation-mongering journalists have tried to make out that Ted Kennedy got away with something that no one else could have gotten away with. On the contrary, he suffered a much greater series of penalties and misfortunes because of who he was.

Had it really been Joe Street and not Ted Kennedy who was driving the car, he would probably have copped to the lesser charge—reckless driving—and gotten a two-*week* suspended sentence, not a two-*month* suspended sentence, as Kennedy did. He would not have been subjected to the ordeal of the inquest. There would have been no exhumation hearing. His career probably would not have been blighted. Joe Street, anonymous affluent American, would have gotten off much easier than Ted Kennedy, scion of the Kennedy family, U.S. senator, and the Kennedy machine's next presidential candidate.

## Justice Done

We have just demonstrated how the crime Kennedy was convicted of and the sentence he received was hardly the least that could have been meted out in the circumstances.

"Cover-up" has been screamed, but we can find only three individuals who engaged in cover-up rather than incompetence and/or stupidity. Those individuals seem to have been acting alone and independently even of each other.

We must distinguish between Kennedy the citizen and Kennedy the politician. Kennedy the citizen took advantage of his right against self-incrimination, his right to counsel, and all those constitutional rights that counsel could secure for him. Most of us would do the same thing and probably would be called stupid if we didn't.

Kennedy the politician must bear the consequences of the actions and advice of the people he relied on.

So, while the Kennedy forces tried to put the best face possible on the situation, they did not succeed in having Kennedy absolved by the courts; nor did they succeed in keeping him a viable presidential candidate.

Since Chappaquiddick Kennedy, while repeatedly being reelected as senator from Massachusetts, has declined to be a presidential candidate except in 1980.

In 1969, just after the tragedy, Kennedy lost his position as Senate Majority Whip. He has not attempted to gain a leadership position in the Senate since. He is now, by virtue of seniority, chairman of the committee on Labor and Human Resources. While not a powerhouse committee, it handles health under the rubric of Human Resources. He also serves on Judiciary and Armed Services committees and is chairman of the subcommittee on Immigration and Refugee affairs.

In 1980 Kennedy chose to run for the Presidential nomination against Jimmy Carter. At the time, because of the Iran hostage crisis, Carter was one of the least popular presidents of the twentieth century. Yet President Carter, in his own words, "whipped [Kennedy's] ass."

The television statement lost Kennedy the press as well. As many Republicans had charged, from 1956 through 1969 the Kennedy family had totally owned the working press in this country. After the accident the owners of media outlets did not change editorial policy markedly, but the active reporters who had been pro-Kennedy almost to a man had become disenchanted.

One journalist who had covered the Kennedys and even written a favorable book about John later ruefully admitted, "They bought us all for Snow's clam chowder and a hot dog, and the access. We all felt like we were part of it."

All that started to end when the reporters were shut out of the Hyannis Port compound in the week following Chappaquiddick. The door closed completely when the speech was broadcast.

Now, whenever Kennedy rises to state or argue a "moral" position, because of Chappaquiddick thousands of people who might otherwise give him a hearing just start laughing.

Health issues seem to be the senator's main interest. Cancer and alcoholism have plagued his own family. Joe, Sr., and his children have logged an amazing amount of hospital time. The Kennedy Institute of Medical Ethics has been established at Georgetown University in Washington, D.C., and many family members work with the Special Olympics and handicapped children. The senator has settled down to being one of those experts in a small field without which the U.S. Senate could not function.

Personally, Kennedy has experienced some of those tragedies that all of us are heir too: a cancer-crippled son, divorce from an alcoholic wife. Little of this can be traced to Chappaquiddick and its aftermath, although Joan herself blames the tragedy for altering her relationship with her husband. But an alcoholic, discovered or denied, married or divorced, still has the disease and the capacity for causing pain to those around her. Chappaquiddick may have changed the timing of her life, but not the reality. Joan's mother was an alcoholic and she could well have inherited the tendency.

Given these facts, has an injustice been done to Kennedy, or even to the public? Has Kennedy been denied deserved chances for advancement? Has the public been denied a chance to vote for or against a public servant who may have made a good president?

First, did Kennedy really deserve the chance for advancement?

Edward Kennedy, married U.S. senator and presidential candidate, could not account for an hour and a half of his time with a young woman not his wife. Gary Hart, presidential candidate, ended his presidential chances with a similar act during which no one was injured and no property was even damaged. Kennedy's judgment must be faulted.

After the accident, Kennedy's hand-picked friends and associates, Paul Markham and Joe Gargan, did not have the sense to call for help or to get Kennedy to a hospital, actions that would definitely have seemed indicated to the average person. Kennedy picked these men. Even if he was completely unable to do anything after the accident, he still bears responsibility for their lack of action. This indicates another flaw in judgment. Giving the television speech, which raised infinitely more political questions than it answered, was another mistake. Even when it has been hand-fed to you by advisors on whom your brother, the president, had relied, it is a mistake. It even turned District Attorney Dinis, a man who had been willing to forget the whole thing, into a man who was asking more questions and demanding the exhumation of Mary Jo Kopechne's body. Some may think the speech won him reelection to the Senate from Massachusetts, but almost anything would have gotten him reelected. Massachusetts voters are not fickle. James Curley was elected from jail.

Ted Kennedy became head of the family by default. He never showed any leadership talent in school or his career. He followed the path of least resistance, attending Harvard and going on to law school. He became a politician because politics had evolved into the family business, thanks to a combination of his father's ambition and his mother's talent. In 1969, no female could have run for president, even one with the Kennedy magic. That left him, the baby, "Fat Stuff" grown up, to take up the family flag and go into political battle.

We don't think Teddy's heart was ever in it. All indications are that the accident at Chappaquiddick, while undeniably tragic, may have been the best thing for him and the country.

Did Kennedy's refusal to run for president in 1969 deny the public a chance to vote for him?

It is now time to make the comparison between Chappaquiddick and Watergate. Usually this is done in terms of self-righteous partisan rhetoric: "Nobody died at Watergate!" "Chappaquiddick was a personal problem, not an attempt to subvert the process!" A better comparison, we think, deals with the wisdom of the American electorate.

Did Nixon, the man who finally ended the Vietnam war, opened relations with China, and presided over reasonable prosperity, deserve to be hounded out of office over a third-rate burglary?

On the other hand, did the imperial presidency started by Roosevelt under the exigencies of depression and war and continued and expanded by all his successors (with the laudable exceptions of Truman and Eisenhower), which caused presidents to make vast treaties and commitments without consulting Congress and to treat federal agencies such as the Federal Bureau of Investigation and the Internal Revenue Service as personal fiefdoms to harass and spy on political opponents, need to be ended?

Did Kennedy, whose actions we have discussed here, deserve

to be pilloried from coast to coast as a drunkard, an adulterer, and a man who escaped justice only because of political pull?

On the other hand, is the man who was primarily responsible, through himself and through his agents, for the fiasco at Chappaquiddick and its aftermath a suitable individual to have his finger on the button?

The electorate is rather like a jury. It may get the facts confused or even wrong, but it tends to come out with a just and reasonable answer.

The other members of the party have fared quite well over the years.

**Jack Crimmins** is retired.

**Paul Markham** is now an associate with Neville & Segalini and Associates in Cambridge, Massachusetts.

**Joseph Gargan** is practicing law on State Street in Boston, Massachusetts. He joined Alcoholics Anonymous and has apparently stayed sober. He stayed Ted Kennedy's very good friend until 1982, when he was accused of "sitting around on his ass all winter" during Kennedy's Senate campaign. He became emotional and stormed out of the campaign office, and the Kennedy people said he had become estranged from the camp over a difference of opinion on abortion. He then ratted out his cousin and former friend to Leo Damore for use in his book *Senatorial Privilege.*

**Raymond LaRosa** is now an executive firefighter.

**Charles C. Tretter** is a lawyer for the New England Governors' Conference in Boston.

None of the women are secretaries.

**Esther Newburgh** became a literary agent for political writers in New York. She has risen through the ranks at Creative Artists Agency, agents for many top writers and performers.

**Rosemary Keough** is a lawyer and married.

**Anne "Nance" Lyons** is a trial lawyer practicing as Nance Lyons on Boston Place, Boston. She always was the powerhouse of the group, and hasn't changed.

**Maryellen Lyons** is a lawyer who for a while practiced with her sister.

**Susan Tannenbaum** became a lobbyist for Common Cause.

**Huck Look** was elected sheriff of Duke's County.

**Edmond Dinis** lost his bid for reelection as District Attorney and is now in private practice in New Bedford.

**Lieutenant Killen** died of cancer in 1979.

**Bernie Flynn** retired from the State Police in 1980. After Leo Damore published *Senatorial Privilege*, Flynn sued him. Flynn claimed that Damore had promised him big money for his story and had failed to pay.

**Judge James Boyle** retired soon after the case.

**Judge Wilfred Pacquet** retired in 1970 and has since died.

**Dr. Robert Watt** has retired.

**Dr. Brougham** died in 1979.

**Edgartown** didn't have a peaceful future from 1969 on. There have been several police chiefs since Arena. In 1974, *Jaws* was filmed there. The full-time medical examiner, Robert Nevin, played himself, and a Silva had a bit part. The entire town suffered the indignities of a Hollywood film crew bullying its way around. Was the money they made worth it? Some think so, some think not. Oddly enough, in 1987 part of *Jaws IV* was also filmed there. Either a lot of people wanted the money very badly, or they forgot the agony.

**The Dyke Bridge** is no longer an old wooden bridge without guard rails. It has been rebuilt as a concrete-and-steel span with guard rails.

**The 1967 Oldsmobile 88** became the property of the insurance company. It was bought back by Kennedy interests, stripped for parts, and compacted to prevent anyone exhibiting it as "The Chappaquiddick Death Car."

**The Kennedy Family** proves to have staying power in the public eye. Ted was not, as some thought, the "last Kennedy." His nephew Joe III, Robert's son, who was present at Edgartown that weekend, is now a congressman from Massachusetts, holding the seat that John held as his first public office and Michael Curley held before him. Young Joe Kennedy's sister Kathleen Townsend ran for Congress from Maryland, where she is now living with her husband. She was defeated, and is now supporting compulsory public service for Maryland students. John Kennedy, Jr., passed his bar exam and joined the prosecutor's office, where many of the family started, though he is in New York and not Boston. He was also voted *People Magazine*'s sexiest man of the year in 1989. Patrick, one of Bobby's sons, is a Rhode Island state legislator. The family suffered another loss when another of Bobby's sons, David, died of a drug overdose in a Florida motel room. Robert Kennedy, Jr., was arrested in 1983 for possession of a gram of heroin. Since he lost a leg to cancer, Ted, Jr., travels around the country showing other young amputees how they can lead full, athletic lives in spite of their handicaps. He has also gone into a twelve-step program. Maria Shriver, daughter of Eunice and Sargent Shriver, is a broadcaster for NBC. She is married to former Mr. America, movie star, and Republican Arnold Schwarzenegger. It may be another kind of justice that Schwarzenegger is now a more recognizable name than Kennedy.

In 1991 William Smith, M.D., son of Jean Kennedy Smith and the late Steven, was charged with rape in Palm Beach, Florida. His Uncle Ted was on the premises, the Kennedy compound south, at the time of the alleged attack. The press had a field day. The Teddy haters, rabid righties, and disappointed lefties sharpened their fangs. But this matter was settled where it should have been—in the court of the State of Florida. Ted really ought to stay away from beaches.

**The Kennedy Family fortune**, a trust known as the Park Agency in 1969 that made possible the careers of John, Robert, and Edward, is suffering. Although it was estimated to be $250 million in 1957, the true figure was probably closer to $100 million. It has not kept up with the Dow Jones or even with inflation. Today it is known as Joseph P. Kennedy Enterprises and estimated to be about $350 million. Its chief holding is the Merchandise Mart in Chicago, a depreciating asset. Since the death of Stephen Smith the management has fallen to a Wharton MBA, Joseph Akim. The continuance of the trust depends on the survival of Pat Kennedy Lawford, Eunice Kennedy Shriver, and Rosemary Kennedy. When the last of those three women dies, the trust will be liquidated and the money distributed. No descendant of Joseph P. Kennedy is a financial tycoon. None appears to be actively engaged in making money. They are all either wage earners, politicians, or volunteers.

**Senator Edward Moore Kennedy** is still serving the citizens of Massachusetts. In the early 1980s, he announced that he would not run for president in 1984 and he and Joan divorced shortly thereafter. Joan was awarded the house on Cape Cod in the divorce settlement and remains close to many Kennedy family friends. In 1992, Senator Kennedy remarried.

**Regatta Footnote.** The summer of 1986 saw the wedding of Caroline Kennedy, President John Kennedy's daughter, at Hyannis Port. Ted Kennedy, Jr., the senator's son, was not in attendance. He was sailing in the Edgartown Regatta ". . . as for thirty years my family has participated . . ."

# APPENDIX A

Friday, July 25, 1969

7:30 P.M.

Live broadcast from the Hyannis Port home of Joseph P. Kennedy

Basic theme worked out with Kennedy

Written by Ted Sorenson, David Burke, Milton Gwirtzman; reviewed by Burke Marshall, Kennedy's personal attorney

My Fellow Citizens:

I have requested this opportunity to talk to the people of Massachusetts about the tragedy which happened last Friday evening. This morning I entered a plea of guilty to the charge of leaving the scene of an accident. Prior to my appearance in court it would have been improper for me to comment on these matters. But tonight I am free to tell you what happened and to say what it means to me.

On the weekend of July 18 I was on Martha's Vineyard Island participating with my nephew Joe Kennedy—as for thirty years my family has participated—in the annual Edgartown sailing regatta. Only reasons of health prevented my wife from accompanying me.

On Chappaquiddick Island, off Martha's Vineyard, I attended on Friday evening, July 18, a cookout I had encouraged and helped sponsor for a devoted group of Kennedy campaign secretaries. When I left the party, about 11:15 P.M., I was accompanied by one of these girls, Miss Mary Jo Kopechne. Mary Jo was one of the most devoted members of the staff of Senator Robert Kennedy. She worked for him for four years and was broken up over his death. For this reason, and because she was such a gentle, kind and idealistic person, all of us tried to help her feel that she still had a home with the Kennedy family.

There is no truth, no truth whatever, to the widely circulated suspicions of immoral conduct that have been leveled at my behavior and hers regarding that evening. There has never been a private relationship between us of any kind. I know of nothing in Mary Jo's conduct on that or any other occasion—the same is true of the other girls at that party—that would lend any substance to such ugly speculation about their character. Nor was I driving under the influence of liquor.

Little over one mile away, the car that I was driving on an unlit road went off a narrow bridge which had no guardrails and was built on a left angle to the road. The car overturned in a deep pond and immediately filled with water. I remember thinking as the cold water rushed in around my head that I was for certain drowning. Then water entered my lungs and I actually felt the sensation of drowning. But somehow I struggled to the surface alive. I made immediate and repeated efforts to save Mary Jo by diving into the strong and murky current but succeeded only in increasing my state of utter exhaustion and alarm.

My conduct and conversations during the next several hours to the extent that I can remember them make no sense to me at all. Although my doctors informed me that I suffered a cerebral concussion as well as shock, I do not seek to escape responsibility for my actions by placing the blame either on the physical, emotional trauma brought on by the accident or on anyone else.

I regard as indefensible the fact that I did not report the accident to the police immediately.

Instead of looking directly for a telephone after lying exhausted in the grass for an undetermined time, I walked back to the cottage where the party was being held and requested the help of my two friends, my cousin Joseph Gargan and Paul Markham, and directed them to return immediately to the scene with me—this was some time after midnight—in order to undertake a new effort to dive down and locate Miss Kopechne. Their strenuous efforts, undertaken at some risks to their own lives, also proved futile.

All kinds of scrambled thoughts—all of them confused, some of them irrational, many of them which I cannot recall and some of which I would not have seriously entertained under normal circumstances—went through my mind during this period. They were reflected in the various inexplicable, inconsistent and inconclusive things I said and did, including such questions as whether the girl might still be alive somewhere out of that immediate area, whether some awful curse did actually hang over all the Kennedys, whether there was some unjustifiable reason for me to doubt what had happened and to delay my report, whether somehow the awful weight of this incredible incident might in some way pass from my shoulders. I was overcome, I'm frank to say, by a jumble of emotion—grief, fear, doubt, exhaustion, panic, confusion and shock.

Instructing Gargan and Markham not to alarm Mary Jo's friends that night, I had them take me to the ferry crossing. The ferry having shut down for the night, I suddenly jumped into the water and impulsively swam across, nearly drowning once again in the effort, and returned to my hotel about 2 A.M. and collapsed in my room. I remember going out at one point and saying something to the room clerk.

In the morning, with my mind somewhat more lucid, I made an effort to call a family legal advisor, Burke Marshall, from a public telephone on the Chappaquiddick side of the ferry and belatedly reported the accident to the Martha's Vineyard police.

Today, as I mentioned, I felt morally obligated to plead guilty to the charge of leaving the scene of an accident. No words on my part can possibly express the terrible pain and suffering I feel over this tragic incident. This last week has been an agonizing one for me and the members of my family, and the grief we feel over the loss of a wonderful friend will remain with us the rest of our lives.

These events, the publicity, innuendo and whispers which have surrounded them and my admission of guilt this morning raise the question in my mind of whether my standing among the people of my state has been so impaired that I should resign my seat in the United States Senate. If at any time the citizens of Massachusetts should lack confidence in their senator's character or his ability, with or without justification, he could not in my opinion adequately perform his duty and should not continue in office.

The people of this state, the state which sent John Quincy Adams and Daniel Webster and Charles Sumner and Henry Cabot Lodge and John Kennedy to the United States Senate, are entitled to representation in that body by men who inspire their utmost confidence. For this reason, I would understand full well why some might think it right for me to resign. For me this will be a difficult decision to make.

It has been seven years since my first election to the Senate. You and I share many memories—some of them have been glorious, some have been very sad. The opportunity to work with you and serve Massachusetts has made my life worthwhile.

And so I ask you tonight, people of Massachusetts, to think this through with me. In facing this decision, I seek your advice and opinion. In making it, I seek your prayers. For this is a decision that I will have finally to make on my own.

It has been written a man does what he must in spite of personal consequences, in spite of obstacles and dangers and pressures, and that is the basis of all human morality. Whatever may be the sacrifices he faces, if he follows his conscience—the loss of his friends, his fortune, his contentment, even the esteem of his fellow man—each man must decide for himself the course he will follow. The stories of past courage cannot supply courage itself. For this, each man must look into his own soul.

I pray that I can have the courage to make the right decision. Whatever is decided and whatever the future holds for me, I hope that I shall be able to put this most recent tragedy behind me and make some further contribution to our state and mankind, whether it be in public or private life.

Thank you and good night.

# APPENDIX B

*Text of the Decision
Closing the Inquest to
the Press*

252 N.E. 2d 201
The Supreme Judicial Court of Massachusetts
Suffolk

Kennedy v. Justice of the District Court of Dukes Co. Mass.
(and two companion cases[1])

Decided Oct. 30, 1969.

Before Wilkens, C.J. and Spalding, Cutter, Spiegel and
Reardon, JJ.

BY THE COURT

These cases originally brought in the County Court for Suffolk
County, are each entitled, "Petition for Writ of Certiorari and
Related Relief Pursuant to G.L. c. 211, section 3." They seek
review of certain acts of the respondent relating to an inquest at

[1]The companion cases are petitions by Joseph Gargan and by John B.
Crimmins and seven other petitioners against the same respondent.

which he was to preside. The cases involve questions not covered by our decisions. To expedite their consideration, the single justice properly reserved and reported the cases, "for such degree as may be appropriate." The record consists of the consolidated petitions, the respondent's return, the transcript of proceedings in the county court, the single justice's order of September 2, 1969, which enjoined the respondent from proceeding with the inquest pending the determination by the full court, and the statement of agreed facts.

We summarize the agreed facts. On or about July 18, 1969, Miss Mary Jo Kopechne of the District of Columbia, formerly a secretary in Washington to the brother of the petitioner Kennedy, died after the automobile in which she was riding and which was operated by the petitioner Kennedy went off "Dyke Bridge" on Chappaquiddick Island in the county of Dukes County. Each of the petitioners and the deceased were in attendance at a social event which took place on Chappaquiddick Island on the evening of July 18.

On July 25 the petitioner Kennedy before the respondent, the justice of the District Court of Dukes County, pleaded guilty to, and was sentenced, upon a complaint under G.L. c. 90, section 24 (II) (a), commonly known as leaving the scene of an accident after causing personal injury.

Later that day the petitioner Kennedy requested and received from the three major Boston television stations and their associated radio station, the opportunity to address the voters of the Commonwealth. The national television and radio networks requested and received from this petitioner and from those Boston television and radio stations, permission to tie in and broadcast his statement, which was later broadcast nationally by television and radio. The statement, which is set forth verbatim in the agreed facts, contains some explanation of his conduct. He in part stated: "These events and the publicity and innuendo and whispers which have surrounded them, and my admission of guilt this morning, raises the question in my mind of whether my standing among the people of my state has been so impaired that

I should resign my seat in the United States Senate." He concluded by appealing to the people of Massachusetts for their advice and opinion to enable him to make a decision on that question.

On August 7 the district attorney of the Southern District by letter to the respondent exercised his authority under G.L. c. 38, section 8 (as amended through St. 1939, c. 30)[2] to require an inquest in the death of Miss Kopechne. On August 8 the respondent designated Sept. 3 as the date for the inquest and announced in open court: "The statutes permit exclusion of all those not required to attend. I have decided to exercise some discretion in that regard and to exclude all except legitimate and accredited members of the press, television, radio and other news media." Subpoenas were served upon 15 witnesses and other subpoenas were issued by the clerk, but not served, on the petitioners in one of the two companion cases. Thereafter the clerk of the District Court drew up and posted a long list of representatives of the news media who would be permitted to attend the inquest. The courtroom, the only one on the island of Martha's Vineyard, has 160 seats, 120 of which are outside the bar enclosure. Because the petitioner Kennedy is a prominent political figure, all events relating to the accident including the scheduled inquest, have been given extensive coverage by the local, national, and international news media.

The petitioner Kennedy, describing himself as "the operator of the motor vehicle," and all the other petitioners, describing themselves as "prospective witnesses," filed motions in substance that they "be permitted the right to be represented by counsel  *   *   * and to have counsel present during the entire proceeding that *   *   * counsel be permitted to examine and cross examine all witnesses and to seek rulings from the court with respect to relevancy  *   *   * of all evidence, to present evidence and to have the power to compel attendance of witnesses *   *   *." There were hearings before the respondent on

[2]See footnote *post.*

August 27 and 28. These motions were denied on August 28, the judge stating: "I am not satisfied that the United States Supreme Court would read the Due Process Clause into our inquest procedure. That is for the United States Supreme Court to say and not for me. *   *   * Witnesses will come into the courtroom singly, may be represented during their appearance in the courtroom by counsel for the sole purpose of advice on constitutional rights against self-incrimination and, where appropriate, [on] privileged communications, and for no other purpose and counsel for that witness will leave the courtroom when the witness leaves the courtroom."

During the hearings the respondent twice declared that it was essential that the petitioner Kennedy, the only eyewitness, be present at the inquest.

At the August 27 hearing, in response to a question by counsel for some petitioners as to "what the ground rules are going to be" the judge had said "That the scope of the proceedings will be such as will enable me to submit the report required" by G.L. c. 38, section 12. "That is, that I must report in writing when, where, and by what means the person met her death, her name, if known, and all material circumstances attending her death and the name, if known, of any person whose unlawful act or negligence appears to have contributed thereto. I will go no further than saying that will be the scope of the inquest. As to physical aspects, I can tell you that there will be no microphones, no cameras, no listening or recording devices allowed in the courtroom. *   *   * The District Attorney has an option to examine and call witnesses, but as I see it, the primary responsibility rests with the judge who may, and in my case would, call any other witnesses, as the evidence develops, he thinks might have something to add to the truth." On the following day at the hearing the judge repeated that he would call "everybody who can be helpful in reaching the required decision."

The petitions for writs of certiorari allege that the rulings of the respondent deprive the petitioners of rights secured to them by the Sixth Amendment to the Constitution of the United States as applied to the states by the Fourteenth Amendment in that (1) the order of August 28 operates to deprive them of the rights to be represented by counsel, to confront and cross-examine witnesses, to present evidence and to compel the attendance of witnesses in "a public and formal judicial proceeding which constitutes the exercise of an accusatory function"; and (2) the ruling of August 8 "sanctions publicity in connection with a hearing of a preliminary nature so widespread as to taint with irremediable prejudice any subsequent judicial proceeding which may arise out of the accident." The petitions allege that the rulings have caused substantial injury and manifest injustice to the petitioners.

In this Commonwealth over a century ago inquests in violent deaths were conducted by coroners with a jury of six. Rev. Sts. (1836) c. 140, sections 1, 2. The coroner had power to summon and swear witnesses (sections 5, 6), whose testimony was reduced to writing by the coroner (section 7). The jury delivered to the coroner their inquisition in which they were to find when, how, and by what means the deceased person came to his death and all the material circumstances. If it appeared that he was murdered, the jurors were to state who was guilty (section 8). The coroner had power to bind over witnesses to the appropriate court (section 9). If any person charged by the inquest with having committed the offense was not in custody, the coroner had power to issue process for his apprehension (section 10).

By St.1850, c. 133, section 1, it was provided that the coroner with the consent of a majority of the jury "may order that a secret inquisition be taken." In such case he might at this discretion exclude all persons other than those required to be present and during the examination of a witness might exclude all the other witnesses, and direct that they be kept separate. By St. 1877, c. 200, the office of the coroner was abolished (section 1), and that of medical examiner was created (section 2). The inquest was to conducted by the court or a trial justice (section 10), who was to make the report (section 12). He had power in certain cases to bind over witnesses "as in criminal prosecutions" to appear and testify at the court in which an indictment might be found (section 13), and to issue process for arrest of persons not in custody (section 14).

The subject of inquests is now covered by G.L. c. 38, sections 8–13.[3]

At the threshold lies a serious question of procedure. It is our opinion that certiorari will not lie. We have been referred to Drowne v. Stimpson, 2 Mass. 441, 445, where proceedings on a bastardy complaint were quashed on writ of error. The last sentence of that opinion drew a distinction from certiorari which, it was there said, would lie at "any stage of the proceedings, at the *discretion* of the court." This statement was not necessary to that decision, and has not been adopted in our practice as a method of reviewing rulings by a quasi-judicial tribunal before any final determination by that tribunal.[4]

We need not now intimate whether there may be a review of an inquest like the present after completion of the proceeding.

We are asked by the petitioners to exercise our extensive powers including those under G.L. c. 211, section 3 (as amended through St.1956, c.707, section 1). This statute recognizes that this court has "general superintendence of the administration of

[3] "* * * The * * * district attorney may * * * require an inquest to be held in case of any death supposed to have been caused by external means. The court or justice shall give seasonable notice of the time and place of the inquest * * * to the department of public works in any case of death in which any motor vehicle is involved. All persons not required by law to attend may be excluded from the inquest. The district attorney * * * may attend the inquest and examine the witnesses, who may be kept separate so that they cannot converse with each other until they have been examined (section 8). "The magistrate shall report in writing when, where, and by what means the person met his death, * * * and the name, if known, of any person whose unlawful act or negligence appears to have contributed thereto. He shall file his report in the superior court for the county where the inquest is held." (section 12). "If a person charged by the report with the commission of a crime is at large, the magistrate shall forthwith issue process for his arrest, returnable before any court or magistrate having jurisdiction. If he finds that murder, manslaughter or an assault has been committed, he may bind over, for appearance in said court, as in criminal cases, such witnesses as he considers necessary, or as the district attorney may designate." (section 13).

[4] Holding an inquest is a quasi-judicial function. LaChapelle v. United Shoe Mach. Corp., 318 Mass. 166, 169, 61 N.E. 2d 8, and cases cited.

all courts of inferior jurisdiction" including the issuance of "such order, directions and rules as may be necessary or desirable for the furtherance of justice, the regular execution of the laws, the improvement of the administration of such courts, and the securing of their proper and efficient administration." We have seldom exercised these powers except as one basis for a rule of general application. Nevertheless, we consider whether there is such risk of serious abuse of the inquest procedure, or of a miscarriage of justice, as to make it appropriate for us to act.

The practice in inquests in the Commonwealth has been to allow the course of the proceedings to remain in the discretion of the District Court. An inquest is not a prosecution of anybody. It is not a trial of anyone. The pertinent statutory provisions exemplify a public policy that the inquest serves as an aid in the achievement of justice by obtaining information as to whether a crime has been committed. See Second and Final Report of Judicature Commission, 6 Mass. L.Q. No. 2, p. 109. Probably most inquests have been closed to the public. Some inquests have been public, usually where the matter was not of general interest.

It never has been expressly provided in legislation in this Commonwealth that inquests must be secret. We cannot attribute that result to the ambiguous statement in Jewett v. Boston Elev. Ry., 219 Mass. 528, 532, 107 N.E. 433, where the authorities cited are statutes which are the ancestors of sections now in G.L. c. 38, relating to medical examiners and inquests, and show that no such interpretation was intended. When the Legislature has intended to have closed proceedings, as in the case of the grand jury, the statutory language has been unmistakable. See G.L. c.277, sections 12, 13.

Few decisions in the Commonwealth discuss the conduct of inquests. Such decisions as there are seem to be consistent with what appears to be the law generally. This is, in effect, that inquests are investigatory in character and not accusatory. State ex rel. Schulter v. Roraff, 39 Wis. 2d 342, 350–351, 159 N.W. 2d 25; Wolfe v. Robinson (1961) Ont. 250, 262, 27 D.L.R. 2d 98; affd. (1962) Ont. 132, 31 D.L.R. 2d 233. They are not part of any crimininal proceedings which may ensue. People v. Coker, 104 Cal.App. 2d 224, 225, 231 P.2d 81; State v. Burnett, 357 Mo. 106, 112, 206 S.W. 2d 345. Cf. LaChapelle v. United Shoe Mach. Corp., 318 Mass. 166, 169–170, 61 N.E. 2d 8. Under statutes resembling our own, in order to initiate a criminal prosecution, there must be subsequent and independent criminal proceedings. Smalls v. State, 101 Ga. 570, 571, 28 S.E. 981, 40 L.R.A. 369; Commonwealth ex rel. Czako v. Maroney, 412 Pa. 448, 450, 194 A. 2d 867. It may be that, to show an admission or confession at an inquest or to prove the prior inconsistent statement of a witness, some evidence at an inquest will be admissible at later criminal proceedings in accordance with usual principles of the law of evidence. The inquest decision itself is not admissible. See Jewett v. Boston Elev. Ry., 219 Mass. 528, 531-33, 107 N.E. 433; Aetna Life Ins. Co. v. Milward, 118 Ky. 716, 725–731, 82 S.W. 364, 68 L.R.A. 285. See also Commonwealth v. Ryan, 134 Mass. 223. There is no inherent right of any witness at an inquest to cross-examine other witnesses or to present evidence of his own. Aetna Life Ins. Co. v. Milward, 118 Ky. 716, 726, 82 S.W. 364, 68 L.R.A. 285; State v. Griffin, 98 S.C. 105, 111, 82 S.E. 254; People v. Collins, 20 How.Prac. 111, 114 (N.Y. Oyer and Terminer). The magistrate holding the inquest has wide discretion in its conduct. Anderson, Sheriffs, Coroners & Constables, section 747. He may permit cross-examination or the presentation of evidence by possibly interested persons when it may be helpful to the magistrate or might serve to diminish the possibility of injustice or to avoid injury to reputation. There is, of course, some practical limit to the number of counsel who helpfully can participate in the same hearing at the same time. He may, we assume, receive and record sworn offers of proof as an aid to determining whether the receipt of testimony will help him in any respect or as a method of affording witnesses the opportunity for amplification or correction of their own testimony or that of others. He should carefully explain to witnesses, if it appears to be necessary or appropriate to do so, their privilege not to incriminate themselves. See State v. Burnett, 357 Mo. 106, 112–14, 206 S.W. 2d 345. See also People v. Ferola, 215 N.Y. 285, 109 N.E. 500.

Cf. Neely v. United States, 79 U.S.App.D.C. 177, 144 F.2d 519, cert. den. 323 U.S. 754, 65 S.Ct. 83, 89 L.Ed. 604. The inquest judge also may close the hearings in whole or in part and at any time in order to avoid unfairness to anyone or to prevent improper prejudice in possible subsequent criminal proceedings. G.L. c. 38, section 8. In so doing he may take into account previous public statements and the relative advantages and risks of public, compared with closed, hearings, including the risk of erroneous rumors.

The inquest here presents unusual problems. It has aroused great public interest, which in turn has stimulated very great efforts by the press, radio, television, and other media to provide news coverage. The petitioners suggest that intensive coverage of the inquest might involve unfortunate pre-trial publicity if the proceedings and the report should lead to action before a grand jury or to a prosecution for some offence. The circumstance that the petitioner Kennedy was the operator of the vehicle and the only available eyewitness has caused him to become what his counsel describes as the focus of the investigation. This has led to the argument that the proceedings have become accusatory as to him and to a demand that he at once be accorded what would be constitutional rights of a defendant in a criminal case. The other petitioners made somewhat similar claims for themselves.

We think that inquest proceedings are not accusatory and that they should be regarded as investigatory. The decisions already cited are controlling in this respect. Nevertheless, if the proceedings are public the activities of the news media may be such as to make it difficult, if not impossible, for a long time to ensure to a defendant a fair trial in any criminal proceedings which may follow the inquest. A public inquest also may tend to limit or delay the inquest investigation.

The difficulties presented are not lessened by the circumstances that the petitioner Kennedy's own resort to television may itself have increased public interest in the events of July 18, 1969, and public demand for a more complete investigation and explanation of those events. The risk of prejudice in possible later proceedings from pre-trial publicity remains.

We shall not make any special rule for a particular case. If it is desirable to prescribe procedural rules for any Massachusetts inquest, those rules must affect all inquests and all participating persons equally. Although few inquests may be likely to arouse public interest as has this one, other situations involving similar risks of prejudice may occur and citizens and others, less well known to the public and less able to protect themselves, affected by, or participating in less conspicuous inquests, must have whatever type of protection, if any, is now to be afforded to these petitioners.

Recent cases in the Supreme Court of the United States discussing the dangers of pre-trial publicity go far in the direction of protecting actual defendants. See e. g. Estes v. Texas, 381 U.S. 532, 85 S.Ct. 1628, 14 L.Ed.2d 543; Sheppard v. Maxwell, 384 U.S. 333, 86, S.Ct. 1507, 16 L.Ed.2d 600. See also Delaney v. United States, 199 F.2d 107, 115 (1st Cir.). See State ex rel. Schulter v. Roraff, 39 Wis.2d 342, 159 N.W.2d 25. They point to the wisdom of taking action to diminish such dangers.

The petitioners also lay great store by Jenkens v. McKeithen, 395 U.S. 411, 89 S.Ct. 1843, 23 L.Ed.2d 404, a 5 to 3 decision of the Supreme Court of the United States dated June 9, 1969, in a controversy between a labor union member and the Labor-Management Commission of Inquiry created by an unusual Louisiana statute. The opinion of three justices appears to rest in large measure upon the ground (pp. 424–425, 89 S.Ct. 1843) that the complaint contained sufficient allegations of injury to the complainant to afford him "standing to challenge" the statute and (pp. 429–431, 89 S.Ct. 1843) to make a hearing in the trial court appropriate to determine whether the complainant was "entitled to declaratory or injunctive relief." Two justices concurred. There was a persuasive dissent in which three justices joined. One justice of the three joining in the first opinion has retired. We are by no means clear what the precise ratio decidendi is, or that the decision (see e. g. p. 430, 89 S.Ct. 1843) has any necessary application to our investigatory inquest procedure, which has a long historical background. We hope that the

*Jenkens* case will be materially clarified before we are again confronted by it.

The cases just cited, although in our opinion not decisive, do suggest general reappraisal of our inquest procedure in the interest of making it conform more closely with certain constitutional views expressed in the decisions, mentioned above, of the Supreme Court of the United States. We think that, to protect the integrity, the investigatory character, and the effectiveness of inquests, it is desirable to prescribe application of the following general principles: (1) All inquests shall be closed to the public and to all news media. (2) Witnesses may be accompanied and advised by counsel while in attendance or testifying at an inquest. (3) In other respects, inquests shall be conducted in the sound discretion of the inquest judge in general in accordance with the principles already discussed above. (4) Upon the completion of the inquest, the inquest documents shall remain impounded and the inquest judge shall transmit his report and a transcript of the evidence received by him to the appropriate clerk of the Superior Court. (5) While these papers remain impounded, access to the report and transcript shall be afforded only to the Attorney General, the appropriate District Attorney, and to counsel for any person who has been stated in the report as having actual or possible responsibility for the decedent's death, except that any witness at the inquest shall be permitted, through counsel or directly, to check the accuracy of the transcript of his own testimony and to file with the inquest judge and the appropriate clerk of the Superior Court any suggested corrections. (6) (a) If the District Attorney shall file with the appropriate clerk of the Superior Court a written certificate that no prosecution is proposed, or (b) if it shall appear that an indictment has been sought and not returned, or (c) if trial of the persons named in the report as responsible for the decedent's death shall have been completed, or (d) if the judge of the Superior Court shall determine that no criminal trial is likely, then upon order of the Superior Court, the report and transcript shall be opened forthwith to public examination.

The principles outlined above should not hinder or delay the pending inquest or any other proper inquest inquiry. Indeed, such inquiries may be substantially facilitated by encouraging witnesses to come forward and to make full disclosure without fear that their testimony will be published in segments or out of context, or published at all (a) until passed upon by the inquest judge in his report and until the events have been considered by the fact finder in any criminal proceeding, and (b) until after probability of criminal proceedings has ceased. These general rules tend to avoid embarrassment, by premature publicity about an investigation conducted in behalf of the Commonwealth, either to the Commonwealth (in seeking or prosecuting indictments or complaints) or to any potential defendant in making a defence. Under the principles stated, all facts concerning the inquiry must eventually be published, and at the earliest possible time consistent with fairness to all parties. Their applications, as has been suggested above, will make the Massachusetts inquest procedure less vulnerable to future constitutional objection if some views expressed in the Jenkens case, 395 U.S. 411, 89 S. Ct. 1843, *supra*, should be expanded.

The District Court judge should not be disqualified on the record before us. The first reason given is that the judge is a party to the present litigation. He was, of course, made a formal party by the petitioners as a method of seeking review of the orders. This is not enough to disqualify him. Kelly v. New York. N. H. & H. R. R., 139 F.Supp. 319, 320 (D.C. Mass.). The petitioners also argue that disqualification will avoid bias or the appearance of bias. An earlier expression of opinion on a matter to be decided is not the kind of bias which disqualifies a judge. King v. Grace, 293 Mass. 244, 247, 200 N.E. 346, and cases cited. The alleged bias and prejudice to be disqualifying must rise from extrajudicial source and not from something learned from participation in the case. United States v. Grinnell Corp., 384 U.S. 563, 583, 86. S. Ct. 1698, 16 L. Ed. 2d 778.

The petitions for writs of certiorari are to be dismissed. The proposed inquest, and all inquests hereafter, shall proceed in compliance with the general principles herein specified.

So ordered.

# APPENDIX C

*Text of Kennedy's Inquest*

*Testimony*

---

## INQUEST HELD JANUARY 5–JANUARY 8, 1970

---

Judge Boyle made an opening statement. References to Mr. Teller are to Thomas Teller, Clerk of the Court.

**THE COURT.** Senator, would you take the witness stand?
**SENATOR KENNEDY.** Yes.
**DINIS.** Please give your name to the court.
**KENNEDY.** Edward Moore Kennedy.
**Q.** And where is your legal residence, Mr. Kennedy?
**A.** Three Charles River Square, Boston.
**Q.** Directing your attention to July 18, 1969, were there plans made by you to have a gathering on Martha's Vineyard Island?
**A.** There were.
**Q.** And what were these plans, Mr. Kennedy?

*A.* There were plans to participate in an annual sailing regatta in Edgartown on the dates of Friday, July 18th, and Saturday, July 19th, and with my cousin Joe Gargan, Mr. Markham, Mr. LaRosa and a number of other people, a number of other individuals.

*Q.* When were these plans made?

*A.* Well, I had planned to participate in the regatta for some period of weeks.

*Q.* And were there any particular arrangements made for this gathering that we have just discussed?

*A.* Well, I had entered my boat in the regatta and had listed my crew. I had made those arrangements through my cousin, Joe Gargan.

*Q.* Were there any arrangements made to rent a house on Chappaquiddick?

*A.* I had made no such arrangements myself.

*Q.* Do you know who did?

*A.* Yes I do.

*Q.* May we have that name?

*A.* Mr. Gargan.

*Q.* Mr. Gargan. When did you arrive on the Island in conjunction with this gathering?

*A.* On July 18th, about one o'clock.

*Q.* One P.M.?

*A.* That is correct.

*Q.* Was there anyone with you?

*A.* No, I arrived by myself.

*Q.* And where did you stay, Senator?

*A.* Well, at the Shiretown Inn.

*Q.* Could you tell the court what your activities were during that afternoon from the time of your arrival?

*A.* Well, I arrived shortly after one o'clock on July 18th, was met by Mr. John B. Crimmins, driven through town, made a brief stop to pick up some fried clams, traveled by ferry to Chappaquiddick Island to a small cottage there where I changed into a bathing suit, later visited the beach on I imagine the east side of that island for a brief swim, returned to the cottage and changed into another bathing suit, returned to the ferry slip and waded out to my boat, the *Victoria* [The court stenographer misheard the name of the boat, *Victura*.], later participated in a race which ended approximately six o'clock.

*Q.* When did you check into the Shiretown Inn that day?

*A.* Sometime after six-thirty, before seven o'clock.

*Q.* Was anyone else in your party staying at the Shiretown Inn?

*A.* My cousin, Joe Gargan.

*Q.* Did your nephew, Joseph Kennedy, stay there?

*A.* Not to my knowledge.

*Q.* Now, following your checking in at the Shiretown Inn, what were your activities after that?

*A.* I returned to my room, visited with a few friends just prior to returning to that room on the porch which is outside the room of the Shiretown Inn, washed up briefly and returned to Chappaquiddick Island.

*Q.* What time did you return to Chappaquiddick Island at that time?

*A.* It was sometime shortly after seven o'clock.

*Q.* And these friends that you had some conversation with at the Shiretown, do you have their names?

*A.* I do.

*Q.* May we have them?

*A.* Well, they are Mr. Ross Richards; I believe Mr. Stanley Moore was there that evening, and perhaps one or two of their crew, maybe Mrs. Richards. I am not familiar with the names. I know the other members of his crew, but I would say a group of approximately five or six.

*Q.* Do you recall the number of the room in which you were staying?

*A.* I believe it was nine. Seven or nine.

*Q.* Now, you say you returned to Chappaquiddick around 7:30 P.M.?

*A.* About seven-thirty.

*Q.* About that time. Now, you were familiar with the island of Chappaquiddick: Had you ever been there before?

*A.* Never been on Chappaquiddick Island before that day.

*Q.* And I believe you did state in one of your prepared statements that you had been visiting this island for about thirty years?

*A.* Martha's Vineyard Island.

*Q.* But you had never been to Chappaquiddick?

*A.* Never been to Chappaquiddick before one-thirty on the day of July 18th.

*Q.* Now, when you left the Shiretown Inn and returned to Chappaquiddick around 7:30 P.M., was there anyone with you?

*A.* Mr. Crimmins.

*THE COURT.* Might I just impose a moment and ask this question? You said you took a swim on Chappaquiddick Island Friday afternoon?

*THE WITNESS.* Yes, I did. If your Honor would permit me, at this time of the afternoon upon arrival on Chappaquiddick Island as at the time I was met at Martha's Vineyard Airport, I was driven by Mr. Crimmins to the cottage and to the beach, returned to the cottage subsequent to the point of rendezvous with the *Victoria* [*sic*].

*Q.* What automobile was being used at that time?

*A.* A four-door Oldsmobile 88.

*THE COURT.* Might I ask you just a question: Who drove you to the beach?

*THE WITNESS.* Mr. Crimmins.

*THE COURT.* Was the car operated over the Dyke Bridge or was it left on the side?

*THE WITNESS.* No, it was operated over the Dyke Bridge.

*Q.* Was there anyone at the cottage when you arrived there at 7:30 P.M.?

*A.* No, I don't believe so.

*Q.* Had there been anyone there when you changed your swimming suits early in the afternoon?

*A.* Not when I first arrived there. Subsequently a group returned to the cottage after the swim.

*Q.* When you returned?

*A.* They were either outside the cottage or in its immediate vicinity. I wasn't aware whether they were inside the cottage or outside at the time I changed.

*Q.* Do you have the names of these persons who were there?

*A.* I can only give them in a general way because I am not absolutely sure which people were there at that particular time and which were in town making arrangements.

*Q.* Were a part of the group there later that evening?

*A.* Yes, they were.

*Q.* Were there any persons other than the crew that participated in the cookout there?

*A.* No.

*Q.* Were there any other automobiles at that house on Chappaquiddick that afternoon?

*A.* Yes, there were.

*Q.* Do you know how many?

*A.* Just two to my best knowledge. One other vehicle, so there were two in total to my best knowledge.

*Q.* Did you have any plans at that time to stay on Chappaquiddick Island?

*A.* No, I did not.

*Q.* Did you plan on staying overnight?

*A.* No, I did not.

*Q.* And how long did you actually stay on Chappaquiddick Island that evening?

*A.* Well, to my best knowledge I would say one-thirty in the morning on July 19th.

*THE COURT.* When you left?

*THE WITNESS.* When I left.

*THE COURT.* When you left.

*Q.* What transpired after you arrived at the cottage after your arrival at 7:30 P.M.?

*A.* Well, after my arrival I took a bath in the tub that was available at the cottage, which was not available at the Shiretown Inn, and soaked my back. I later was joined by Mr. Markham who arrived some time about eight o'clock, engaged in conversations with Mr. Markham until about eight-thirty, and the rest of the group arrived at eight-thirty or shortly thereafter. During this period of time Mr. Crimmins made me a drink of rum and Coca-Cola.

*Q.* Now, did you have dinner at the cottage?

*A.* Well, at eight-thirty the rest of the group arrived and were made to feel relaxed and at home, enjoyed some hors d'oeuvres, were served a drink, those who wanted them, and steaks were cooked on an outdoor burner by Mr. Gargan at about approximately quarter of ten, I would think.

*Q.* Did you recall who did the cooking? Was there any cooking at that time?

*A.* Yes, there was.

*Q.* And do you recall who performed the job?

*A.* Well, principally Mr. Gargan. I think the young ladies did some of the cooking of the hors d'oeuvres and some of the gentlemen helped in starting the charcoal fire, and also the cooking of the steaks, the making of the salad and so forth.

*Q.* Were there any drinks served, any cocktails?

*A.* There were.

*Q.* Did anyone in particular tend bar or have charge of this particular responsibility?

*A.* Well, I tried initially to respond to any of the requests of the guests when they arrived and then I think most of the individuals made their drinks after that, what they wanted.

*Q.* And I believe you said earlier that Mr. Gargan was in charge of the arrangements of renting the cottage and making the preparation for the cookout, as far as you know?

*A.* That is correct. I would say the other gentlemen did some of the purchasing of the food and others got the stuff for the cookout.

*Q.* Did you have occasion to leave the cottage at any time during the evening?

*A.* That is correct.

*Q.* Did you leave more than once?

*A.* That is correct.

*Q.* Well, will you please give us the sequence of events with regard to your activities after 8:30 P.M.?

*A.* Well, during the course of the evening, as I mentioned, I engaged in conversation and recollections with those that were attending this group which were old friends of myself and our families. Some alcoholic beverages were served.

**THE COURT.** Excuse me. Read the question back to me.

(Question read.)

**Q.** How many times did you leave the cottage that evening, Senator?

**A.** Two different occasions.

**Q.** Would you please tell us about the first time?

**A.** The first time I left at approximately eleven-fifteen the evening of July 19 and I left a second time, sometime after midnight, by my best judgement, it would be approximately twelve-fifteen for the second time. On the second occasion I never left the cottage itself, I left the immediate vicinity of the cottage which was probably fifteen or twenty feet outside the front door.

**Q.** And when you left the second time, did you then return to Edgartown?

**A.** Sometime after I left the second time, I returned to Edgartown. I did not return immediately to Edgartown.

**Q.** Now, when you left on the first occasion, were you alone?

**A.** I was not alone.

**Q.** And who was with you?

**A.** Miss Mary Jo Kopechne was with me.

**Q.** Anyone else?

**A.** No.

**Q.** And did you use the 88 Oldsmobile that was later taken from the river?

**A.** I used—yes, I did.

**Q.** What time did Miss Kopechne arrive at the cottage that evening?

**A.** My best knowledge approximately eight-thirty.

**Q.** At 8:30 P.M.?

**A.** That is correct.

**Q.** Do you know how she arrived?

**A.** To my best knowledge she arrived in a white Valiant that brought some of the people to that party.

*Q.* Do you know who owned that car?

*A.* I believe it was a rented car.

*Q.* Do you know who rented it?

*A.* No. One of the group that was there, I would say . . . I'm not sure.

*Q.* When you left the party at eleven-fifteen with Miss Kopechne, had you had any prior conversation with her?

*A.* Yes, I had.

*Q.* Will you please give that conversation to the court?

*A.* At eleven-fifteen, I was talking with Miss Kopechne perhaps for some minutes before that period of time. I noticed the time, desired to leave and return to the Shiretown Inn and indicated to her that I was leaving and returning to town. She indicated to me that she was desirous of leaving, if I would be kind enough to drop her back at her hotel. I said, well, I'm leaving immediately; spoke with Mr. Crimmins, requested the keys for the car and left at that time.

*Q.* Does Mr. Crimmins usually drive your car or drive you?

*A.* On practically every occasion.

*Q.* On practically every occasion?

*A.* Yes.

*Q.* Was there anything in particular that changed those circumstances at this particular time?

*A.* Only to the extent that Mr. Crimmins, as well as some of the other fellows that were attending the cookout, were concluding their meal, enjoying the fellowship, and it didn't appear to me to be necessary to require him to bring me back to Edgartown.

*Q.* Do you know whether or not Miss Kopechne had her pocketbook with her at the time you left?

*A.* I do not.

*Q.* Mr. Kennedy, how were you dressed at the time you left the first time at eleven-fifteen?

*A.* In a pair of light slacks and a dark jersey and I believe shoes, moccasins, and a back brace.

*Q.* Do you know how Miss Kopechne was dressed, do you recall that?

*A.* Only from what I have read in the—I understand, slacks and a blouse, sandals, perhaps a sweater; I'm not completely—

*Q.* And when you left the house at Chappaquiddick at eleven-fifteen, you were driving?

*A.* That is correct.

*Q.* And where was Miss Kopechne seated?

*A.* In the front seat.

*Q.* Was there any other person—was there any other person in the car at that time?

*A.* No.

*Q.* Was there any other item, thing or object in the car at that time of any size?

*A.* Well, not to my knowledge at that particular time. I have read subsequently in newspapers that there was another person in that car, but that is only what I have read about and to my knowledge at that time there wasn't any other object that I was aware of.

*Q.* Well, Senator, was there any other person in the car?

*A.* No, there was not.

*Q.* And on leaving the cottage, Senator—Mr. Kennedy, where did you go?

*A.* Well, I traveled down, I believe it is Main Street, took a right on Dyke Road and drove off the bridge at Dyke Bridge.

*Q.* Did you at any time drive into Cemetery Road?

*A.* At no time did I drive into Cemetery Road.

*Q.* Did you back that car up at that time?

*A.* At no time did I back that car up.

*Q.* Did you see anyone on the road between the cottage and the bridge that night?

*A.* I saw no one on the road between the cottage and the bridge.

*THE COURT.* Did you stop the car at any time?

*THE WITNESS.* I did not stop the car at any time.

*Q.* (By Mr. Dinis) Did you pass any other vehicle at that time?

*A.* I passed no other vehicle and I saw no other person and I did not stop the car at any time between the time I left the cottage and went off the bridge.

*Q.* Now, would you describe your automobile to the Court?

*A.* Well, it is a four-door black sedan, Oldsmobile.

*Q.* Do you recall the registration plate?

*A.* I do not recall the registration plate.

*Q.* Senator, I show you a photograph and ask whether or not you can identify that?

*A.* I believe that to be my car.

*Q.* Your automobile?

*A.* Yes.

*MR. DINIS.* This is the automobile that the senator identifies as his.

*THE COURT.* I think we ought to have a little more. This location is—

*THE WITNESS.* I have no—

*THE COURT.* Mr. Kennedy says this is his automobile after the accident and he doesn't know the location of where the automobile is or when this picture was taken. Mark that Exhibit 1.

(The picture was marked Exhibit No. 1.)

*Q.* (By Mr. Dinis.) I show you two photographs. Are you able to identify the automobile in the photographs?

*A.* In my best judgment that is my automobile that went off the bridge.

*Q.* In examining the registration, would that help you at all?

*A.* I believe that is my vehicle.

*MR. DINIS* If your Honor pleases, these are photographs that have been taken of the car which had been removed from the water.

*THE COURT.* Well, are you going to have any witness testify when these were taken?

*MR. DINIS.* Yes, your Honor, we can have that.

*THE COURT.* And where they were taken?

*MR. DINIS.* Yes, your Honor.

*THE COURT.* You identify the car as being your car?

*THE WITNESS.* I do, your Honor, it is my best judgment that it is my car. I don't think there is really much question.

**THE COURT.** I would prefer that you wait until you put on the witness that is going to say—

**MR. DINIS.** May it be allowed de bene [provisionally], your Honor? The sequence in presenting this evidence is for the purpose of—we couldn't—all I want to establish is that the Senator says they look like his car and then we will later have testimony as to where they were taken.

**THE COURT.** Well, I would rather not get into the trial technique.

**MR. DINIS.** I appreciate that.

**THE COURT.** De bene. I prefer you wait until you have the witness to identify it. I want to avoid as much as possible, Mr. Dinis, any trial technique.

**THE WITNESS.** I would just say to the best of my knowledge that those are pictures of my car that were shown to me.

*Q.* (By Mr. Dinis) In your conversation with Miss Kopechne prior to your leaving at eleven-fifteen, did she indicate to you any necessity for returning to Martha's Vineyard or to Edgartown?

*A.* Prior to that conversation, no.

*Q.* Well, when she left with you, where was she going?

*A.* Back to her hotel.

*Q.* Now, when you left at eleven-fifteen do you know how many persons remained at the house on Chappaquiddick?

*A.* To my best judgment most of them were in the cottage when I left. I didn't make a count of who was there, but I think most of them were there.

**THE COURT.** Well, do you know of anyone having left before?

**THE WITNESS.** No, I don't except on one occasion where—

**THE COURT.** No, I mean having left permanently.

**THE WITNESS.** No, no.

*Q.* (By Mr. Dinis) Did anyone else have access to your automobile that afternoon or that evening?

*A.* Oh, yes.

*Q.* And who might that have been?

*A.* Well, Mr. Crimmins certainly had access that afternoon and I believe Mr. Tretter borrowed the car to return to Edgartown briefly. I couldn't say of my own knowledge that he used that car rather than the Valiant, but he may very well have, and I would say during the course of the afternoon it was generally available to any of the group to use for transportation.

*Q.* Do you recall how fast you were driving when you made the right on Dyke Road?

*A.* No, I would say approximately seven or eight miles an hour.

*Q.* And what were the lighting conditions and weather conditions that evening?

*A.* Well, as you know, there are no lights on that road. The road was dry. There was a reasonable amount of humidity. The night was clear, extremely dark.

*Q.* Were the windows of the automobile open or closed?

*A.* Some of the windows were open and some were closed.

*Q.* Do you have an air-conditioner in that car?

*A.* No, I don't.

*THE COURT.* Could we know which were opened and which were closed?

*THE WITNESS.* I read, your Honor—

*THE COURT.* No, no, of your own knowledge.

*THE WITNESS.* Of my own knowledge?

*THE COURT.* What about the window on your side?

*THE WITNESS.* I would expect it was open.

*THE COURT.* You don't remember that?

*THE WITNESS.* I don't remember that.

*THE COURT.* How about the windows on the passenger's side?

*THE WITNESS.* I really don't remember.

*THE COURT.* Was it a warm night?

*THE WITNESS.* I would think it was cool at that hour, but I really have no personal knowledge as to which windows were open or closed. I have read subsequently which ones were open or blown open, but at that time I really don't recall.

*Q.* (By Mr. Dinis) Well, Mr. Kennedy, was the window on the driver's side open?

*A.* Yes, it was.

*Q.* Do you recall whether or not the window in the car seat behind the driver was open?

*A.* I don't recall.

*Q.* And you have no recollection as to the windows on the passenger's side of the vehicle?

*A.* No, I really don't.

*Q.* How fast were you driving on Dyke Road?

*A.* Approximately twenty miles an hour.

*Q.* Were the brakes of your Oldsmobile in order at that time?

*A.* I believe so. There is no reason to assume otherwise. Mr. Crimmins takes very good care of the car.

*Q.* Well, were you aware at the time that you were driving on a dirt road when you hit, when you turned into Dyke Road?

*A.* Well, sometime during the drive down Dyke Road I was aware that I was on an unpaved road, yes.

*Q.* At what point, Mr. Kennedy, did you realize that you were driving on a dirt road?

*A.* Just sometime when I was—I don't remember any specific time when I knew I was driving on an unpaved road. I was generally aware sometime during the going down that road that it was unpaved, like many of the other roads here in Martha's Vineyard and Nantucket and Cape Cod.

*Q.* When you left the house at eleven-fifteen, what was your destination?

*A.* The Katama Shores, the ferry slip, the Katama Shores, Shiretown.

*Q.* Now, had you been over that road from the ferry slip to the cottage more than once that day?

*A.* Yes, I had.

*Q.* Did you recall at the time that you noticed you were driving on a dirt road, that road from the ferry slip to the house had been paved?

*A.* Well, Mr. Dinis, I would say that I, having lived on Cape Cod and having visited these islands, I am aware some roads are paved.

*THE COURT.* I am sorry, that is not quite responsive. The

question is whether or not you realized the road from the ferry slip to the cottage was paved.

**MR. DINIS.** That is correct.

**THE WITNESS.** Yes.

**THE COURT.** That is, did you become aware of it during your trips?

**THE WITNESS.** Well, I would just say it was not of particular notice to me whether it was paved or unpaved.

**THE COURT.** Were you driving the car either one of those times?

**THE WITNESS.** I was not.

**Q.** (By Mr. Dinis) Well, while you were driving down Dyke Road and after you noticed it was a dirt road and you were driving at twenty miles an hour, what happened, Mr. Kennedy?

**A.** Well, I became—

**THE COURT.** I'm going to ask one question. At any time after you got on the unpaved road, the so-called Dyke Road, did you have a realization that you were on the wrong road?

**THE WITNESS.** No.

**THE COURT.** Do you remember the question?

**THE WITNESS.** After I realized it was an unpaved road, what did I become aware of?

**Q.** (By Mr. Dinis) Well, after you realized it was an unpaved road, and that you were driving at twenty miles an hour, what happened then?

**A.** I went off Dyke Bridge or I went off a bridge.

**Q.** You went off a bridge into the water?

**A.** That is correct.

**Q.** Did you apply the brakes of that automobile prior to going off into the water?

**A.** Perhaps a fraction of a second before.

**Q.** What prompted you to do that?

**A.** Well, I was about to go off a bridge and I applied the brakes.

**Q.** Were there any lights in that area?

**A.** Absolutely no lights in that area I noticed other than the lights on my vehicle.

*Q.* Did you realize at that moment that you were not heading for the ferry?

*A.* At the moment I went off the bridge, I certainly did.

*Q.* Do you recall whether or not the—strike that question—well, what happened after that, Senator?

*A.* Well, I remembered the vehicle itself just beginning to go off the Dyke Bridge and the next thing I recall is the movement of Mary Jo next to me perhaps hitting or kicking me and I, at this time, opened my eyes and realized I was upside down, that water was crashing in on me, that it was pitch black. I knew that and I was able to get a half a gulp, I would say of air, before I became completely immersed in the water. I realized that Mary Jo and I had to get out of the car.

I can remember reaching what I thought was down to try to get the doorknob of the car and lifting the doorhandle and pressing against the door and it was not moving. I can remember reaching what I thought was down, which was really up, to where I thought the window was and feeling along the side to see if the window was closed, and I can remember the last sensation of being completely out of air and inhaling a lung full of water and assuming that I was going to drown and the full realization that no one was going to be looking for us that night until the next morning and that I wasn't going to get out of the car alive and then somehow I can remember coming up to the last energy of just pushing, pressing, and coming up to the surface.

*Q.* Senator, how did you realize that you were upside down in the car?

*A.* Because—that was a feeling that I had as soon as I became aware that—the water rushing in and the blackness, I knew that I was upside down. I really wasn't sure of anything, but I thought I was upside down.

*Q.* Were you aware that the windows on the passenger's side were blown out of the car, were smashed?

*A.* I have read that subsequently. I wasn't aware of it at the time.

*Q.* Were you aware that there was any water rushing in on the passenger's side?

*A.* There was complete blackness. Water seemed to rush in from every point, from the windshield, from underneath me, above me. It almost seemed like you couldn't hold the water back even with your hands. What I was conscious of was the rushing of the water, the blackness, the fact that it was impossible to even hold it back.

*Q.* And you say at that time you had a thought to the effect that you may not be found until morning?

*A.* I was sure that I was going to drown.

*Q.* Did you make any observations of the condition of Miss Kopechne at that time?

*A.* At what time?

*Q.* At that particular moment when you were thrashing around in the car?

*A.* Well, at the moment I was thrashing around I was trying to find a way that we both could get out of the car and at some time after I tried the door and the window I became convinced I was never going to get out.

*Q.* Was the window closed at that time?

*A.* The window was open.

*Q.* On the driver's side?

*A.* That's correct.

*Q.* And did you go through the window to get out of the car?

*A.* I have no idea in the world how I got out of that car.

*Q.* Do you have any recollection as to how the automobile left the bridge and went over into the water?

*A.* How it left the bridge?

*Q.* Yes. What particular path did it take?

*A.* No.

*Q.* Did it turn over?

*A.* I have no idea.

**THE COURT.** I would like to inquire, Mr. Dinis, something about the operation of the car, if you are finished.

**MR. DINIS.** Go right ahead, your Honor.

**THE COURT.** You are driving along the dike sandy road and you are approaching the Dyke Bridge. Now, you can describe to me what you saw, what you did, what happened from the point when you first saw the bridge?

**THE WITNESS.** I would estimate the time to be a fraction of a second from the time that I first saw the bridge and was on the bridge.

**THE COURT.** Did you have on your high beams, do you remember?

**THE WITNESS.** I can't remember.

**THE COURT.** It is your custom to use high beams when you are driving?

**THE WITNESS.** I rarely drive. I really couldn't tell you. I may have.

**THE COURT.** It is recommended.

**THE WITNESS.** It is recommended, but sometimes if there is a mist you see better with low beams.

**THE COURT.** Did you see the bridge before you actually reached it?

**THE WITNESS.** The split second before I was on it.

**THE COURT.** Did you see that it was at an angle to the road?

**THE WITNESS.** The bridge was at an angle to the road?

**THE COURT.** Yes.

**THE WITNESS.** Just before going on it I saw that.

**THE COURT.** Did you make any attempt to turn your wheels to follow that angle?

**THE WITNESS.** I believe I did, your Honor. I would assume that I did try to go on the bridge. It appeared to me at that time that the road went straight.

**THE COURT.** Were you looking ahead at the time you were driving the car, at that time?

**THE WITNESS.** Yes, I was.

**THE COURT.** Your attention was not diverted by anything else?

**THE WITNESS.** No, it wasn't.

**THE COURT.** I don't want to foreclose you, Mr. Dinis, I want to go into the question of alcoholic beverages. Perhaps you had that in mind later?

**MR. DINIS.** Yes, your Honor.

*THE COURT.* All right.

*Q.* Going back to the cottage earlier in the day, you stated, you volunteered the information that you had a rum and Coca-Cola?

*A.* That is right.

*Q.* Did you have more than one?

*A.* Yes, I did.

*Q.* How many did you have?

*A.* I had two.

*THE COURT.* What time was this?

*THE WITNESS.* The first was about eight o'clock.

*THE COURT.* I would like to go back before that. I think you said you visited some friends at the Shiretown Inn?

*THE WITNESS.* That is right.

*THE COURT.* Did you do some drinking then?

*THE WITNESS.* I had about a third of a beer at that time.

*THE COURT.* And you had nothing further until this?

*THE WITNESS.* No, I had nothing further.

*Q.* And when did you have the second rum and Coke?

*A.* The second some time later on in the evening. I think before dinner, sometime about nine-fifteen. It would be difficult for me to say.

*Q.* Now, during the afternoon of the eighteenth did you have occasion to spend some time with your nephew, Joseph Kennedy?

*A.* I might have greeted him a brief greeting, but otherwise, no. I knew he was concerned about where he was going to stay; that he had some reservations and that somehow they had gotten cancelled, but I would say other than a casual passing and a greeting, I would say no.

*Q.* He was at this time on Chappaquiddick Island?

*A.* Not to my knowledge. I never saw him at Chappaquiddick.

*Q.* Did you see him at the Shiretown Inn?

*A.* I might have seen him in inquiring whether he could stay at the Shiretown Inn.

*Q.* Did he stay with you in your room?

*A.* No, he did not.

**THE COURT.** I would like to ask some questions. You said you had a portion of beer late in the afternoon at the Shiretown Inn?

**THE WITNESS.** That is correct.

**THE COURT.** Then you had two rums and Coke at this cottage at Chappaquiddick Island sometime after you arrived at about eight-thirty?

**THE WITNESS.** That is right.

**THE COURT.** Who poured those drinks?

**THE WITNESS.** Mr. Crimmins poured the first one. I poured the second one.

**THE COURT.** What amount of rum did you put in?

**THE WITNESS.** It would be difficult, your Honor, to estimate.

**THE COURT.** Well, by ounces.

**THE WITNESS.** By ounces? I suppose two ounces.

**THE COURT.** I mean, some people pour heavy drinks. Some pour light drinks.

**THE WITNESS.** Yes.

**THE COURT.** When did you take the last one?

**THE WITNESS.** I would think about nine o'clock. The only way I could judge that, your Honor, would be that I ate about ten and it was sometime before I ate.

**THE COURT.** You had nothing alcoholic to drink after eating?

**THE WITNESS.** No, I didn't.

**THE COURT.** How much liquor was at this cottage?

**THE WITNESS.** There were several bottles so that I wouldn't be able to tell specifically.

**THE COURT.** Not a large supply?

**THE WITNESS** I wouldn't be able to tell how much. There was an adequate supply.

**THE COURT.** Was there a sustained amount of drinking by the group?

**THE WITNESS.** No, there wasn't.

**THE COURT.** By any particular person?

**THE WITNESS.** Not that I noticed. There wasn't prior to the time I left.

**THE COURT.** Mr. Hanify, you have advised your client of his constitutional rights?

*MR. HANIFY.* Yes, I have, your Honor.

*THE COURT.* Were you at any time that evening under the influence of alcohol?

*THE WITNESS.* Absolutely not.

*THE COURT.* Did you imbibe in any narcotic drugs that evening?

*THE WITNESS.* Absolutely not.

*THE COURT.* Did anyone at the party to your knowledge?

*THE WITNESS.* No, absolutely not.

*THE COURT.* In your opinion were you sober at the time that you operated the motor vehicle to the Dyke Bridge?

*THE WITNESS.* Absolutely sober.

*Q.* Senator Kennedy, what did you do immediately following your release from the automobile?

*A.* I was swept away by the tide that was flowing at an extraordinary rate through that narrow cut there and was swept along by the tide and called Mary Jo's name until I was able to make my way to what would be the east [nearer the ocean] side of that cut, waded up to about my waist and started back to the car, at this time I was gasping and belching and coughing. I went back just in front of the car.

Now the headlights of that car were still on and I was able to get what I thought was the front of the car, although it was difficult—and I was able to identify the front of the car from the rear of the car by the lights themselves. Otherwise I don't think I would be able to tell.

*Q.* How far were you swept along by the current?

*A.* Approximately thirty to forty feet.

*Q.* Did you pass under the bridge?

*A.* The vehicle went over the bridge on the south side and rested on the south side, and that was the direction the water was flowing, and I was swept I would think to the south or probably east, which would be the eastern shore.

*Q.* Some thirty feet?

*A.* I would think thirty to forty feet.

*Q.* Now, in order to get back to the car was it necessary for you to swim?

*A.* I couldn't swim at that time because of the current. I waded into—swam to where I could wade and then waded along the shore up to where I could go to the front of the car and start diving in an attempt to rescue Mary Jo.

*Q.* Was the front of the car facing a westerly direction?

*A.* I would think it was facing in a northerly direction.

*Q.* Well, in regard to the bridge could you describe the location of the automobile with relation to the bridge?

*A.* Well, your Honor, in the direction of north and south. I will do the best I can.

**THE COURT.** We don't have any map, do we?

**MR. TELLER.** The bridge runs north and south, fairly close to north and south. [Actually, it runs east and west.]

**THE COURT.** That is coming towards Edgartown would be north and towards the ocean would be south?

**MR. TELLER.** Yes, sir.

**MR. DINIS.** May we use the chalk, your Honor?

**THE COURT.** Yes, if it is helpful.

*Q.* Would that be helpful, Mr. Kennedy?

*A.* It may be.

*Q.* I believe there is a board behind you. Assuming the bridge is north and south—

*A.* Yes.

(Witness draws sketch on blackboard.)

I would bet that the bridge runs more east–west than north–south.

**MR. TELLER.** Not directly north, but southeast–northwest.

*Q.* Will you indicate, Mr. Kennedy, Edgartown?

*A.* I would rather have counsel draw and respond. I will be delighted to do whatever the court desires.

**THE COURT.** It is only for the purpose of illustration.

**THE WITNESS.** I suppose the road runs something like this.

**THE COURT.** You are trying to get the relation of the car to the bridge?

**MR. DINIS.** Yes, your Honor.

*Q.* As you went off the bridge?

*A.* I think it was like this.

***THE COURT.*** All right, Mr. Dinis.

*Q.* Mr. Kennedy, after you emerged from the automobile you say you were swept some thirty feet away from the car, is that correct?

*A.* In this direction. (Indicating)

*Q.* And how much time did it take you after you left the automobile to be swept down to about thirty feet, down the river?

*A.* By the time I came up I was, the best estimate would be somewhere over here, which would be probably eight to ten feet, it is difficult for me to estimate specifically, and I think by the time I was able at least to regain my strength, I would say it is about thirty feet after which time I swam in this direction until I was able to wade, and wade back up here to this point here, and went over to where the front of the car was, and crawled over to here, dove here, and the tide would sweep out this way there, and then I dove repeatedly from this side until, I would say, the end, and then I was swept away the first couple of times, again back over to this side, I would come back again and again to this point here, or try perhaps the third or fourth time to gain entrance to some area here until at the very end when I couldn't hold my breath any longer. I was breathing so heavily it was just a matter of seconds. I was just able to hold on to the metal undercarriage here, and the water itself came right out to where I was breathing, and I could hold on, I knew that I just could not get under water any more.

*Q.* And you were fully aware at that time of what was transpiring?

*A.* Well, I was fully aware that I was trying to get the girl out of that car and I was fully aware that I was doing everything I possibly could to get her out of the car and I was fully aware at that time that my head was throbbing and my neck was aching and I was breathless, and at that time, the last time, hopelessly exhausted.

*Q.* You were not confused at that time?

*A.* Well, I knew that there was a girl in that car and I had to get her out. I knew that.

*Q.* And you took steps to get her out?

*A.* I tried the best I thought I possibly could to get her out.

*Q.* But there was no confusion in your mind about the fact that there was a person in the car and that you were doing the best you could to get that person out?

*A.* I was doing the very best I could to get her out.

*THE COURT.* May I ask you some questions about the depth of the water?

*THE WITNESS.* Yes.

*THE COURT.* You were not able to stand up at any point around any portion of that car?

*THE WITNESS.* No, it was not possible to stand. The highest level of the car to the surface were the wheels and undercarriage itself. When I held on to the undercarriage and the tide would take me down, it was up to this point. (Indicating)

*Q.* Mr. Kennedy, how many times if you recall did you make an effort to submerge and get into the car?

*A.* I would say seven or eight times. At the last point, the seventh or eighth attempts were barely more than five- or eight-second submersions below the surface. I just couldn't hold my breath any longer. I didn't have the strength even to come down even close to the window or the door.

*A.* And do you know how much time was used in these efforts?

*A.* It would be difficult for me to estimate, but I would think probable fifteen to twenty minutes.

*Q.* And did you then remove yourself from the water?

*A.* I did.

*Q.* And how did you do that?

*A.* Well, in the last dive, I lost contact with the vehicle again and I started to come down this way here and I let myself float and came over to this shore and I came onto this shore here, and I sort of crawled and staggered up some place in here and was very exhausted and spent on the grass.

*Q.* On the west bank of the river?

*A.* Yes.

*Q.* As indicated by that chart?

*A.* Yes, that's correct.

*Q.* And how long did you spend resting?

*A.* Well, I would estimate probably fifteen to twenty minutes trying to get my—I was coughing up the water and I was exhausted and I suppose the best estimate would be fifteen or twenty minutes.

*Q.* Now, did you say earlier you spent fifteen to twenty minutes trying to recover Miss Kopechne?

*A.* That is correct.

*Q.* And you spent another fifteen or twenty minutes recovering on the west side of the river?

*A.* That is correct.

*Q.* Now, following your rest period, Senator, what did you do after that?

*A.* Well, I—

*Q.* You may remain seated.

*A.* All right, after I was able to regain my breath, I went back to the road and I started down the road and it was extremely dark and I could make out no forms or shapes or figures, and the only way I could even see the path of the road was looking down the silhouettes of the trees on the two sides and I started going down that road, walking, trotting, jogging, stumbling as fast as I possibly could.

*Q.* Did you pass any houses with lights on?

*A.* Not to my knowledge; never saw a cottage with a light on.

*Q.* And did you then return to the cottage where your friends had been gathered?

*A.* That is correct.

*Q.* And how long did that take you to make that walk, do you recall?

*A.* I would say approximately fifteen minutes.

*Q.* And then you arrived at the cottage as you did, is that true?

*A.* That is true.

*Q.* Did you speak to anyone there?

*A.* Yes, I did.

*Q.* And with whom did you speak?

*A.* Mr. Ray LaRosa.

*Q.* And what did you tell him?

*A.* I said, get me Joe Gargan.

*Q.* And was Joe Gargan there?

*A.* He was there.

*Q.* He was at the party?

*A.* Yes.

**THE COURT.** Excuse me a moment. Did you go inside the cottage?

**THE WITNESS.** No, I didn't go inside.

*Q.* (By Mr. Dinis) What did you do? Did you sit in the automobile at that time?

*A.* Well, I came up to the cottage, there was a car parked there, a white vehicle, and as I came up to the back of the vehicle, I saw Ray LaRosa at the door and I said Ray get me Joe, and he mentioned something like right away, and as he was going in to get Joe, I got in the back of the car.

*Q.* In this white car?

*A.* Yes.

*Q.* And now, did Joe come to you?

*A.* Yes, he did.

*Q.* And did you have conversation with him?

*A.* Yes I did.

*Q.* Would you tell us what the conversation was?

*A.* I said, you had better get Paul, too.

*Q.* Did you tell him what happened?

*A.* At that time I said, better get Paul, too.

*Q.* What happened after that?

*A.* Well, Paul came out, got in the car. I said, there has been a terrible accident, we have got to go, and we took off down the road, the main road there.

*Q.* How long had you known Mr. LaRosa prior to this evening?

*A.* Eight years, ten years, eight or ten years.

*Q.* Were you familiar with the fact or—strike that—did you have any knowledge that Mr. LaRosa had some experience in skindiving?

*A.* No, I never did.

*Q.* Now, before you drove down the road, did you make any further explanations to Mr. Gargan or Mr. Markham?

*A.* Before driving? No, sir. I said there has been a terrible accident, let's go, and we took off—

*Q.* And they went—

*A.* Driving.

*Q.* And they drove hurriedly down?

*A.* That is right.

*Q.* And where did you stop the white automobile that you were riding in?

*A.* Mr. Gargan drove the vehicle across the bridge to some location here (indicating) and turned it so that its headlights shown [sic] over the water and over the submerged vehicle. (Indicating on blackboard)

*Q.* And what happened after the three of you arrived there?

*A.* Mr. Gargan and Mr. Markham took off all their clothes, dove into the water, and proceeded to dive repeatedly to try to save Mary Jo.

*Q.* Now, do you recall what particular time this is now when the three of you were at the . . .

*A.* I think it was twelve-twenty, Mr. Dinis, I believe that I looked at the Valiant's clock and believe that it was twelve-twenty.

*Q.* Now, Mr. LaRosa remained at the cottage?

*A.* Yes, he did.

*Q.* Was Mr. LaRosa aware of the accident?

*A.* No, he hadn't heard—no, I don't believe so.

*Q.* No one else at the cottage was told of the accident?

*A.* No.

*Q.* How many times did you go back to Dyke Bridge that night?

*A.* Well, that was the only—

*Q.* After the accident, that was the only occasion?

*A.* The only time, the only occasion.

*Q.* Now, how long did Mr. Markham and Mr. Gargan remain there with you on that particular occasion?

*A.* I would think about forty-five minutes.

*Q.* And they were unsuccessful in entering the car?

*A.* Well, Mr. Gargan got halfway in the car. When he came out he was scraped all the way from his elbow, underneath his arm was all bruised and bloodied, and this is the one time that he was able to gain entrance I believe into the car itself.

*Q.* And did he talk to you about his experience in trying to get into the car?

*A.* Well, I was unable to, being exhausted, to get into the water, but I could see exactly what was happening and made some suggestions.

*Q.* So that you were participating in the rescue efforts?

*A.* Well, I was fully aware that Joe Gargan and Paul Markham were trying to get in that car and rescue that girl, I certainly would say that.

*Q.* Did you know at the time or did you have any idea how long Mary Jo had been in the water?

*A.* Well, I knew that some time had passed.

*Q.* Well, you testified earlier that you spent some fifteen or twenty minutes of—

*A.* Well, Mr. District Attorney, I didn't add up the time that I was adding to rescue her and time on the beach, the shore, and the time to get back and the time it took back and calculate it.

*Q.* Was it fair to say that she was in the water about an hour?

*A.* Yes, it was.

*Q.* Was there any effort made to call for assistance?

*A.* No, other than the assistance of Mr. Gargan and Mr. Markham.

*Q.* I know, but they failed in their efforts to recover—

*A.* That is right.

*Q.* Miss Kopechne?

*A.* That is correct.


This concludes Day One of the inquest.

# DAY TWO OF TESTIMONY

**MR. DINIS.** I believe, your Honor, before the witness left the courtroom the question was whether or not any assistance had been asked for.

**THE COURT.** I think the answer had been no.

**Q.** (By Mr. Dinis) And now may I ask you, Mr. Kennedy, was there any reason why no additional assistance was asked for?

**A.** Was there any reason?

**Q.** Yes, was there any particular reason why you did not call either the police or the fire department?

**A.** Well, I intended to report it to the police.

**THE COURT.** That is not quite responsive to the question.

**Q.** Was there any reason why it did not happen at that time?

**THE COURT.** Call for assistance.

**THE WITNESS.** I intended to call for assistance and to report the accident to the police within a few short moments after going back into the car.

**Q.** I see, and did something transpire to prevent this?

**A.** Yes.

**Q.** What was that?

**A.** With the Court's indulgence, to prevent this, if the Court would permit me I would like to be able to relate to the Court the immediate period following the time that Mr. Gargan, Markham, and I got back in the car.

**THE COURT.** I have no objection.

**MR. DINIS.** I have no objection.

**THE WITNESS.** Responding to the question of the District Attorney—

**MR. DINIS.** Yes.

**THE WITNESS.** —at some time, I believe it was about forty-five minutes after Gargan and Markham dove they likewise became exhausted and no further diving efforts appeared to be of any avail and they so indicated to me and I agreed. So they came out of the water and came back into the car and said to me, Mr. Markham and Mr. Gargan at different times as we drove down the road towards the ferry, that it was necessary to report this accident. A lot of different thoughts came into my mind at that time about how I was going to really be able to call Mrs. Kopechne at some time in the middle of the night to tell her that her daughter was drowned, to be able to call my own mother and my own father, relate to them, my wife, and I even—even though I knew that Mary Jo Kopechne was dead and believed firmly that she was in the back of that car, I willed that she remained alive.

As we drove down that road I was almost looking out the front window and windows trying to see her walking down that road. I related this to Gargan and Markham and they said they understood this feeling, but it was necessary to report it. And about this time we came to the ferry crossing and I got out of the car and we talked there just a few minutes.

I just wondered how all of this could possibly have happened. I also had some sort of a thought and the wish and desire and the hope that suddenly this whole accident would disappear, and they reiterated that this has to be reported and I understood at the time I left that ferry boat, left the slip where the ferry boat was, that it had to be reported and I had full intention of reporting it, and I mentioned to Gargan and Markham something like "You take care of the girls, I will take care of the accident"—that is what I said and I dove into the water.

Now, I started to swim out into that tide and the tide suddenly became, felt an extraordinary shove and almost pulling me down again, the water pulling me down and suddenly I realized at that time even as I failed to realize before I dove into the water—that I was in a weakened condition, although as I had looked over that distance between the ferry slip and the other side, it seemed to me an inconsequential swim; but the water got colder, the tide began to draw me out and for the second time that evening, I knew I was going to drown and the strength continued to leave me. By this time I was probably fifty yards off the shore and I remembered being swept down toward the direction of the Edgartown Light and well out into darkness, and I continued to attempt to swim, tried to swim at a slower pace and be able to regain whatever kind of strength that was left in me.

And some time after, I think it was about the middle of the channel, a little further than that, the tide was much calmer, gentler, and I began to get my—make some progress, and finally was able to reach the other shore, and all the nightmares and all the tragedy and all the loss of Mary Jo's death was right before me again. And when I was able to gain this shore, this Edgartown side, I pulled myself on the beach and then attempted to gain some strength.

After that I walked up one of the streets in the direction of the Shiretown Inn. By walking up one of the streets I walked into a parking lot that was adjacent to the inn and I can remember almost having no further strength to continue, and leaning against a tree for a length of time, walking through the parking lot, trying to really gather some idea as to what happened, and feeling that I just had to go to my room at that time, which I did by walking through the front entrance of the Shiretown Inn up the stairs.

*Q.* Do you have any idea what time you arrived at the Shiretown Inn?

*A.* I would say some time before two o'clock.

*Q.* Can you tell us now how great a distance you swam when you left the ferry slip?

*A.* I left just adjacent to the ferry slip here, I would say on the north side of it and I was swept down for a number of yards and then across. I don't think I can estimate the terms of the yardage.

*Q.* When you arrived at the Shiretown Inn, did you talk to anyone at that time?

*A.* I went to my room and I was shaking with chill. I took off all my clothes and collapsed on the bed, and at this time, I was very conscious of a throbbing headache, of pains in my neck, of strain on my back, but what I was even more conscious of is the tragedy and loss of a very devoted friend.

*Q.* Now, did you change your clothes?

*A.* I was unable really to determine, detect the amount of lapse of time and I could hear noise that was taking place. It seemed around me, on top of me almost in the room, after a period of time I wasn't sure whether it was morning or afternoon or nighttime, and I put on—and I wanted to find out and I put on some dry clothes that were there: a pants and a shirt, and I opened the door and I saw what I believed to be a tourist, someone standing under the light off the balcony and asked what time it was. He mentioned to me it was, I think, two-thirty, and went back into the room.

*Q.* Had you known Miss Kopechne prior to July 18th?

*A.* Well, I have known her—my family has known her for a number of years. She has visited my house, my wife. She has visited Mrs. Robert Kennedy's house. She worked in the Robert Kennedy Presidential campaign, and I would say that we have known her for a number of years.

*Q.* Now, directing your—

*A.* If the question is, have I ever been out with Mary Jo—

*Q.* No, that is not the question. The question was whether you have known her socially prior to this event.

*A.* Well, could I give you a fuller explanation of my knowledge of Mary Jo, your Honor?

*MR. DINIS.* I have no objection.

*THE COURT.* Go ahead.

*THE WITNESS.* I have never in my life, as I have stated on television, had any personal relationship with Mary Jo Kopechne. I never in my life have been either out with Mary Jo Kopechne nor have I ever been with her prior to that occasion where we were not in a general assemblage of friends, associates, or members of our family.

*Q.* (By Mr. Dinis) Directing your attention to the nineteenth at around 7:30 A.M., did you have any conversation with anyone at that time?

*A.* Could I hear the question, please?

*A.* The nineteenth, which was that morning at around 7 A.M., 7:30 A.M.—

*A.* Yes.

*Q.* Did you meet anyone at your room?

*A.* Not at seven-thirty, I did not.

*Q.* Did you meet anyone at any time that morning in your room?

*A.* Yes, I did.

*Q.* And whom did you meet there?

*A.* If your Honor would permit me to give—I would like to be specifically responsive, and I can, I think. It might be misleading to the Court if I just gave a specific response to it. Whatever the Court wants.

*Q.* Well, the point is, what time did you get up that morning?

*A.* I never really went to bed that night.

*Q.* I see. After that noise at two-thirty in the morning, when did you first meet anyone, what time?

*A.* It was sometime after eight.

*Q.* And whom did you meet?

*A.* Sometime after eight I met the woman that was behind the counter at the Shiretown Inn and I met Mr. Richards and Mr. Moore, very briefly Mrs. Richards, and Mr. Gargan and Mr. Markham, and I saw Mr. Tretter, but to be specifically responsive as to who I met in my room, which I believe was the earlier question, Mr. Markham and Mr. Gargan.

*Q.* What time was this, sometime around eight o'clock?

*A.* I think it was close to eight-thirty.

*Q.* Did you have any conversation with Mr. Moore or Mrs. Moore or Mr. Richards or Mrs. Richards?

*A.* It is my impression that they did the talking.

*Q.* Well, what was the conversation, do you recall?

*A.* Mr. Moore was relating about how I believe some members of his crew were having difficulty with their housing arrangements.

*Q.* Now, what time did Mr. Markham and Mr. Gargan arrive?

*A.* About a few—I would think about eight-thirty, just a few minutes after I met Mr. Moore probably.

*Q.* And do you recall how they were dressed?

*A.* To the best of my knowledge, a shirt and slacks.

*Q.* Do you recall at this time the condition of their dress?

*A.* Well, they had an unkempt look about them.

*Q.* Nothing further, nothing more than that?

*A.* Well, I mean it was not pressed; it was messy looking. It was unkempt looking.

*Q.* Did you have any conversation with Mr. Markham or Mr. Gargan or both at that time?

*A.* Yes, I did.

*Q.* Can you give the Court what the conversation was?

*A.* Well, they asked, had I reported the accident, and why I hadn't reported the accident; and I told them about my thoughts and feeling as I swam across that channel and how I always willed that Mary Jo still lived; how I was hopeful even as that night went on and as I almost tossed and turned, paced that room and walked around that room that night that somehow when they arrived in the morning that they were going to say that Mary Jo was still alive. I told them how I somehow believed that when the sun came up and it was a new morning that what had happened the night before would not have happened and did not happen, and how I just couldn't gain the strength within me, the moral strength to call Mrs. Kopechne at two o'clock in the morning and tell her that her daughter was dead.

*Q.* Now, at some time did you actually call Mrs. Kopechne?

*A.* Yes, I did.

*Q.* And prior to calling Mrs. Kopechne, did you cross over on the Chappaquiddick Ferry to Chappaquiddick Island?

*A.* Yes, I did.

*Q.* And, was Mr. Markham and Mr. Gargan with you?

*A.* Yes, they were.

*Q.* Now, did you then return to Edgartown after some period of time?

*A.* Yes, I did.

*Q.* Did anything prompt or cause you to return to Edgartown once you were on Chappaquiddick Island that morning?

*A.* Anything prompt me to? Well, what do you mean by prompt?

*Q.* Well, did anything cause you to return? You crossed over to Chappaquiddick?

**A.** Other than the intention of reporting the accident, the intention of which had been made earlier that morning.

**Q.** But you didn't go directly from your room to the police department?

**A.** No, I did not.

**Q.** Did you have a particular reason for going to Chappaquiddick first?

**A.** Yes, I did.

**Q.** What was that reason?

**A.** It was to make a private phone call to one of the dearest and oldest friends that I have and that was to Mr. Burke Marshall. I didn't feel that I could use the phone that was available outside of the dining room at the Shiretown Inn, and it was my thought that once I went to the police station, that I would be involved in a myriad of details and I wanted to talk to this friend before I undertook that responsibility.

**Q.** You mean that—

**THE COURT.** Excuse me, Mr. Dinis, we are now at one o'clock.

**MR. DINIS.** The recess.

**THE COURT.** I think we will take the noon luncheon recess.

# AFTERNOON SESSION

**THE COURT.** All right, Mr. Dinis.

**Q.** (By Mr. Dinis) Mr. Kennedy, you said that you made a phone call to a friend, Mr. Burke Marshall?

**A.** I made a phone call with the intention of reaching Mr. Burke Marshall.

**Q.** Did you not reach him?

**A.** No, I did not.

**Q.** And then I believe the evidence is that you left Chappaquiddick Island, crossed over on the ferry, and went over to the local police department?

A. That is correct.

Q. There you made a report to Chief Arena?

A. That is correct.

Q. And you arrived at the police station at approximately 10 A.M.?

A. I think it was sometime before ten.

Q. And you made a statement in writing, is that correct?

A. That is correct.

Q. Did the chief reduce this to a typewritten statement, do you know?

A. No, he did not.

Q. Now, I have in my hand what purports to be the statement that you made to Chief Arena at that time, and I would like to give you a copy of that, and in this statement you say—well, would you read first, Senator?

A. Yes, that is correct.

Q. Now, Senator, prior to the phone call you made, the effort you made to contact Burke Marshall by phone, did you make any other phone calls?

A. Yes, I did.

Q. Where did you make these phone calls?

A. I made one call after eight o'clock in the morning from the public phone outside of the restaurant at the Shiretown Inn.

Q. One call?

A. That is all. This was made sometime after eight.

Q. And to whom did you make this call?

A. I was attempting to reach Mr. Stephen Smith, the party that I felt would know the number.

Q. Were you alone in the police station?

A. No. At certain times I was, but if the thrust of the question is did I arrive at the police station with someone with me, I did.

Q. And who was that?

A. Mr. Markham.

Q. Mr. Markham.

A. Yes.

*Q.* With regard to the statement that you made at the police station, Senator, you wind up saying, "When I fully realized what had happened this morning, I immediately contacted the police." Now is that in fact what you did?

*THE COURT.* Mr. Dinis, are you going to ask the statement be put in the record?

*MR. DINIS.* Yes, your Honor.

*THE COURT.* Mr. Kennedy already said this was a copy of the statement he made. He already testified as to all his movements. Now, won't you let the record speak for itself?

*MR. DINIS.* All right, your Honor.

*THE COURT.* This will be Exhibit—

*MR. TELLER.* Two.

*THE COURT.* Two.

(Statement given to Chief Arena by Senator Kennedy marked Exhibit 2.)

*Q.* (By Mr. Dinis) Senator, you testified earlier that when you arrived at the cottage you asked Mr. LaRosa to tell Mr. Markham you were outdoors, outside of the house, when you arrived back at the house?

*A.* No, that is not correct.

*Q.* Did you ask someone to call Mr. Markham?

*A.* I asked Joe Gargan when he entered the vehicle to call for Mr. Markham.

*Q.* Well, did you at that time ask anyone to take you back to Edgartown at that time when you arrived back at the house after the accident?

*A.* No, I asked Mr. Gargan to go to the scene of the accident.

*Q.* But you didn't ask anyone to take you directly back to Edgartown?

*A.* I asked them to take me to Edgartown after their diving.

*Q.* After the diving?

*A.* After their diving.

*Q.* I show you, Mr. Kennedy, what purports to be a copy of the televised broadcast which you made approximately a week after the accident. Would you read the statement and tell me whether or not this is an exact copy of what you said?

*A.* (Witness complied.) Yes. After a quick reading of it, I would say that that is accurate.

*MR. DINIS.* Your Honor, may I introduce this statement made by Senator Kennedy in a televised broadcast?

*THE COURT.* You may, Exhibit No. 3. (Statement made by Senator Kennedy in a televised broadcast marked Exhibit 3.)

*Q.* Now, Senator, in that televised broadcast you said and I quote, "I instructed Gargan and Markham not to alarm Mary Jo's friends that night," is that correct?

*A.* That is correct. I would like to—

*Q.* Look at it?

*A.* —look at it. I believe that is correct.

*Q.* It would be on page 3.

(Witness examined the document.)

*A.* That is correct.

*Q.* Can you tell the Court what prompted you to give you this instruction to Markham and Gargan?

*A.* Yes, I can.

*Q.* Will you do that, please?

*A.* I felt strongly that if those girls were notified that an accident had taken place and that Mary Jo had in fact drowned, which I became convinced of by the time that Markham and Gargan and I left the scene of the accident, that it would only be a matter of seconds before all of those girls who were long and dear friends of Mary Jo's to go to the scene of the accident and dive themselves and enter the water with, I felt, a good chance that some serious mishap might have occurred to any one of them. It was for that reason that I restrained—asked Mr. Gargan and Mr. Markham not to alarm the girls.

*MR. DINIS.* I have no further questions of Mr. Kennedy.

*THE COURT.* And I have no further questions. Would you be available in the event we needed you back for anything?

*THE WITNESS.* I will make myself available, your Honor.

*THE COURT.* Well, were you planning to stay in Hyannis Port or some place near?

*THE WITNESS.* Well, I will. I will be glad to be available.

*THE COURT.* Otherwise you would go back to Boston?

*THE WITNESS.* No, I would return to Cape Cod tonight and I would hope to be able to return to Washington sometime this week, but I would be glad to remain available to the Court if the Court so desired.

*THE COURT.* Well, it is difficult for me to say right now.

*THE WITNESS.* Well, then, I will remain available as long as—

*THE COURT.* We will try to give you as much notice as possible if we felt it essential to have you back.

*MR. DINIS.* Your Honor, I think we could make it an overnight notice, so if the Senator had to be in Washington, we would arrange for his arrival the next day, if necessary, which may not be.

*THE COURT.* All right, subject to that, you are excused.

*THE WITNESS.* Your Honor, could I talk to my counsel before being released, just on one point that I might like to address the bench on?

*THE COURT.* Go ahead.

(Off-the-record discussion.)

*THE COURT.* And I think we can put in the record this question. Why did you not seek further assistance after Mr. Markham and Mr. Gargan had exhausted their efforts in attempting to reach Mary Jo? Now, you give the answer.

*THE WITNESS.* It is because I was completely convinced at that time that no further help and assistance would do Mary Jo any more good. I realized that she must be drowned and still in the car at this time, and it appeared a question in my mind at that time was, what should be done about the accident.

*THE COURT.* Anything further? Off the record.

(Discussion off the record.)

*THE WITNESS.* Since the alcoholic intake is relevant; there is one further question, your Honor, and although I haven't been asked it, I feel that in all frankness and fairness and for a complete record that it should be included as a part of the complete proceedings, and that is that during the course of the race that afternoon that there were two other members of my crew and I shared what would be two beers between us at different points in the race, and one other occasion in which there was some modest intake of alcohol would be after the race at the slip in which Ross Richards' boat was attached, moored, that I shared a beer with Mr. John Driscoll. The sum and substance of that beer would be, think, less than a quarter of one, but I felt that for the complete record that at least the Court should at least be aware of these instances as well.

THE COURT.    Anything more?

THE WITNESS.    There is nothing further.

THE COURT.    Anything more, Mr. Dinis?

MR. DINIS.    No, your Honor.

THE COURT:    All right, you are excused subject to further recall. Off the record.

(Discussion off the record.)

THE COURT.    All right, your next witness, Mr. Dinis.

This is the end of Mr. Kennedy's testimony. The remainder will not fit into a single book, but would take at least two fat volumes. For a condensation, see appendix H.

# APPENDIX D

*Text of the Findings of*

*the Inquest*

Inquest re Mary Jo Kopechne            Docket No. 15220

**REPORT**

James A. Boyle, Justice

I, James A. Boyle, Justice of the District Court for the County of Dukes County, in performance of the duty required of me by Section 12 of Chapter 38 of the General Laws of Massachusetts, in the matter of the inquest into the death of Mary Jo Kopechne, holden at Edgartown January 5, 1970 to January 8, 1970, inclusive, herewith submit my report. There are 763 pages of transcript and 33 numbered exhibits. Although most testimony was given orally, some was accepted by affidavit and included as exhibits. It is believed that, to aid in understanding this report, certain names and places should first be relatively located and some measurement shown:

(1)    The town of Edgartown, which is one of six towns on Martha's Vineyard, includes a small, sparsely settled island named Chappaquiddick. (Map, Exhibit 32)

(2) The mainland of Edgartown is separated from Chappaquiddick by Edgartown Harbor, the distance between being approximately five hundred feet, and transportation of vehicles and persons is provided by a small motor ferry which plies two ferry slips or landings. The ferry slip on the Edgartown side is near the center of town. (Exhibit 19)

(3) Chappaquiddick has few roads. At the ferry slip, begins a macadam paved road called Chappaquiddick Road, the main road of the island, with a white center line which is partly obliterated at the curve. The road is approximately twenty feet wide, running in a general easterly direction for two and one-half miles, whence it curves south and continues in that direction past the cottage to the southeast corner of the island. Chappaquiddick Road is sometimes referred to in the testimony as Main Street and, after it curves, as School Road or Schoolhouse Road, because a schoolhouse formerly stood on that portion of it. (Exhibits 16, 19)

(4) At the curve, and continuing easterly, begins Dyke Road, a dirt and sand road, seventeen to nineteen feet wide, which runs a distance of seven-tenths miles to Dyke Bridge, shortly beyond which is ocean beach. (Exhibits 15, 16, 17)

(5) Dyke Bridge is a wooden structure, ten feet, six inches wide, has timber curbs on each side four inches high by ten inches wide, no other guard rails, and runs at an angle of twenty-seven degrees to the left of the road. There are no signs or artificial lights on the bridge or its approach. It spans Poucha Pond. (Exhibits 7, 8, 9, 10)

(6) The Kennedy Oldsmobile is eighteen feet long and eighty inches wide. (Exhibits 1, 33)

(7) Poucha Pond is a salt water tidal pond, and has a strong current where it narrows at Dyke Bridge. (Exhibits 10, 18)

(8)   Cemetery Road is a single car–width private dirt road, which runs northerly from the junction of Chappaquiddick and Dyke Roads. (Exhibits 16, 22)

(9)   The Lawrence Cottage (herein called Cottage) is one-half mile from the junction of Chappaquiddick and Dyke Roads and approximately three miles from the ferry slip. (Exhibit 20)

(10)  Proceeding northerly from the Cottage, on the east side of Chappaquiddick Road, a distance of one-tenth mile before the curve, is a metal sign with an arrow pointing toward the ferry landing.

(11)  Katama Shores Motor Inn (called Katama Shores) is located approximately two miles from the Edgartown ferry slip.

(12)  Shiretown Inn (called Shiretown) is a very short distance from the Edgartown ferry slip, approximately one block.

Although the testimony is not wholly consistent, a general summary of the material circumstances is this: A group of twelve persons, by invitation of Edward M. Kennedy, a United States Senator, from Massachusetts, were gathered together in Edgartown to attend the annual sailing regatta held on Friday and Saturday, July 18 and 19, 1969. They were:

| | |
|---|---|
| John B. Crimmins | Rosemary Keough |
| Joseph Gargan | Mary Jo Kopechne |
| Edward M. Kennedy | Ann (also called Nance) Lyons |
| Raymond S. LaRosa | Maryellen Lyons |
| Paul F. Markham | Esther Newburgh |
| Charles C. Tretter | Susan Tannenbaum |

*(All hereafter referred to by surnames)*

The six young women, in their twenties, had been associated together in Washington, D.C. and were quite close friends. Kopechne shared an apartment with Ann Lyons. Reservations had been made for them to stay at Katama Shores, in three double rooms. Kopechne roomed with Newburgh. Crimmins, chauffeur for Kennedy when he was in Massachusetts, drove Kennedy's black Oldsmobile sedan from Boston to Martha's Vineyard on Wednesday, July 16. He brought a supply of liquor with him and stayed at the Cottage. Tretter, who brought some of the young women, arrived late Thursday and stayed at Shiretown. LaRosa, who brought his Mercury car, came Thursday and shared the room with Tretter. Gargan and Markham sailed Kennedy's boat to Edgartown on Thursday and roomed together at Shiretown. Kennedy arrived by plane on Friday, July 18, was met by Crimmins at the airport and was driven to the Cottage. Kennedy shared a room at Shiretown with Gargan. The Lyons sisters arrived Friday morning and were driven by Gargan to Katama Shores. Markham, who stayed at Shiretown Thursday night, moved to the Cottage to stay with Crimmins for Friday and Saturday nights.

Kennedy, with Gargan, was entered to sail his boat in the regatta on Friday and Saturday.

The Cottage became headquarters for the group and a cook-out was planned for Friday night. Three cars were available for general transportation; LaRosa's Mercury, Kennedy's Oldsmobile 88, and a rented white Valiant.

Thursday night those present, including Kopechne, visited the Cottage; Friday morning, they, including Kopechne, traveled over Dyke Bridge to the beach to swim; Friday evening, they, including Kopechne, traveled to the Cottage for the cook-out. Kennedy who arrived at 1:00 P.M. Friday and was driven by Crimmins to the Cottage, was then driven by Crimmins over Dyke Road and Dyke Bridge to the beach to swim; he was driven back to the Cottage to change, to the ferry slip to sail in the race, and, after the race, was driven back to the Cottage. There were other trips between Edgartown and the Cottage, but not including Kopechne or Kennedy. These are set forth to indicate the use of, and increasing familiarity with, the roads of Chappaquiddick.

The Cottage is small, contains a combination of kitchen-living room, two bedrooms and bath, has an open yard, no telephone, and is near to and visible from Chappaquiddick Road, which had little traffic. The entire group of twelve had assembled there by approximately 8:30 P.M. on Friday. Two cars were available for transportation on Chappaquiddick, the Oldsmobile and Valiant. LaRosa's Mercury was at the Shiretown. Activities consisted of cooking, eating, drinking, and conversation, singing and dancing. Available alcoholic beverages consisted of vodka, rum, scotch, and beer. There was not much drinking and no one admitted to more than three drinks; mostly only to two or less.

During the evening, Tretter, with Keough, drove to Edgartown in the Oldsmobile to borrow a radio. Keough left her pocketbook in the vehicle on that trip.

Only Crimmins and Markham planned to stay the night at the Cottage. The others intended to return to their respective hotels in Edgartown. It was known that the last ferry trip was about midnight, but that a special arrangement for a later trip could be made.

Between 11:15 and 11:30 P.M., Kennedy told Crimmins (but no other person) that he was tired, wanted to return to Shiretown to bed, that Kopechne did not feel well (some conflict here—see pages 32 and 346) and he was taking her back to Katama Shores, requested and obtained the car keys to the Oldsmobile, and both he and Kopechne departed. Kopechne told no one, other than Kennedy, that she was leaving. Kopechne left her pocketbook at the Cottage.

Kennedy stated he drove down Chappaquiddick Road toward the ferry, that when he reached the junction of Dyke Road, instead of bearing left on the Curve to continue on Chappaquiddick Road, he mistakenly turned right onto Dyke Road, realized at some point he was on a dirt road, but thought nothing of it, was proceeding at about twenty miles per hour when suddenly Dyke Bridge was upon him. He braked but the car went off the bridge into Poucha Pond and landed on its roof. The driver's window was open and he managed to reach the surface and swim to shore. It was extremely dark, there was a strong current, and repeated efforts by him to extricate Kopechne from the car were unsuccessful. Exhausted, he went to shore and, when recovered, walked back to the Cottage, not noticing any lights or houses on the way. He summoned Gargan and Markham, without notifying the others, and they returned in the Valiant to the bridge, where Gargan and Markham unsuccessfully attempted to recover Kopechne.

The three drove back to the ferry landing. After much discussion, it was decided that Kennedy would return to Edgartown (no mention how) to telephone David Burke, his administrative assistant, and Burke Marshall, an attorney, and then report the accident to the police. Kennedy advised Gargan and Markham to return to the Cottage, but not to tell the others of the accident. Suddenly and unexpectedly, Kennedy left the car, dove into the harbor and swam across to Edgartown. Gargan and Markham finally returned to the Cottage, but did not then tell the others what had occurred.

After Kennedy and Kopechne had left the Cottage, their purported destination unknown to anyone except Crimmins, the social activities gradually diminished. The absence of Kennedy and Kopechne was noticed but it was presumed they had returned to Edgartown. Some persons went walking. Only LaRosa saw Kennedy return at about 12:30 A.M., some were sleeping and the others, realizing they would not return to Edgartown that night, then slept or tried to. There not being sufficient beds, some slept on the floor.

In the morning, those in the Cottage returned to Edgartown at different times. The young women eventually reached Katama Shores and were then told what had happened, although some of them had previously been made aware that Kopechne was missing.

Kennedy, after swimming across to Edgartown, went to his room, took off his wet clothes, lay on the bed, then dressed, went outside and complained to someone (later identified as the innkeeper, Russell Peachy) of noise and to inquire the time. He was told it was 2:24 A.M. He returned to his room and remained there until 7:30 A.M. when he went outside, met Richards, a sailing competitor, chatted with him for one-half hour, when Gargan and Markham appeared and the three retired to Kennedy's room. When Kennedy informed them he had failed to report the accident, they all went to Chappaquiddick to use the public telephone near the ferry slip and Kennedy called David Burke, his administrative assistant, in Washington. (But Exhibit 4, list of calls charged to Kennedy, does not show this call.) Gargan returned to the Cottage to tell those there about the accident. Kennedy and Markham went to Edgartown Police Station, and were later joined by Gargan.

At about 8:20 A.M. Police Chief Arena, receiving notice of a submerged car at Dyke Bridge, hurried to the scene, changed into swim trunks, and made several futile attempts to enter the Oldsmobile. Farrar, a scuba diver, was summoned, found and retrieved the body of Kopechne from the car, and also found in the car the pocketbook of Keough. The car was later towed to shore.

Dr. Robert Mills of Edgartown, Associate Medical Examiner, was summoned and arrived about 9:15 A.M., examined the body and pronounced death by drowning, and turned it over to Eugene Frieh, a mortician, who took the body to his establishment at Vineyard Haven. The clothing and a sample of blood from the body were turned over to the State Police for analysis. No autopsy was performed and the body was embalmed and flown to Pennsylvania on Sunday for burial.

When Kennedy and Markham arrived at the Police Station, Chief Arena was at Dyke Bridge. He returned to the station at Kennedy's request. Kennedy stated he was the operator of the car and dictated a statement of the accident as Markham wrote it down. Chief Arena then typed the statement which Kennedy said was correct but did not sign. (Exhibit 2)

On July 25, 1969, Kennedy pleaded guilty in this Court to, and was sentenced on, a criminal charge of "leaving the scene of an accident after causing personal injury, without making himself known." That same night, Kennedy made a television statement to the voters of Massachusetts. (Exhibit 3)

A petition by District Attorney Edmund Dinis in the Court of Common Pleas for Luzerne County, Pennsylvania, for exhumation and autopsy on the body of Kopechne, was denied after hearing. Expert evidence was introduced that chemical analysis of the blouse worn by Kopechne showed blood stains, but medical evidence proved this was not inconsistent with death by drowning. (Exhibit 31)

Christopher F. Look, Jr., a deputy sheriff then living on Chappaquiddick, was driving easterly on Chappaquiddick Road to his home about 12:45 A.M. on July 19. As he approached the junction of Dyke Road, a car crossed in front of him and entered Cemetery Road, stopped, backed up, and drove easterly on Dyke Road. He saw two persons in the front seat, a shadow on the shelf back of the rear seat which he thought could have been a bag, article of clothing or a third person. The car was dark colored with Massachusetts registration plate L7 _____ 7. He was unable to remember any other numbers or how many there were intervening. Later that morning, he saw the Kennedy Oldsmobile when it was towed to shore, but he cannot positively identify it as the same car he saw at 12:45 A.M. During the inquest, a preliminary investigation was initiated through the Registry of Motor Vehicles to determine whether a tracking of the location on July 18 and 19, 1969, of all dark-colored cars bearing Massachusetts plates with any and all combinations of numbers beginning with L7 and ending in 7, would be practicable. The attempt was disclosed that it would not be feasible to do this since there would be no assurance that the end result would be helpful and, in any event, the elimination of all other cars within that registration group (although it would seriously affect the credibility of some of the witnesses) would not alter the findings of this report.

A short distance before Dyke Bridge, there is a small house called "Dyke House," then occupied by a Mrs. Malm and her daughter. (Exhibit 18) Both heard a car sometime before midnight but are not sure of its direction. The daughter turned off her light at midnight.

Drs. Watt and Brougham examined Kennedy on July 19 and 22. Diagnostic opinion was "concussion, contusions and abrasions of the scalp, cervical strain. Impairment of judgment and confused behavior are consistent with this type of injury." (Exhibit 27)

Eugene D. Jones, a professional engineer, testified by affidavit as to the condition of Dyke Road and Dyke Bridge and concluded that the site is well below approved engineering standards and particularly hazardous at night. (Exhibits 29, 30)

Donald L. Sullivan, an employee of Arthur D. Little, Inc. testified by affidavit as to a road test conducted on or about October 10, 1969, describing the factors involved in a motor vehicle, on high beam light, approaching Dyke Bridge at night, with film showing the results of such test. (Exhibit 28)

State Police Chemist McHugh, who analyzed the blood sample taken from the body of Kopechne, testified the alcoholic content was .09 percent, the equivalent of three and one-half to five ounces of eighty or ninety proof liquor consumed by a person, weighing about one hundred ten pounds, within an hour prior to death, or a larger amount if consumed within a longer period.

This concluded in substance, the material circumstances as testified to by the witnesses.

The failure of Kennedy to seek additional assistance in searching for Kopechne, whether excused by his condition, or whether or not it would have been of any material help, has not been pursued because such failure, even when shown, does not constitute criminal conduct.

Since there was no evidence that any air remained in the immersed car, testimony was not sought or allowed concerning how long Kopechne might have lived, had such a condition existed, as this could only be conjecture and purely speculative.

As previously stated, there are inconsistencies and contradictions in the testimony, which a comparison of individual testimony will show. It is not feasible to attempt to indicate each one. I list my findings as follows:

I.   The decedent is Mary Jo Kopechne, 28 years of age, last resident in Washington, D.C.

II.  Death probably occurred between 11:30 P.M. on July 18, 1969 and 1:00 A.M. on July 19, 1969.

III. Death was caused by drowning in Poucha Pond at Dyke Bridge on Chappaquiddick Island in the Town of Edgartown, Massachusetts, when a motor vehicle, in which the decedent was a passenger, went off Dyke Bridge, overturned and was immersed in Poucha Pond. The motor vehicle was owned and operated by Edward M. Kennedy of Boston, Massachusetts.

The statute states that I must report the name of any person whose unlawful act or negligence *appears* to have contributed to Kopechne's death. As I stated at the commencement of the hearing, the Massachusetts Supreme Court said in its decision concerning the conduct of this inquest, "the inquest serves as an aid in the achievement of justice by obtaining information as to whether a crime has been committed." In *La Chappelle vs. United States Machinery Corporation*, 318 Mass. 166, decided in 1945, the same Court said, "It is designed merely to ascertain facts for the purpose of subsequent prosecution" and ". . . the investigating judge may himself issue process against a person whose probable guilt is disclosed."

Therefore, in guiding myself as to the proof herein required of the commission of any unlawful act, I reject the cardinal principle of "proof beyond a reasonable doubt" applied in criminal trials but use as standard the principle of "probable guilt."

I have also used the rule, applicable to trials, which permits me to draw inferences, known and presumption of facts, from the testimony. There are several definitions and I quote from the case of *Commonwealth vs. Green*, 295 Pa. 573: "A presumption of fact is an inference which a reasonable man would draw from certain facts which have been proven. The basis is in logic and its source of probability." Volume 29 *American Jurisprudence*, 2nd Evidence Section 161, states in part, "A presumption of fact or an inference is nothing more than a probable or natural explanation of facts . . . and arises from the commonly accepted experiences of mankind and the inference which reasonable men would draw from experiences."

I find these facts:

A.    Kennedy was the host and mainly responsible for the assembly of the group at Edgartown.

B.  Kennedy was rooming at Shiretown with Gargan, his cousin and close friend of many years.

C.  Kennedy had employed Crimmins as Chauffeur for nine years and rarely drove himself. Crimmins drove Kennedy on all other occasions herein set forth, and was available at the time of the fatal trip.

D.  Kennedy told only Crimmins that he was leaving for Shire-town and requested the car keys.

E.  The young women were close friends, were on Martha's Vineyard for a common purpose as a cohesive group, and staying together at Katama Shores.

F.  Kopechne roomed with Newburgh, the latter having in her possession the key to their room.

G.  Kopechne told no one, other than Kennedy that she was leaving for Katama Shores and did not ask Newburgh for the room key.

H.  Kopechne left her pocketbook at the Cottage when she drove off with Kennedy.

I.  Ten of the persons at the cook-out did not intend to remain at the cottage overnight.

J.  Only the Oldsmobile and the Valiant were available for transportation of those ten, the Valiant being the smaller car.

K.  LaRosa's Mercury was parked at the Shiretown and was available for use.

I infer a reasonable and probable explanation of the totality of the above facts is that Kennedy and Kopechne did not intend to return to Edgartown at that time; that Kennedy did not intend to drive to the ferry slip and his turn onto Dyke Road was intentional. Having reached this conclusion, the question then arises as to whether there was anything criminal in his operation of the motor vehicle.

From two personal views, which corroborate the Engineer's statement (Exhibit 29), and other evidence, I am fully convinced that Dyke Bridge constitutes a traffic hazard, particularly so at night, and must be approached with extreme caution. A speed of even twenty miles per hours, as Kennedy testified to, operating a car as large as this Oldsmobile, would at least be negligent and, possibly, reckless. If Kennedy knew of this hazard, his operation of the vehicle constituted criminal conduct.

Earlier on July 18, he had been driven over Chappaquiddick Road three times, and over Dyke Road and Dyke Bridge twice. Kopechne had been driven over Chappaquiddick Road five times and over Dyke Road and Dyke Bridge twice.

I believe it probable that Kennedy knew of this hazard that lay ahead of him on Dyke Road but that, for some reason not apparent from the testimony, he failed to exercise due care as he approached the bridge.

IV.   I, therefore, find there is probably cause to believe that Edward M. Kennedy operated his motor vehicle negligently in a way or in a place to which the public have a right of access and that such operation appears to have contributed to the death of Mary Jo Kopechne.

February 18, 1970


JAMES A. BOYLE
Justice

# APPENDIX E

*Text of the Findings of
the Pennsylvania Exhumation
Hearing*

In the Court of Common Pleas of Luzerne County, Pennsylvania
In Re: Kopechne            Criminal 1114 of 1969

## DECISION

This matter comes before the court upon petition and the amended petition for exhumation and autopsy of the body of Mary Jo Kopechne. The petitioners are Edmund Dinis, District Attorney for the Southern District of Massachusetts, and Robert W. Nevin, M.D., Medical Examiner for Dukes County, Massachusetts. The amended petition sets forth the following allegations of fact:

1. The death of Mary Jo Kopechne on July 18 or 19, 1969.

2. Her burial in Larksville, Luzerne County, Pennsylvania.

3. A search of July 19, 1969 which resulted in the recovery of the body of Mary Jo Kopechne from a submerged car off Dyke Bridge, Edgartown, Dukes County, Massachusetts.

4. A determination by Dr. Mills that the death of Mary Jo Kopechne was caused by asphyxiation by immersion (i.e. drowning); that the cause of death was determined without benefit of autopsy; that Dr. Mills did not perform an autopsy because he found no external signs of violence or foul play; that the body of the deceased had been submerged eight hours before his observation; that it was assumed Mary Jo Kopechne was not only the driver of the car, but was its sole occupant; and that death occurred five to eight hours prior to 9:30 A.M.

5. That the operator of the motor vehicle in which the deceased's body was found did not report the accident to the police until approximately ten hours after he said it occurred; that said operator reported that the accident happened at 11:15 P.M. on July 18, 1969; that there is a witness who claims to have seen the car at 12:40 A.M. on July 19, 1969, with two or possibly three persons in it.

6. That said operator pleaded guilty to a motor vehicle law infraction.

7. That the report of the accident made to the Chief of Police of Edgartown, Massachusetts, by the operator on July 19, 1969, differed from a report of the accident broadcast by the operator on July 25, 1969.

8. That the broadcast and police reports are silent on many important details.

9. That persons who were not directly involved in the accident but who were cognizant of it, did not call the authorities.

10. That there appear on the white shirt worn by the de-

ceased "washed out" stains that give a positive benzidine reaction, an indication of the presence of residual
traces of blood.

11.  That there was present a certain amount of blood in both
     the deceased's mouth and nose which may not be incon-
     sistent with death by drowning.

12.  That the information in paragraph 10 and 11 (5-I and
     5-J) was not available to the petitioners until after
     interment.

13.  That the public interest and proper administration of
     justice requires confirmation of Dr. Mills's original de-
     termination of the cause of death which can be accom-
     plished only by an autopsy.

14.  The passage of time from the date of death on July 18 or
     19, 1969, has not diminished to any significant degree
     the findings which could be made from an autopsy con-
     ducted at the present time.

15.  There is now pending in Dukes County, Massachusetts,
     an inquest into the death of Mary Jo Kopechne.
         The petitioners also allege, although they are mostly
     conclusions of law, the following:

16.  That the purpose of the inquest is to determine whether
     or not there is any reason sufficient to believe that the
     sudden death of Mary Jo Kopechne may have resulted
     from the act or negligence of a person or persons other
     than the deceased.

17.  That in order that the circumstances of death be clearly
     established and the doubt and suspicion surrounding the
     death be resolved, an exhumation and autopsy will be
     required.

18.  That once Dr. Mills's determination of the cause of death
     is confirmed by an autopsy, the inquest can proceed with
     certainty that Mary Jo Kopechne's death was caused by

drowning. However, if the autopsy should disclose that her death resulted from some cause other than drowning, the inquest may then proceed in the direction appropriate in light of the information thus revealed.

19. That in either event, an autopsy would further serve the public interest and promote administration of justice in that it will disclose either the presence or absence of other conditions beside the cause of death having a critical bearing on the events and circumstances culminating in the death of Mary Jo Kopechne.

20. That the public interest in general and the proper administration of justice in particular require that all facts relative to the inquest be established with the utmost attainable degree of certainty.

The basic law on this subject was cited on pages 2 and 3 of the court's decision in this matter dated October 9, 1969. Since its applicability is equally cogent to the present matter, it is again cited:

Courts have never hesitated to have a body exhumed where the application under the particular circumstances appeared reasonable and was for the purpose of eliciting the truth in the promotion of justice.

On the other hand, an application for disinterment for the purpose of performing an autopsy should not be granted where there is no basis or justification for an order. Disinterment for the purpose of examination or autopsy should not be ordered unless it is clearly established that good cause and urgent necessity for such action exist. An order should not be made except on a strong showing that the facts sought will be established by an examination or autopsy. In the search for truth, the problems of religion, the wishes of decedent, the sensitivities of loved ones and friends, or even the elements of public health and welfare, should not be disregarded. The law will not reach into the grave in search of the facts except in the rarest of cases, and not even then unless it is clearly necessary and there is reasonable probability that such a violation of the sepulchre will establish that which is sought.

The positive criteria in law are then that the application for exhumation and autopsy:

1. Must be reasonable under the circumstances.

2. Its purpose is to elicit the truth in the promotion of justice.

3. It must be clearly established that:
   (a) good cause and
   (b) urgent necessity for such action exist.

4. There must be a strong showing that the facts sought will be established by an exhumation and autopsy.

5. That the law will reach into the grave in:
   (a) only the rarest of cases and
   (b) not even then, unless clearly necessary, and
   (c) where there is a reasonable probability that such a violation of the sepulchre will establish that which is sought.

Let us now turn to the facts established at the hearing on the petition for exhumation and autopsy.

Essentially, they must be examined in two categories. First, from the purely legal point of view as they obtain to the eliciting of the truth in the promotion of justice and the good cause and urgent necessity that must exist to warrant an exhumation and autopsy; and, second, from the medical-legal aspect that there must be a strong showing that the facts sought will be established by an autopsy and the reasonable probability that the violation of the sepulchre will establish that which is sought.

As to the former, we are obviously referring to such facts as would cause one in authority to conclude that the death of Mary Jo Kopechne resulted from a cause other than drowning.

A review of the record of testimony, in light of the allegations of the petition from Edmund Dinis, reveals that there is some question as to whether the vehicle in question departed to Dyke Bridge at about 11:15 P.M., July 18, 1969, or about 12:40 A.M., July 19, 1969. That the driver of the vehicle failed to report the incident until some ten hours after it happened. That the report given by the driver to the Edgartown police varied from his broadcast on July 25, 1969, and that the police report and broadcast are silent on many important details of the accident. That persons not directly involved in the accident, who were cognizant of it, did not call the authorities. That there were washed-out stains on the back of the blouse of the deceased which, when exposed to a benzidine test, indicated the presence of blood and that there was present a certain amount of blood in both the deceased's mouth and nose which may or may not be inconsistent with death by drowning. That a witness saw the car in question July 19, 1969 at about 12:40 A.M. in which there appeared to be a man and a woman in the front seat and a person or a sweater or pocketbook or something on the back seat and that this car stopped and, upon approach by the witness, left hurriedly and that this was the same car that was found in Poucha Pond off the Dyke Bridge the following morning. That the witness also saw two other unidentified girls and a man that night near the scene. That there is an inquest now pending in Edgartown, Massachusetts, and that an autopsy is necessary to resolve the circumstances surrounding the death of Mary Jo Kopechne.

Starting with the premise that the purpose of this autopsy is to establish the cause of death of Mary Jo Kopechne, are there any credible facts of record here that could objectively cause one to conclude that a reasonable probability exists that the cause of death was other than death by drowning?

Let us first consider the fact that the driver failed to report the accident until ten hours after it occurred. Disposition of same need not be considered here since the Massachusetts authorities have accepted the driver's plea of guilty to leaving the scene of the accident. Furthermore, the fact that the vehicle operated by the driver may have entered the water at 12:40 A.M., July 19,

1969, rather than at 11:15 P.M., July 18, 1969, does not suggest a cause of death other than death by drowning.

Reference is then made to the difference between the driver's broadcast and the police report. Essentially, there are but two basic differences between the two. First, in the broadcast the driver made reference to seeking aid from Joseph Gargan and Paul Markham. In the police report, no reference was made to them. Second, in the police statement, he said he went back to the party and had someone (unidentified) drive him back to Edgartown, while in his broadcast he refers to the aforesaid Gargan and Markham assisting him. These discrepancies do not alter the determination of the cause of death.

The next reference is that the police report and the broadcast are silent on many important details of the accident. While this is possibly so, proper subpoenaing of witnesses may or may not have substantiated this, but at the moment this court is not at liberty to speculate as to what those details might be.

Again, reference is made to witnesses who had knowledge of the accident and did not call the authorities. The court is unable to determine from the record who these witnesses were, to what they would testify, or why they were not subpoenaed.

One of the most substantial references in the petition was concerning the evidence of blood on the back of the deceased's blouse, as well as in her mouth and nose. Yet, the only positive testimony as to these was that this evidence was wholly consistent with death by drowning.

Equally significant was the testimony of Christopher Look, Jr., who testified as the presence of the car of the driver near the bridge at about 12:40 A.M. on July 19, 1969 with a man and a woman in the front and a person or a sweater in the back, which left the scene hurriedly when his presence was evident and that this was the same car found in Poucha Pond that same day; also that he saw two unidentified girls and a man nearby. Again, this course of conduct by the driver does not suggest a cause of death other than as has been found.

With this in mind, let us examine the testimony in the petitioners' case that refutes their own contentions. In Chief Dominick

Arena's police report, he states: "It was felt that because of the evidence at the scene, condition of the roadway and accident scene that there was no negligence on the part of the operator in the accident." The testimony of John N. Farrar, the scuba driver, is that at the scene there was nothing outstanding about the body other than that she was attractively dressed and fully clothed. That the submerged car had its ignition on, the car was in drive, the brake off, the light switch on, and it was full of gas. Also that the window on the driver's side was down and the door was locked. Dr. Robert Mills's testimony, reference to which will be made at length in the legal-medical portion of this opinion, was that he found no signs of foul play or any criminal conduct. Finally, Eugene Frieh, the mortician, testified that in cleansing the body of Mary Jo Kopechne, he found no bruises, contusions or abrasions, except on a knuckle of her left hand.

In view of the above, it is difficult for this court to conclude that exhumation and autopsy are warranted. If there is testimony available to the petitioners that might establish the relief they seek, it has not been presented here.

Let us now address ourselves to the medical-legal aspect of this matter. As stated before, the petitioners must establish by a strong showing that the facts sought will be established by an exhumation and autopsy and there must be reasonable probability that a violation of the sepulchre will establish those facts.

In cases of death resulting from unnatural causes, autopsies before burial are performed as a matter of course. After interment, the legal test recited on pages four and five of this decision controls. As stated in this court's decision of October 9, 1969, ". . . It must not be overlooked that the Massachusetts authorities had the statutory right and opportunity to perform an autopsy prior to interment of the body of Mary Jo Kopechne, but once burial is complete, the aforementioned legal principles as to exhumation and autopsy must be considered."

Let us first review the medical testimony offered by the pathologists for the petitioners, that of Doctors Joseph W. Spellman, George G. Katsas, and Cyril H. Wecht. They all testified that if the body of Mary Jo Kopechne were exhumed and an autopsy performed, an interpretation of results would be more difficult but it would be entirely possible to make observations and draw valid conclusions. In the instance of Dr. Spellman, he testified he has performed autopsies on bodies interred for a period of five years. They also testified autopsies have frequently revealed causes of death not revealed by external examination, such as fractured sculls, hemorrhages within the brain, broken necks, broken ribs, ruptured internal organs and natural disease processes. In the case of Dr. Spellman, he testified that he attaches little significance to froth about the mouth or nose of a victim since it is found in other kinds of deaths such as heart failure, overdose of drugs, and death from respiratory depression. Dr. Katsas referred specifically to tests that might confirm death by drowning such as the presence of foreign material deep in the trachea or bronchi, hemorrhage in the middle ear and presence of diatoms and algae in the bones and remote areas of the body. However, on cross-examination, he testified that if all three tests proved negative, he would conclude that the cause of death was by drowning if he didn't find any other evidence of disease or injury in the remainder of the body. The only reference to reasonable medical certainty developed in the testimony of Dr. Wecht, who after reciting many general areas of causes of death, stated: "There would be an excellent opportunity to arrive at a quite substantial valid medical opinion that could be rendered by any competent pathologist with more than a reasonable degree of certainty." But of what? Even if we assume that an autopsy would reveal a broken neck or any other bone in the body, a fractured skull, the rupture of an internal organ, none of these would be incompatible with the manner in which the accident occurred. To consider any other cause of death at this time would give loose rein to speculation unsupported by any medical facts of record.

When we weigh this evidence with that of Dr. Robert Mills, who was also called on behalf of the petitioners, we immediately find an inconsistency within the petitioners' cause. Dr. Mills, after examination of the body of Mary Jo Kopechne, concluded and issued the death certificate with the cause of death as:

"Asphyxiation by immersion—(overturned submerged automobile)" i.e. death by drowning. His examination included a view of the body, finding a dead girl, well nourished, fully clothed, in total *rigor mortis*. He opened her blouse, put a stethoscope to her heart, percussed her chest with slight pressure and water came out of her nose and mouth. There was a fine white froth about her nose and mouth which was present before percussion. There were little cobwebs of blood on the foam which went directly to a little capillary just on the left hand edge of her nostril. She obviously had much water in her respiratory tract since he applied pressure a number of times in varying degrees and each time water would well up and out. This pressure was on the chest, not the stomach. He saw no evidence of trauma of any kind after feeling her legs, arms, skull and back. That although he did not disrobe her, he did open her blouse and pulled her slacks down over her abdomen. To him, it was an "obvious case of drowning" since the foam about the nose and mouth, the cobwebs of blood from her nostril, the splashing sound of water in her chest and the emission of water from deep down are all common concomitants of drowning. It was his opinion that for all practical purposes his external examination excluded other causes of death. He also added that there was no evidence of foul play or any criminal conduct. To this we add the report of the blood test of the blood of the deceased which was negative as to barbiturates and evidence of the consumption of only a small amount of alcoholic beverages.

While this may actually belong to the first category of consideration, the eliciting of truth in the promotion of justice, the fact is that after his examination Dr. Mills released the body to Mr. Frieh, the mortician, with a caveat that there should be no embalming until he cleared with the District Attorney's Office and the State Police. Only after it had been determined that there was no necessity for an autopsy did Dr. Mills then direct Mr. Frieh to embalm the body. This testimony of the delay in embalming was corroborated by Mr. Frieh, also a witness for the petitioners.

Turning to the testimony of Dr. Werner Spitz, the pathologist testifying for the respondents, while his colleagues in his field did not attach particular significance to pinkish foam about the nose and mouth in drowning cases, he explained that when water enters the lungs under pressure, particularly salt water, there is a rupture of very small vessels and the blood from the rupture gives the foam a pinkish appearance. That when resuscitation stops, foam develops and being lighter than water, comes up. While there may be differences of opinion among pathologists, it would be illogical for this court not to accept that which is a logical explanation in view of all the attending circumstances. In addition, Dr. Spitz gave the only explanation as to the presence of blood on the back of the blouse of the deceased. He stated that when this pinkish foam begins to form, it runs down the face along the neck and makes a puddle behind the head and hence the blood on the back of the blouse. He said he couldn't imagine a drowning victim looking any different. He concedes that he would like to have had an autopsy when the body was first removed from the water, but that an exhumation and autopsy would be but of academic importance and added that, in his opinion, within medical certainty, Mary Jo Kopechne died from drowning.

The testimony of Dr. Henry C. Freimuth, a toxicologist, lends verity to the testimony of Drs. Mills and Spitz in that the stains on the blouse of the decedent were characteristic of the stains produced by pinkish foam from drowning victims.

In evaluating this medical testimony as it relates to the law of the Commonwealth of Pennsylvania, it must be concluded that the petitioners have failed to meet their burden of proof by a "strong showing that the facts sought will be established by an exhumation and autopsy" and that there is a "reasonable probability" that that which is sought warrants a violation of the sepulchre. *A fortiori*, from the testimony before this court, every reasonable probability leads to a conclusion that supports the original finding of the cause of death of Mary Jo Kopechne, asphyxiation by immersion, i.e. death by drowning.

In view of the testimony and law considered herein, and bearing in mind that courts are not reluctant to grant autopsies in given cases, we must be mindful that Joseph A. Kopechne and Gwen L. Kopechne, the parents of Mary Jo Kopechne, have indicated that they are unalterably opposed to exhumation and autopsy. Thus, it is incumbent that this court give weight to their objections. While their disapproval is not an absolute bar to an exhumation and autopsy, in view of the facts presented to this court, their objections are well taken.

It is the conclusion of this court that the facts presented herein are insufficient to support a finding of the cause of death by Mary Jo Kopechne other than asphyxiation by immersion.

Therefore, we enter the following:

# ORDER

Now this 8th day of December, 1969, at 11:55 A.M., EST, it is hereby ordered and decreed that the objections of Joseph A. Kopechne and Gwen L. Kopechne, parents of Mary Jo Kopechne, are hereby sustained and the petitioners' request for exhumation and autopsy of the body of Mary Jo Kopechne is hereby denied.

BY THE COURT

—P. J.

# APPENDIX F

*Brief  Discussion  of
Judicial  Decisions  in
Cases  Growing  Out  of  the
Accident  and  the  Later
Litigation*

*Lipman v. Commonwealth of Massachusetts*

The text of the three cases titled *Lipman* v. the *Commonwealth* would take up approximately sixteen pages. They deal largely with issues that have nothing to do with the events on Chappaquiddick, but as their subject was the transcript of the inquest, we summarize them here.

Normally in Massachusetts court reporters sell copies of their transcripts to the parties in the case and anyone else who is interested. They pay for reproduction, charge a reasonable profit for their efforts, and keep the money.

Because of the great interest in the Chappaquiddick inquest, the Clerk of the Superior Court, without consulting the court reporters, made arrangements to reproduce and sell copies of the transcript at $75 each, less than the court reporters would normally have charged for such a voluminous work.

Sidney R. Lipman and Harold T. McNeil brought an action in the Federal District Court against Judge Boyle, Edward V. Keating, Clerk of the Superior Court, and the Commonwealth of Massachusetts alleging that they had been the court reporters on the Kopechne inquest and that practice and usage was that court reporters sold the transcripts of inquests or any other proceedings at their normal rate. In this case, however, transcripts had been sold by the clerk of the Superior Court at a lower price than the court reporters would have charged. The original case was in the form of a request for injunctive relief to stop this sale. There was great interest in the Kopechne inquest transcript, 111 copies of which the clerk eventually sold. This would have represented a substantial profit to the court reporters.

In the first case, *Lipman* v. *Commonwealth* 311 F. Supp. 593 (1970), injunctive relief was denied.

The case was appealed to the Federal Circuit Court, which ordered a trial on the merits, in other words on the witnesses and evidence, not merely on the legal principles. Trial was then held in 1972—345 F. Supp. 523 (1972). Lipman and McNeil lost again.

By this time transcripts had been sold; because the action was in litigation, the profit over reproduction that the Superior Court received for the transcripts was being held in escrow. The amount was $3,325.

After their defeat in August 1972, Lipman and McNeil appealed to the United States Court of Appeals for the First Circuit. That court found that it was the Massachusetts custom to give court reporters the right to sell transcripts for all proceedings but that the lower court had been correct in ruling that the court reporters had no common-law copyright in the transcripts of the proceedings, which were public documents. In essence, the plaintiffs had the right to sell transcripts, but the court had the right to control the price at which they were sold. The fund that was being held in escrow was paid over to Lipman and McNeil. This case, 475 F. 2d. 565 (1973), was the last legal gasp of the events that took place on July 19, 1969.

# APPENDIX G

*Applicable Laws of the Commonwealth of Massachusetts*

Massachusetts Laws Applied in the Various Cases, Actions, and Theories Arising from the Accident on Chappaquiddick

## Traffic

Chapter 90 of the Annotated Laws of Massachusetts in effect July 19, 1969, titled Motor Vehicles and Aircraft:

# SECTION 24. RECKLESS, UNAUTHORIZED, DRUNKEN, ETC., DRIVING; FRAUD IN CONNECTION WITH LICENSE; NOT STOPPING AFTER COLLISION; PROSECUTION FOR SECOND OFFENSE; PENALTIES.

(1)*(a)* Whoever, upon any way or in any place to which the public has a right of access, or upon any way or in any place to which members of the public have access as invitees or licensees, operates a motor vehicle while under the influence of intoxicating liquor or narcotic drugs, as defined in section one hundred and ninety-seven of chapter ninety-four, or under the influence of barbiturates, amphetamines, or other hypnotic or somnifacient drugs, or under the influence of the vapors of glue, carbon tetrachloride, acetone, ethylene, dichloride, toluene, chloroform, zylene or any combination thereof, shall be punished by a fine of not less than thirty-five nor more than one thousand dollars, or by imprisonment for not less than two weeks nor more than two years, or both. A court or magistrate, before imposing sentence upon a person found guilty of a violation of this paragraph, shall ascertain by inquiry of the office of the registrar or of the board of probation, or of both of said offices, what records or other information said office has tending to show that said person has been convicted of a like offense by a court or magistrate of the commonwealth within a period of six years immediately preceding the commission of the offense with which he is charged. (Amended by 1961, 347, approved April 10, 1961, effective 90 days thereafter; 1961, 422, Section 2, approved May 3, 1961, effective 90 days thereafter; 1962, 394, section 2, approved May 1, 1962, effective 90 days thereafter; 1963, 369, section 2, approved May 6, 1963, effective 90 days thereafter.)

*(b)* A conviction of a violation of the preceding paragraph of this section shall be reported forthwith by the court or magistrate to the registrar, who shall revoke immediately the license

or the right to operate of the person so convicted, and no appeal, motion for new trial or exceptions shall operate to stay the revocation of the license or right to operate. (Amended by 1964, 200, section 1, approved March 23, 1964, effective 90 days thereafter.

*(c)* The registrar, after having revoked the license or the right to operate of any person under the preceding paragraph of this section, shall not issue a new license or reinstate the right to operate to such person, except in his discretion if the prosecution of such person has terminated in favor of the defendant, until five years after a conviction of a violation of paragraph *(a)* hereof committed within six years after conviction of a violation of said paragraph, nor until one year after a conviction of any violation of said paragraph other than one committed within six years as aforesaid; but notwithstanding the foregoing, no new license shall be issued or right to operate be reinstated by the registrar to any person convicted of a violation of paragraph *(a)* of subdivision (1) of this section until ten years after the date of conviction in case the registrar determines upon investigation and after hearing that the action of the person so convicted in committing such offense caused an accident resulting in the death of another, nor at any time after a subsequent conviction of such an offense, whenever committed, in case the registrar determines in the manner aforesaid that the action of such person, in committing the offense of which he was so subsequently convicted, caused an accident resulting in the death of another. (Amended by 1955, 198, section 1, approved March 22, 1955, effective 90 days thereafter; 1964, 200, section 2, approved March 23, 1964, effective 90 days thereafter.)

*(d)* For the purposes of subdivision (1) of this section, a person shall be deemed to have been convicted if he pleaded guilty or nolo contendere or was found or adjudged guilty by a court of competent jurisdiction, whether or not he was placed on probation without sentence or under a suspended sentence or the case was placed on file, and a license may be revoked under paragraph *(b)* hereof notwithstanding the pendency of a prosecution upon appeal or otherwise after such a conviction. Where

there has been more than one conviction in the same prosecution, the date of the first conviction shall be deemed to be the date of conviction under paragraph *(c)* hereof. (Amended by 1955, 198, section 2, approved March 22, 1955, effective 90 days thereafter.)

*(e)* In any prosecution for a violation of paragraph (1) *(a)* of this section, evidence of the percentage, by weight, of alcohol in the defendant's blood at the time of the alleged offense, as shown by chemical test or analysis of his blood or as indicated by chemical test or analysis of his breath, shall be admissible and deemed relevant to the determination of the question of whether such defendant was at such time under the influence of intoxicating liquor; provided, however, that if such test or analysis was made by or at the direction of a police officer, it was made with the consent of the defendant, the results thereof were made available to him upon his request, and the defendant was afforded a reasonable opportunity, at his request and at his expense, to have another such test or analysis made by a person or physician selected by him. Evidence that the defendant failed or refused to consent to such test or analysis shall not be admissible against him in any civil or criminal proceeding. Blood shall not be withdrawn from any such defendant for the purposes of any such test or analysis except by a physician. If such evidence is that such percentage was five one hundredths or less, there shall be a presumption that such defendant was not under the influence of intoxicating liquor; if such evidence is that such percentage was more than five one hundredths but less than fifteen one hundredths, there shall be no presumption; and if such evidence is that such percentage was fifteen one hundredths or more, there shall be a presumption that such defendant was under the influence of intoxicating liquor. (Added 941, 340, approved April 10, 1961, effective 90 days thereafter.)

(2)*(a)* Whoever upon any way or in any place to which the public has a right of access, or any place to which members of the public have access as invitees or licensees, operates a motor vehicle recklessly, or operates such a vehicle negligently so that the lives or safety of the public might be endangered, or upon a bet or wager or in a race, or whoever operates a motor vehicle for the purpose of making a record and thereby violates any provision of section seventeen or any regulation under section eighteen, or whoever without stopping and making known his name, residence and the register number of his motor vehicle goes away after knowingly colliding with or otherwise causing injury to any other vehicle or property, or whoever loans or knowingly permits his license to operate motor vehicles to be used by any person, or whoever makes false statements in an application for such a license or falsely impersonates the person named in such an application or procures such false impersonation whether of himself or of another, or whoever in an application for registration of a motor vehicle or trailer gives as his name or address or the place where such vehicle is principally garaged a false name, address or place, shall be punished by a fine of not less than twenty dollars nor more than two hundred dollars or by imprisonment for not less than two weeks nor more than two years, or both; and whoever uses a motor vehicle without authority knowing that such use is unauthorized shall be punished by a fine of not less than fifty dollars nor more than five hundred dollars or by imprisonment for not less than thirty days nor more than two years, or both; and whoever operates a motor vehicle upon any way or in any place to which the public has a right of access, or upon any way or in any place to which members of the public have access as invitees or licensees, and, without stopping and making known his name, residence and the register number of his motor vehicle, goes away after knowingly colliding with or otherwise causing injury to any person shall be punished by imprisonment for not less than two months nor more than two years. A summons may be issued instead of a warrant for arrest upon a complaint for a violation of any provision of this paragraph if in the judgment of the court or justice receiving the complaint there is reason to believe that the defendant will appear upon a summons. (Amended by 1964, 200, section 3, approved March 23, 1964, effective 90 days thereafter; 1966, 316, approved May 31, 1966, effective 90 days thereafter.)

*(b)* A conviction of a violation of the preceding paragraph of

this section shall be reported forthwith by the court or magistrate to the registrar, who may in any event, and shall unless the court or magistrate recommends otherwise, revoke immediately the license or right to operate of the person so convicted, and no appeal, motion for new trial or exceptions shall operate to stay the revocation of the license or right to operate. If it appears by the records of the registrar that the person so convicted as the owner of a motor vehicle or has exclusive control of any motor vehicle as a manufacturer or dealer or otherwise, the registrar may revoke the certificate of registration of any or all motor vehicles so owned or exclusively controlled. (Amended by 1964, 200 section 4, approved March 23, 1964, effective 90 days thereafter.)

*(c)* The registrar, after having revoked the license or right to operate of any person under the preceding paragraph of this section, in his discretion may issue a new license or reinstate the right to operate to him, if the prosecution of such person in the superior court has terminated in favor of the defendant, or, after an investigation or upon hearing, may issue a new license or reinstate the right to operate to a person convicted in any court of the violation of any provision of paragraph *(a)* of subdivision (2) of this section; provided, that no new license or right to operate shall be issued by the registrar to any person convicted of going away without stopping and making known his name, residence, and the register number of his motor vehicle after having, while operating such vehicle after upon any way or in any place to which the public has a right of access, or any place to which members of the public have access as invitees or licensees, knowingly collided with or otherwise caused injury to any person, or to any person convicted of using a motor vehicle knowing that such use is unauthorized, or to any person adjudged a delinquent child by reason thereof under the provisions of section fifty-eight B of chapter one hundred and nineteen, until one year after the date of his original conviction or adjudication if for a first offense or until two years after the date of any subsequent conviction or adjudication, or to any person convicted of violating any other provision of paragraph *(a)* of subdi-

vision (2) of this section until sixty days after the date of his original conviction if for a first offense, or one year after the date of any subsequent conviction within a period of three years. But the registrar, after investigation, may at any time rescind the revocation of a license or right to operate revoked because of a conviction of operating a motor vehicle upon any way or in any place to which the public has a right of access, or any place to which members of the public have access as invitees or licensees, negligently so that the lives or safety of the public might be endangered. (Amended by 1955, 198, section 3, approved March 22, 1964, effective 90 days thereafter; 1964, 200, section 5, approved March 23, 1964, effective 90 days thereafter; 1966, 191, section 1, approved April 21, 1966, effective 90 days thereafter.)

# MEDICAL EXAMINER, AUTOPSIES, AND INQUESTS

Chapter 38, titled "Medical Examiner":

## SECTION 6. DUTIES OF EXAMINERS; AUTOPSY, WHEN AUTHORIZED.

When any person in the commonwealth is supposed to have died by violence or by the action of chemical, thermal or electrical agents or following abortion, or from diseases resulting from injury or infections related to occupation, or suddenly when not disabled by recognizable disease, or when any person is found dead, it shall be the duty of any person having knowledge of such death immediately to notify the medical examiner of the district of the county wherein the body lies of the known facts concerning the time, place, manner, circumstances, and cause of such death. A physician who, having knowledge of such a death, fails to notify the medical examiner shall be punished by a fine of not more than one hundred dollars. Immediately upon receipt of such notification, the medical examiner shall carefully inquire into the cause and circumstances of the death and if, as a result of such inquiry, he is of the opinion that death may have resulted from violence or unnatural causes, he shall go to the dead body and take charge of the same. Upon taking charge of the dead body and before moving the same the medical examiner shall carefully note the appearance, the condition and position of the body and record every fact and circumstance tending to show the cause and manner of death with the names and addresses of all known witnesses and subscribe the same and make such record a part of his report as provided in section seven. If on view of the dead body and after personal inquiry into the cause and manner of death, the medical examiner considers a further examination necessary in the public interest, he shall immediately notify the district attorney of the district and county within whose jurisdiction the body lies of his intention to make such further examination. The body shall not be moved from the place where it lies until it has been viewed by the district attorney or his representative if, at the time he is notified of its existence by the medical examiner, the district attorney gives notice of his desire to view the same. After the district attorney or his representative has viewed the body or has given notice that he does not desire to do so, the medical examiner on his own authority [Except see section 7] may and, if he be so requested by the district attorney or the attorney general, shall make or cause to be made in his presence an autopsy on the aforesaid body. Such an autopsy shall be performed in the presence of two or more discreet persons whose attendance the medical examiner may compel by subpoena. If a medical examiner considers it necessary to have a physician present as a witness at an autopsy, such physician shall receive a fee of five dollars. Other witnesses, except officers named in section fifty of chapter two hundred and sixty-two [various appointed state officers], shall be allowed two dollars each. A clerk may be employed to record the results of such a view or autopsy and shall receive not more than five dollars per day therefor. Upon written order of the district attorney of the district where the body lies, or of the attorney general, a medical examiner shall also make, or cause to be made in his presence, an autopsy under like conditions of any dead body within his county. The medical examiner may on his own authority, and shall if so requested by the district attorney of the county where the body lies, employ the services of a pathologist, a chemist or other expert to aid in the examination of the body or of substances supposed to have caused or contributed to death, and if the aforesaid pathologist, chemist or other expert is not already employed by the commonwealth or by the city or county where the body lies for the discharge of such services he shall, upon written authorization of the medical examiner and of the district attorney, if such employment and services were requested by him, be allowed reasonable compensation, payable by the county in the manner provided in section nineteen. The medical examiner shall, at the time of the autopsy, record or cause to be recorded each fact and circumstance tending to show the condition of the body and cause and manner of death, with the names and addresses of said witnesses, which record he shall subscribe. The medical examiner may allow reasonable compensation, payable by the county in the manner provided in section nineteen, for the transportation of such bodies as need to be moved to a place where they can be more satisfactorily examined, and for the use of such quarters as may be needed for the performance of an autopsy.

## SECTION 7. REPORT TO DISTRICT ATTORNEY AND COURT; CERTIFICATE TO TOWN CLERK AND DEPARTMENT OF INDUSTRIAL ACCIDENTS

He shall forthwith file with the district attorney for his district a report of each autopsy and view and of his personal inquiries,

*with a certificate that, in his judgment, the manner and cause of*
*death could not be ascertained by view and inquiry and that an*
*autopsy was necessary.* [Emphasis added.] If the autopsy was
requested or ordered by the district attorney as provided in
section six, he shall so certify to the commissioners of the county
where the same was held or, in Suffolk county, to the auditor of
Boston. If upon such view, personal inquiry or autopsy, the
medical examiner is of the opinion that the death may have been
caused by the act or negligence of another, he shall at once notify
the district attorney and a justice of a district court within whose
jurisdiction the body was found, if the place where found and the
place of the said act or negligence are within the same county, or
if the latter place is unknown; otherwise, the district attorney
and such a justice within whose district or jurisdiction the said
act or negligence occurred. He shall also file with the district
attorney thus notified, and with the justice or in his court, an
attested copy of the view and his personal inquiries and a copy of
the record of the autopsy made as provided in section six. He
shall in all cases forthwith certify to the town clerk or registrar in
the place where the deceased died, and to the department of
industrial accidents in cases where death, in his opinion, was
caused by or related to the occupation of the deceased, and to the
registrar of motor vehicles in cases where death, in his opinion,
was caused by or related to the operation of a motor vehicle, his
name and residence, if known; otherwise a description as full as
may be, with the cause and manner of death.

# SECTION 8. INQUEST

The court or justice may thereupon hold an inquest. The
attorney general or the district attorney may, notwithstanding
the fact that no action has been taken by the medical examiner
under section six, or that no notification that the death may have
been caused by the act or negligence of another has been given to
the court or justice under section seven, require an inquest to be

held in case of any death supposed to have been caused by external means. The court or justice shall give seasonable notice of the time and place of the inquest to the department of public utilities in any case of death by accident upon a railroad, electric railroad, street railway, or railroad for private use, and in any case of death in which a motor vehicle of a common carrier of passengers for hire by motor vehicle is involved. All persons not required by law to attend may be excluded from the inquest. The district attorney or any person designated by him may attend the inquest and examine the witnesses, who may be kept separate so that they cannot converse with each other until they have been examined.

# MURDER

Chapter 265, Crimes Against the Person:

## SECTION 1. MURDER DEFINED

Murder committed with deliberately premeditated malice aforethought, or with extreme atrocity or cruelty, or in the commission or attempted commission of a crime punishable with death or imprisonment for life, is murder in the first degree. Murder which does not appear to be in the first degree is murder in the second degree. Petit treason shall be prosecuted and punished as murder. The degree of murder shall be found by the jury.

# Adultery

Chapter 272, Crimes Against Chastity, Morality, etc.:

## SECTION 14. ADULTERY

A married woman who has sexual intercourse with a man not her husband shall be guilty of adultery or an unmarried man who has sexual intercourse with a married woman shall be guilty of adultery and shall be punished by imprisonment in the state prison for not more than three years or in jail for not more than two years or by a fine of not more than five hundred dollars.

# Loss of Elected Office Through Conviction for a Felony

Chapter 279, Judgment and Execution:

## SECTION 30, OFFICES FORFEITED BY SENTENCE TO STATE PRISON, ETC.

If a convict sentenced by a court or commonwealth or of the United States to imprisonment in the state prison or by a court of the United States to a federal penitentiary for a felony holds an office under the constitution or laws of the commonwealth at the time of sentence, it shall be vacated from the time of sentence. If the judgment against him is reversed upon writ of error he shall be restored to his office with all its rights and emoluments; but, if pardoned, he shall not by reason thereof be restored unless it is so expressly ordered by the terms of the pardon.

# APPENDIX H

*Annotated Bibliography*

## A NOTE ON YELLOW JOURNALISM

A difficulty that historians encounter when trying to do research is slanted journalism. Probably the most infamous example is the story of Richard III. Made out to be a child murderer by Shakespeare and others writing under the Tudors, Richard III has been exonerated repeatedly over the years, yet he remains an ogre in the minds of most British schoolchildren and adults.

We had to dig through a lot of yellow journalism when researching this book.

Only Jack Olsen in *The Bridge at Chappaquiddick* and Leo Damore in *Senatorial Privilege* seem to have been even slightly objective. Olsen interviewed many of the people involved and reported on what they said. It was a simple, straightforward job of journalism until he started speculating about what "really happened." Damore reinterviewed everyone twelve to eighteen years after the event, brought much up to date, and added his local knowledge.

Certain journalists writing for right-wing newspapers did their best to make Kennedy appear to be an evil killer. We encountered at least two cases of what appear to have been deliberate distortions of the truth. The *Manchester Union Leader* appears to have misstated some details on some telephone calls in an apparent effort to put the senator in a bad light. Kenneth Kappel in *Chappaquiddick Revealed* cites a nonexistent *New York Times* article to demonstrate a legal point.

The Tedrows, in *Death at Chappaquiddick*, ignored or obscured information in order to make their point. Zad Rust, in the suggestively titled *Teddy Bare*, is the very worst of the lot. He implies that Ted Kennedy is such a giant of a figure that he couldn't be without deep, dark motives. He really compliments Kennedy by doing this. Rust assumes Kennedy couldn't be just an ordinary guy thrust into public life who had an unfortunate accident.

On the other hand, journalists writing for the left-wing newspapers did their best to find excuses for Kennedy. Favorable biographers downplay the whole incident, and many other incidents of the senator's past, to emphasize the positive qualities and present another picture: a wonderful, fatherly figure whose only concern is the welfare of family and country.

The pertinent works referred to for this book were:

Armstrong, Neil; Collins, Michael; and Aldrin, Edwin E., Jr. *First on the Moon.* New York: Little, Brown and Company, Inc., 1970. An account of the voyage of *Apollo 11* by the men who made the trip. A reminder of what else was going on at the time of Chappaquiddick.

Anderson, Jack. "Grand Jury Needed in Kennedy Probe," *Washington Post*, August 22, 1969.

———."'Mary Jo Rescue Possible,' Diver Says," *Washington Post*, September 1, 1969.

———."Kennedy Clung to Hope Girl Escaped," *Washington Post*, September 25, 1969.

Barron, John. "Chappaquiddick, the Still Unanswered Questions," *Reader's Digest*, February 1980. Excellent journalistic account by a good investigative reporter (*KGB, Breaking the Ring*, etc.) written with a view to the 1980 elections. This contains the accounts of the tidal studies commissioned by the *Reader's Digest*. The timing of the tide tables contains a glaring error; otherwise it is a good article directed more toward asking questions than giving answers.

Burns, James MacGregor. *Edward Kennedy and the Camelot Legacy*. New York: W. W. Norton & Co., 1976. A sycophantic paean by a Kennedy loyalist. He ran unsuccessfully for Congress in the fiefdom, served as convention delegate. He has no explanation for Kennedy's behavior and cheerfully accepts the senator perjuring himself at the inquest.

Chellis, Marcia. *The Joan Kennedy Story—Living with the Kennedys*. New York: Simon & Schuster, 1985; New York: Berkely Publishing, 1986. Popular Confessions trash with an Alcoholics Anonymous moral. Interesting for the fact that Ted was apparently kept as far away from Joan as from the press during the aftermath. The book mentions that Joan intercepted a telephone call where Ted told his then-current girlfriend about the accident before he told his wife.

Cutler, R (obert) B (radley). *You the Jury . . . In Re: Chappaquiddick*. Danvers, MA: Betts & Mirror Press, 1973 (original Self-published paperback). Cutler is a known conspiracoid, who has also woven webs around the John Kennedy assassination and the shooting down of Korean Air Flight 007. He would have us believe that some outside force conspired to set Ted Kennedy up. Forensic medicine? Analysis of physical evidence? They would get in the way of the theories. This is a hard book to find. The Library of Congress doesn't have it, but the Assassination Archives and Research Center in Washington, D.C., has two copies. No index. Poor photo credits.

Dallas, Rita, and Radcliffe, Jeanira. *The Kennedy Case*. New York: G.P. Putnam Sons, 1973; New York: Popular Library, 1974 (paperback). An account by the nurse during Joseph P. Kennedy's last illness. One more vote for a head injury from one of the few trained medical persons to see Ted Kennedy after the accident. Dallas mentions Gargan's changed behavior at the compound during the aftermath.

Damore, Leo. *In His Garden*. New York: Arbor House, 1981. The exhaustively detailed story of serial murderer Antone "Tony" Costa, who was being investigated by the same lawmen as Kennedy at the same time the Chappaquiddick incident took place.

———. *Senatorial Privilege*. Washington, D.C.: Regnery Gateway, 1988; New York: Dell, 1989 (paperback). A heavily researched retelling with some weak backup by Kennedy cousin and former friend Gargan of the old Jack Anderson story that Ted Kennedy tried to get Gargan to take the rap for driving the car in which Mary Jo Kopechne died. This time Kennedy wants Mary Jo to have been driving. The problem is that Damore believes people. He believes lawyers who tell him what the law is without researching the law. He provides cites to every interview but cites to only two legal cases. He believes the stories of various witnesses without testing these stories against other evidence. He believes self-confessed accomplice Bernie Flynn, who later sued him. His forensic science is weak.

David, Lester. *Joan, the Reluctant Kennedy*. New York: Warner Paperback Library, 1975. Quickie paperback with a view to the 1976 elections. From what we know now, Mr. Lester didn't have a clue to Chappaquiddick. Companion to the following volume.

———. *Ted Kennedy, Triumphs and Tragedies*. New York: Award Books, 1975. Largely fawning account written for Kennedy fans with a view to the 1976 elections. Again, the author cheerfully accepts the idea that Ted perjured himself.

Farago, Ladislas. *Worse Than a Crime*. Never published but originally on Avon's 1980 book list. Farago's account largely follows the so-called Republican National Committee theory, that Kennedy and Keough were in the car with Mary Jo crashed out in the backseat. Kennedy gets out of the car, and Keough drives off the bridge but escapes death. Neither realized Kopechne was missing until they counted heads later. Farago is an intelligence expert and claims to have had access to FBI and other records. The problem is that since the principals have never talked, these records would merely be base speculation marked "High-level Evaluation." Its failure to be published is not really suspicious. After being defeated for the Democratic nomination by Carter in 1980, Teddy was no longer hot copy.

Farrell, Jane. "Memories of Mary Jo," *Ladies' Home Journal*, vol. 106, no. 7, July 1989. Supposedly new, but at least the fourth interview with the Kopechnes offering no new information and demonstrating that, unfortunately, they have not yet come to terms with their daughter's death.

Goodwin, Doris Kearns. *The Fitzgeralds and the Kennedys: An American Saga.* New York: Simon & Schuster, 1987. Heavily researched, largely favorable story of the Fitzgerald and Kennedy families from 1848 to 1960. Tends to whitewash Joseph P.'s actions in England, which, for an obvious lefty (from her description of the Spanish civil war), must have been an intellectual tussle. Nice index.

Helpern, Milton, M.D., and Knight, Bernard, M.D. *Autopsy.* New York: St. Martin's Press, 1977; New York: Signet, 1979 (paperback). Helpern's autobiography in which he devotes a page or so to Chappaquiddick, stressing the need for autopsies in all case of questionable death. Contains other useful medicolegal information.

Hersh, Burton. *The Education of Edward Kennedy.* New York: William Morrow & Co., 1972. Hersh, although another fawning apologist for the Kennedy clan, is an excellent writer. Some think he overwrites, but his prose has flavor. He comes closest to our diagnosis of the situation, although he attributes Kennedy's state of mind to psychological stress rather than physical trauma. He also cheerfully accepts perjury on the part of a U.S. senator. Well indexed.

Jereski, Laura. "Shirtsleeves to Shirtsleeves," *Forbes*, October 21, 1991. The dwindling Kennedy fortune.

Kappel, Kenneth. *Chappaquiddick Revealed.* New York: Shapolsky Publishers Inc., 1989; New York: St. Martin's Paperbacks, 1991. This book shows what a man who does not know the history of blood tests, the principles of fluid dynamics, the crummy construction of American cars during the 1960s, the difference between an inquest and a trial, the difference between an order for an autopsy and an order for exhumation, or the physiology of drowning can do if he tries. A wonderful argument for the licensing of typewriters. Surprisingly, indexed and with a bibliography.

Kopechne, Mrs. Joseph; as told to James, Suzanne. "The Truth About Mary Jo," *McCall's*, September 1970. This article was the only source for information about Mary Jo for most of the other books cited here. The anecdotes from it are all repeated in these books, often without citation.

Lange, Jim. "Medical Evidence," *Mensa Bulletin*, October 1984. The trial of Spencer Cowper in 1699.

Lerner, Max. *Ted and the Kennedy Legend.* New York: St. Martin's Press, 1980. This account convicts Ted of panic and paralysis of will, perjury, and receiving favored treatment from the judiciary, but it tells his faithful audience to take heart because Ted will remain a "symbol of the alternative road" through the 1990s. No one can fault Lerner for scholarship. This book has the finest index, chapter notes, and bibliography of any in the collection.

Lippman, Theo. *Senator Ted Kennedy: The Career Behind the Image.* New York: W. W. Norton and Co., 1976. Lippman, writing basically and favorably about the Senate career of Ted Kennedy, reduces the entire Chappaquiddick affair to two paragraphs. Even in these, he convicts Kennedy of attempting to cover up his involvement in the episode.

McCahill, Tom. "In-Between Olds," *Mechanix Illustrated*, April 1967. A road test of the car in the case.

Oates, Joyce Carol. *Black Water.* New York: Dutton, 1992. A declared work of fiction based on Chappaquiddick. Its most interesting point is that the author had the Mary Jo character fail to rescue herself not because she failed to think of it but specifically because her foot was caught. Otherwise if this is as far as women have come, why did we have women's liberation?

Olsen, Jack. *The Bridge at Chappaquiddick.* New York: Ace Books, 1970 (paperback). Probably the best account of the happenings of the days before and the week after the accident that was published. Olsen simply interviewed everybody and wrote it down. These were fresh accounts, near the time of the accident. The only flaws are the awkward organization, some internal contradictions, and the lack of an index. Olsen wrote and published this account even before the inquest. Unfortunately, he didn't stop at recording his interviews. Instead, he went on to theorize, missing some important points to conclude that Kennedy was not in the car at the time of the accident.

Reybold, Malcolm. *The Inspector's Opinion,* New York: E. P. Dutton and Company, 1975; paperback edition also published. A work of fiction in the style of Ellery Queen's *A Study in Scarlet* (Queen's backward-looking analysis of Sherlock Holmes's Jack the Ripper investigation). Reybold's analyses of times are quite good, but his psychology is a miss and he reaches a version of the same tired, unlikely theory that others reached (Ted wasn't in the car). The whole book is cluttered up with an idealistic June–September love affair.

Rust, Zad. *Teddy Bare.* Belmont, MA: Western Islands Press, 1971 (original Self-published paperback). A real hatchet job. This book is wonderful in its own way, with Teddy as a conscious agent of the Communist Conspiracy, Mary Jo as a pregnant murder victim, judges and investigators as boobs and lackeys (here the book comes a little closer to reality). Some of these "Hidden Forces" theories are wonderful products of a fertile imagination.

Zad Rust is the anagram of Sturdza (Prince Michael), a former Romanian diplomat and known sponsor of right-wing causes. Western Islands Press is owned by Robert Welch, the founder of the John Birch Society. [There is a rust remover called Zud Rust.]

Sherrill, Robert. *The Last Kennedy.* New York: Dial Press, 1976.

Taken from his July 1974 *New York Times Magazine* article and expanded to book length. This is a whine from the press and an attack on Kennedy from the left. Unlike Rust's commie or most everyone's darling liberal, Ted is Sherrill's crusty old reactionary whose only liberal positions are political expediency. He tries to put the story in narrative form, but his expressions of disbelief every few lines make it hard to follow. He is the chief exponent of the "drunk-as-a-skunk" theory. The book is a good example of post-Vietnam, post-Watergate disillusionment and the outraged *amour propre* of a press Ted hasn't talked to. The same ground is covered much more fairly and with new evidence in Barron's *Reader's Digest* article.

Spitz, Werner U., M.D., Ed., and Fisher, Russell S., M.D., Ed. *Medicolegal Investigation of Death.* Springfield, IL: Charles C. Thomas, 1980. The definitive text on forensic pathology. Profusely illustrated. This is the standard textbook, used, along with Helpern's text and a British work, by all practicing forensic pathologists and responsible coroners and medical examiners. It includes, unfortunately, some circular reasoning. Spitz quotes his own testimony at the Kopechne exhumation hearing in Pennsylvania to prove that foam at the mouth is specific to death by drowning.

Staff of the New York Times. "Supreme Court Reaffirms Public's Right of Access to Criminal Trials," *New York Times,* June 24, 1982. The article that Kappel miscited and misquoted.

Stevenson, William. *A Man Called Intrepid.* New York: Harcourt Brace Jovanovich, 1976; New York: Ballatine Books, 1977 (paperback). This excellent account of Sir William Stephenson's World War II career is useful for its information on the America First sentiments of Joseph P. Kennedy.

Tedrow, Thomas L., and Tedrow, Richard L. *Death at Chappaquiddick.* Gretna, LA: Pelican Publishing Co., 1976, 1980 (original Self-published paperback). This book raises in a legitimate format many of the questions addressed by *Teddy Bare.* The elder Tedrow is a former chief commissioner, U.S. Court of Military Appeals, and does have a trained legal mind. He may be a whiz on the Uniform Code of Military Justice, but it is obvious he has not been down to the autopsy room and the local courts where we try traffic accidents and drunken drivers every day. Nor does he understand the difference between an order for an autopsy and an order for an exhumation. Had he laid off *American Jurisprudence* and *Corpus Juris Secundum* and done a little work in the *State Reporter*, he would never have made certain blanket statements. He seems to have difficulty reconciling the real and the ideal. The younger Tedrow has recently become embroiled in a controversy regarding writing the "Days of" Laura Ingalls Wilder series. No notes, no index.

Thomas, Jo. "Gaps Found in Chappaquiddick Phone Data," *New York Times*, March 12, 1980.

————."Withholding of Chappaquiddick Phone Data Denied," *New York Times*, March 13, 1980.

Note: Kennedy's whine about privacy, origin United Press International, was printed by the *Times* as a sidebar to the March 13 story.

Thorwald, Jügen; translated by Richard and Clara Winston. *Crime and Science: The New Frontier in Criminology.* New York: Harcourt, Brace & World, 1967. The history of blood tests. The book verifies that the benzidine test was considered unreliable and out of date even in 1969.

Ulasewicz, Tony, with McKeever, Stewart A. *The President's Private Eye.* Westport, CT: MACSAM Publishing Company, 1990. Ulasewicz was one of Nixon's White House Plumbers. He has a chapter on Chappaquiddick. If he had written "they sent me to Edgartown, and I didn't find out crap," it would have been one of the most refreshing and truthful things ever written on the subject. Unfortunately he goes on about phone calls and still thinks Ted wasn't in the car.

Whitty, C.W.M., D.M. F.R.S.P., Ed., and Zangwill, O.L., MA, F.R.S., Ed. *Amnesia: Clinical, Psychological and Medicolegal Aspects.* London: Butterworths, 1977. An excellent text, containing information unavailable at the time of the accident. Biochemistry and biophysiology of the brain are the leading edge of research, even today. Much of the information in this book was gathered during treatment of head wounds in Vietnam. It was in this book, looking for the duration of retrograde amnesia, that we found the description of posttraumatic amnesia that fit the accounts of Kennedy's symptoms recounted by assorted witnesses who had never read this work. It was our final breakthrough.

Ziegler, Henry, ed. *Inquest.* New York: Tower Books, 1970 (original paperback). A quickie paperback containing the important points gleaned from the five volumes of inquest testimony. No table of contents, let alone index. The work that prompted *Lippman* v. *the Commonwealth* 1, 2, and 3.

*Annotated Laws of Massachusetts* (Michie/Law. Co-Op)

*Atlantic Digest*

*Atlantic Reporter*

*Féderal Reporter*

*Northeastern Reporter*

*U.S. Reports*

We also consulted innumerable textbooks, almanacs, and other works for facts and information. They were standard works, most of them indexed or at least categorized, and we are grateful to the Montgomery County, Maryland, Public Library system for having them readily available to refresh or confirm our knowledge; also the Montgomery County Circuit Court Library, Rockville, Maryland, and Washington College of Law Library, American University, Washington, D.C.

In addition to consulting books we conducted some telephone interviews.

We would like to thank authors Leo Damore, John Barron, and a few other people—most of whom would rather remain nameless.

All these interviews were for fact checking and source checking. Any errors of fact or opinions in this book are solely our responsibility.

# A NOTE ON THE DEDICATION

William of Ockham (1285–1349), also known as *Doctor Invincibilis, Venerabilis Inceptor*, is the author of Ockham's Razor: "Entities must not be unnecessarily multiplied." This statement is usually held to mean that, when dealing with unknowns, the theory that requires the fewest assumptions is most correct.

# Index